The Unconscious Roots of Creativity

EDITED BY KATHRYN MADDEN

With Articles by

Linda Carter • Anna Maria Costantino • Carol Thayer Cox
Leonard Cruz • Lisa Raye Garlock • James Hollis
Naomi Ruth Lowinsky • Ian Livingston
Kathryn Madden • Jordan S. Potash
Susan Rowland • Murray Stein
Ann Ulanov • Tjeu van den Berk
Robin van Löben Sels • Heidi S. Volf

CHIRON PUBLICATIONS • ASHEVILLE, NORTH CAROLINA

www.ChironPublications.com

978-1-63051-369-6 paperback

978-1-63051-370-2 Hardcover

978-1-63051-371-9 ebook

Cover design and typesetting by Nelly Murariu
Printed in the United States of America.

Library of Congress Cataloging-in-Publication Data
Names: Madden, Kathryn Wood, editor.
Title: The unconscious roots of creativity / edited by Kathryn Madden ; with
    articles by Linda Carter and 14 others.
Description: Asheville, N.C. : Chiron Publications, 2016. | Includes
    bibliographical references and index.
Identifiers: LCCN 2016025902 (print) | LCCN 2016034118 (ebook) | ISBN
    9781630513856 (pbk. : alk. paper) | ISBN 9781630513863 (hardcover : alk.
    paper) | ISBN 9781630513870 (electronic) | ISBN 9781630513870 (E-book)
Subjects: LCSH: Creative ability.
Classification: LCC BF408 .U53 2016 (print) | LCC BF408 (ebook) | DDC
    153.3/5--dc23
LC record available at https://lccn.loc.gov/2016025902

Table of Contents

Foreword

by Leonard Cruz, MD

As I look back, I suspect that no matter how I turned the lyre, I played the same tune.

Just as the Muses were the offspring of *Mnemosyne*, the goddess of memory, our memories are the ancestors of our creativity that finds its multifaceted expression in the written word, image, theater, dance, and music. *The Unconscious Roots of Creativity* seeks to push the investigation into that domain of memory that is beyond our conscious reach.

Just beyond the pale of conscious autobiography will be found creative expression that the creator easily recognizes to be autobiographical in nature. Beyond that domain lies art that the artist would not recognize as autobiographical but that others clearly would. A region whose origins are even more obscure exists in the next zone. This is where psychoanalysis, and in particular analytical psychology, has much to offer. This is the vast territory of the unconscious where memory is stored. That spring is fed by our personal experiences and from a deep aquifer of the collective unconscious that C. G. Jung helped reveal.

The great diversity of experience and creative talent assembled by Dr. Kathryn Madden, the editor of this volume, is impressive. We know that contributors drew from their personal experience as well as their experience of the collective unconscious. This brings me to the origins of this book you hold in your hands. On one level, this book was born from a question posed by Dr. Madden in an online discussion forum hosted by the LinkedIn Group, Jungian (Analytical) Psychology. But, if we propose that the moment of conception occurred nearly two years ago in a LinkedIn discussion, before long we discover something akin to Heisenberg's Uncertainty Principle. This principle of quantum mechanics reveals that the more precisely the position of a subatomic particle is determined, the less precisely the momentum is known. The LinkedIn discussion is too precise and concrete a locus to account for the full story. Perhaps the moment of conception occurred when the group formed 5-6 years earlier, or when Dr. Madden first conceived the idea that lay dormant until she and I spoke of compiling an edited volume. Of course, without the pioneering work of Freud and Jung this book might not be in your hands at all, the moment of conception is with them.

If you have done any creative writing or created anything informed by the Muses, you know that the unconscious roots of creativity extend wide and far and deep. From that deep aquifer of the unconscious each of us draws inspiration that manifests in art, architecture, literature and the life we compose. These living waters are teaming with memories that have yet to be recovered and integrated.

You hold a book in your hand that has been through a long period of Advent. Like a child that was knit in the womb, it has passed through the birth canal of the contributors and editors. The staff of Chiron attended its birth like a caring midwife, making sure it would arrive in your hands ready for the life that awaits it. The essence of this foundling will not be discovered in the sinew, the bones, and the viscera that came together as *The Unconscious Roots of Creativity*. The greatest mystery is that you the reader complete the circle. It is our sincere desire that this book may *inform* you and that you may be *formed in* this book.

This is the first of a series of books being planned by Chiron Publications. We are humbled by the creative process that culminates in this volume. We hope that you will be enriched and that as you meet the words on this page a burst of creativity may overtake you. If the unconscious roots of the contributors to this book were to intermingle with the vast unconscious of every reader, then our supplications to the Muses will have been answered.

Len Cruz, MD, ME
Editor-in-Chief of Chiron Publications
Asheville, NC

References

Murray, Donald M. "All Writing Is Autobiography." College Composition and Communication 42.1 (1991): 66. Web. 5 Mar. 2016.

Jung, Collected Works vol. 7 (1953), "The Structure of the Unconscious" (1916), ¶437–507 (pp. 263–292).

Introduction

by Kathryn Madden

When we say someone is creative or has a creative personality, what is it that we mean exactly? Are we referring to a trait that has been genetically inherited? Is it more of a psychological disposition? Could it be that creativity is a skill or combination of skills? If so, can it be taught and learned by anyone? Is it possible for a tendency toward creativity to be predicted by a personality typology test such as the Myers-Briggs Type Indicator (MBTI©) that might, for example, suggest an intuitive feeler (NF) type would be more likely suited to an artistic career?

As anyone who has studied a musical instrument can attest, you either "take to it or you don't." This would imply, then, some kind of predisposition or inherited musical talent. The phrase "musically inclined" comes to mind. However, having a musical inclination without the willingness or ability to put in the hours of study and practice required to master the instrument of choice will render yours an unrealized inclination, a hidden talent. Even if you take the trouble to study your instrument, unless you become fluent in its capabilities, your playing will likely never rise above a mere recitation of notes on a page—certainly nothing that one would recognize as inspiring or creative.

So then, from whence spring the sparks of creativity? It is to this very question that the field of depth psychology—especially that of C.G. Jung and his intellectual descendants—has much to contribute. This is of particular importance to me because the subject bridges my two, somewhat intersecting, professional interests. Soon after graduating from the University of Maryland, my first professional pursuits were directed to the performing arts—music and theatre, to be precise. I began to teach and direct theatre at the junior high and high school level. Within a couple of years, I had moved to New

York City where I pursued my own performing career, appearing first in experimental theatre as well as in other off-off-Broadway and off-Broadway productions. Later I was cast in a leading role in a hit Broadway show which kept me busy in New York City and throughout the country for five years. When I finally returned from the road to my New York City apartment and had some time to reflect, I soon found myself pulled in the direction of new and deeper relationships, connection with community, and, unexpectedly but inexorably, a new professional vocation. That new vocation turned out to be my other field of interest: depth psychology. Over the next several years, I proceeded to earn my doctorate in the field of psychology and religion under the mentorship of Prof. Ann Belford Ulanov at Union Theological Seminary (UTS), now part of Columbia University. After a period of supervised clinical training, I opened a practice in New York where a number of individuals from the arts began to find their way to my consulting room. I began lecturing at conferences, various Jung societies across the country, and at two graduate institutions. One of these graduate schools is my alma mater, UTS. The other is the Pacifica Graduate Institute in Carpinteria, CA. Among the subjects that interest me and that I have taught include—perhaps not unsurprisingly by now—the roots of theatre in myth, archetype, and ritual. This has led me into a further exploration of the contribution of the unconscious—especially what Jung called the "collective unconscious"—to theatrical and other artistic expression.

A little over a year ago, I raised a question concerning the question of the unconscious roots of creativity in an online Jungian discussion group. Surprisingly, this sparked an energetic, free-wheeling exploration of the topic. Participation in this discussion led to my introduction to Dr. Len Cruz, the moderator of that group as well as the Editor-In-Chief of Chiron Publications. At some point, during the twists and turns of the discussion group, Len invited me to contribute to and edit a book on the topic we were exploring. Thus was born *The Unconscious Roots of Creativity*, the book.

A call for articles was sent to Jungian practitioners and scholars, and again, this topic seemed to have touched a chord. We received far more excellent offerings than could be included in this volume. The articles that follow, then, are on such a wide range of topics falling under the rubric of "the unconscious roots of creativity" as: the imagination as an "aperture" into the psyche and its expression in such diverse areas as quantum physics and poetry; an exploration of Erich Neumann's extensive work in the field of "psyche's creativity;" the experience of sitting for a portrait that now hangs in a seminary's hall as a legacy to a career of service to the school and its students; imaginal expression and healing; the devotional relationship between an artist and her art; the compensatory nature of "art-making;" the spiritual calmness and path to self experience in the surrender of the Butoh dancer's "dance of being;" a consideration of the "impossible troika" of art, aesthetics, and ethics; a look at the various intersection points of theatre and the unconscious; a contribution on poetry; one on dreams; and a clinical case study.

The "red thread" running through each of the offerings in this volume is that, whatever its ultimate expression, the creative impulse has its roots deep in the psyche. As I was doing research for this introduction, I came across a marvelous quote in an article by author E.M. Forster in the November 1925 issue of *The Atlantic Monthly* with the somewhat opaque title, "Anonymity: An Inquiry." When you read Forster's quote below, however, along with one from Jung's article, "On the Relation of Analytical Psychology to Poetry," published in *The Spirit in Man, Art, and Literature* (CW 15), I believe you will also be struck by the concurrence of ideas, if expressed in very different styles. It caused me to wonder whether Forster had actually corresponded with Jung. They were contemporaries after all. I found no evidence of a correspondence in any online research I conducted nor in copies of Jung's letters. It does not rule out the possibility that they met and spoke. More likely Forster read some of Jung's work. We do know that Jung's aforementioned article was originally published in 1922, a full three years before Forster's piece on "Anonymity" appeared and that Jung's theories on the collective unconscious were first introduced in 1916. So, regardless of the source, Forster appears familiar with Jung's concept of the collective unconscious as distinct with the Freudian notion of the personal unconscious.

Just as words have two functions—information and creation—so each human mind has two personalities, one on the surface, one deeper down. The upper personality has a name. It is called S.T. Coleridge or William Shakespeare... It is conscious and alert, it does things like dining out, answering letters, and so forth, and it differs vividly and amusingly from other personalities. The lower personality is a very queer affair. In many ways it is a perfect fool, but without it there is no literature, because unless a man dips a bucket down into it occasionally he cannot produce first-class work. There is something general about it. Although it is inside S.T. Coleridge, it cannot be labeled with his name. It has something in common with all other deeper personalities, and the mystic will assert that the common quality is God, and that here, in the obscure recesses of our being, we near the gates of the Divine. It is in any case the force that makes for anonymity. As it came from the depths, so it soars to the heights, out of local questionings; as it is general to all men, so the works it inspires have something general about them, namely beauty. The poet wrote the poem, no doubt, but he forgot himself while he wrote it, and we forget ourselves while we read.

> — E.M. Forster (1925. "Anonymity: An Inquiry,"
> *The Atlantic Monthly*. p. 592)

And in "On the Relation of Analytical Psychology to Poetry," Jung describes the concept of the creative process in similar terms.

The unborn work in the psyche of the artist is a force of nature that achieves its end either with tyrannical might or with the subtle cunning of nature herself, quite regardless of the personal fate of the man who is its vehicle. The creative urge lives and grows in him like a tree in the earth from which it draws its nourishment. We would do well, therefore, to think of the creative process as a living thing implanted in the human psyche.

> In the language of analytical psychology this living
> thing is an autonomous complex. It is a split-off portion
> of the psyche, which leads a life of its own outside the
> hierarchy of consciousness.
>
> — C.G. Jung (CW 15, para. 115)

Forster, then, sees the creative urge as coming from a deep "well" of the "lower personality," while Jung says "it lives and grows in [the artist] like a tree in the earth." If, according to Jung, it is like a "living thing planted in the human psyche" that he sees as "outside the hierarchy of consciousness," then "this tree" must have its roots somewhere else. While the lower personality may exist in the artist the two are not equivalent. Great art, says Forster, can only be derived from the artist dipping "a bucket down into it occasionally." This lower personality to which he refers can be none other than the collective unconscious. He says that "[i]t has something in common with all other deeper personalities;" that it can be located in the "obscure recesses of our being;" and it is the "force that makes for anonymity." In other words, it is deeper than or beyond what Forster calls the "upper personality" or what Jung would call the level of the ego. If the poet has been able to tap into this level of the psyche while writing the poem, Forster concludes that, "he forgot himself while he wrote it." And, as significantly, "we forget ourselves while we read [it]."

These statements from two contemporaries—one from the field of literature and one from analytical psychology—are succinct, parallel testimonials to the unconscious roots of creativity. The articles within this volume shine further light on this theme through the prism of a diversity of backgrounds and interests. I truly hope you will learn from and enjoy their perspectives.

Acknowledgements

As the Volume Editor, I would like to express much gratitude to the Series Editor, Len Cruz, M.D., whose vision for this book synchronistically coincided with my own. Eliciting excitement from the froth of the above-mentioned online conversations, Len intuitively observed that there was a collective urge for more contemporary writing on this subject matter. His invitation to Edit the Volume took me by surprise, but the hope most likely already was lingering not too far beneath the surface of my psyche, waiting to be summoned. So, I am most grateful to Len Cruz, and Chiron publisher, Steve Buser, who opened the door for this work to become incarnate.

The authors who have contributed to this volume are profoundly equipped and display much diversity in their perspectives and methodologies: whether theoretical, phenomenological, or experiential. The notion of "unconscious roots" implied that even the authors were summoned to a new charge. The flow and exchange between editor and authors was extremely open.

This book contains many figures, photos, and illustrations. Two artists, in particular, I would like to extend special appreciation for permission to use their remarkable works. Thank you to Susan Crehan-Hostetler, Owner and Director of the David Hostetler Gallery on Nantucket Island, for use of her late-husband David Hostetler's painting, entitled "Head or Heart," opposite my chapter, "Theatre and the Unconscious." Thank you also to Colette Calascione for the use of her painting, "Coincidental Gathering," in my chapter, and for the use of two other works, "Traveling Hermit" and "Internal Landscape," in Ian Livingston's chapter, "Witnesses of the Other."

I also wish to acknowledge Jennifer Fitzgerald at Chiron for her presence and constancy of being there for queries or requests from authors and editor alike. She worked far beyond her role in assisting authors with permissions and other details, and I am especially grateful for her assistance.

Finally, I am always grateful for the assistance of Ron Madden who has consistently availed himself to be a listening ear to the creative process of the Editor. He has also given generously of his time to help with the organization of the manuscript for submission to Chiron Publications.

This book is dedicated to Ron Madden, my best friend and husband.

Kathryn Madden, PhD
February 2016
New York City

Book Cover Credits

The profound art of Butoh is represented on the cover photo, "Dialogue of Self and Soul" © international artist Maureen Fleming, 2016. Ms Fleming is renowned for her original form of visual theatre and invents surreal movement poetry with the discipline of a classicist and the imagination of an iconoclast.

Among numerous accolades in response to her performances, the *New York Times* said of her work: "she seemed to transcend the material world and enter a realm of pure spirit...[a] wondrous choreographic metamorphosis."

Her works have received international acclaim in Italy's Spoleto and Milan's *Oltre* Festivals, Japan's Butoh Festival, Iceland's Reykjavik Arts Festival, France's *Maison des Cultures* in Paris, Colombia's *Contemporanea* International Festival, Korea's Seoul Performing Arts Festival, Brazil's FILO and Mercado Cultural, Cleveland Museum of Art, and Boston's Emerson Majestic Theatre. Additionally, she is esteemed at the Institute of Contemporary Art, Jacob's Pillow Festival, Fall for Dance Festival at City Center, and the Women of Substance at the O'Shaughnessy. Her innovative work has achieved numerous awards including fellowships from the National Endowment for the Arts, the National Performance Network, the NEFA National Dance Project, and the Rockefeller MAP Fund.

Further, she has received awards and fellowships from the NY Foundation for the Arts, the Japan U.S. Friendship Commission, the Japan Foundation, and the Fulbright in Colombia, Korea and Ireland. Ms. Fleming's works *After Eros* (1996), *Decay of the Angel* (2004), *Waters of Immortality* (2007) and *B. MADONNA* (2013, 2015) include collaborations with playwright David Henry Hwang, composer Philip Glass, and light and visual designer Christopher Odo. www.maureenfleming.com

Chapter 1

All is Fire: the Imagination as Aperture into Psyche

by James Hollis

> "The imagination lends to airy nothing a local habitation and a name."
>
> W. Shakespeare

> "Perhaps creating something is nothing but an act of profound remembrance."
>
> R. M. Rilke

Pre-Socratic philosopher Heraclitus once observed that "all is fire," a lambent metaphor for the flickering, energetic transformation of material forms: creating, disassembling, devouring itself, process personified. From the archaic realms of imagination to the discoveries of quantum physics, we intuit what dismays our senses—that nothing is substantial, below *Dinglichkeit*, materiality, floats no-thingness. All phenomena, *natura naturans*, nature naturing, appear to such epiphenomena as mind, sensibility, consciousness, as stable, fixed, and objectified. But all things are transforming, composing and decomposing, even as the human ego, that most fragile barque of all, would fix them, hold them, control them. Every appearance to our sensibility is an instant only, a snap-shot of the already-disappearing, or as Apollonaire's "*Cors de Chaisse*," hunting horns whose sound dies out along the wind. Or G. M. Hopkins's nomination that nature is a Heraclitean fire. Or Rilke's glimpse of the gods in passing, always passing, "*nur ein Spur*," only a trace, and then the no-thingness. *Natura naturans* quickly becoming *nature naturata*, nature naturing *cum* nature natured.

And for all the transience of material forms, how much more insubstantial the *psyche*, that strange word we translate as *soul* but which has wind, breathing, and transformation of pupae into butterfly in its etymological ancestry. So it is, the most fleeting is apprehended by, perceived by, construed, animated, turned, torqued and tortured by us—by something still more fleeting. As Rilke notes in his *Ninth Duino Elegy*, the evanescent world is rendered conscious by us, "the most fleeting of all," this *Sein-zum-Tode*, spinning toward its imminent dissolution, death, dismemberment, and decay. So the world is lent a local habitation and a name by this creature whose sand is running through the glass, and as G. M. Hopkins notes, sand which at first seems "at the wall fast / but mined with a motion that crowds and combs to a fall" (Hopkins, 1918, "*The Wreck of the Deutschland*").

When Hume, Kant, and others declared that we cannot know the *Thing* in its thingness, but only our experience of the thing, metaphysics died, perhaps much theology too, and obliged the birth of phenomenology and depth psychology. Phenomenology studies the conditions of experience, its limitations and capacities, and refrains from absolute pronouncements lest it be bewitched by its own legerdemain as so much theology, political rhetoric, and sloganeering has succumbed. Without a sustained, disciplined analysis of the conditions of, and limitations, of experience, we slip into the oldest of semantic and delusional heresies: idolatry. We mistake our constructs, our metaphors, our fictive intimations for the thing itself and thus become servant to our construing rather than sustain a radical openness to mystery. So, the image, the trace, *ein Spur*, left behind by the passing god, is worshipped, deified, reified, while the departed divinity is already elsewhere. And how many have died in the name of ossified metaphors? How many tortured by the literalism of the single-minded. "O Lord us keep," as Blake reminded, "from Single Vision, and Newton's sleep" (*cf. Letter to Thomas Butts,* December 22, 1802).

Depth psychology, too, is tasked with the formidable: to bring us into relationship with the invisible world, to track its peregrinations and permutations, and to render conscious what is unconscious. The problem with the unconscious is that it is unconscious, and therefore we can say nothing about it definitively. We project that it exists because of several daily facts: "stuff" keeps spilling into our world without our intending it to; we experience multiple autonomous phenomena which are clearly emanating from us: patterns, dreams, symptoms; and sooner or later we are stunned by the world's abrasive reminders to account for our presence and apparent choices, and the wake of consequences we leave behind us.

We can only gain momentary purchase on that invisible realm when psyche informs image in matter, in mind, in imagination—"Lends to airy nothing a local habitation and a name"—(Shakespeare, A Mid-Summer Night's Dream, Act V, Sc. I, ll. 17-18). Newton could track the informing of matter and derive from it "laws" which allow us to weigh, shape, direct, predict, and control the movement of matter. In so doing, he believed he was reading the mind of God in an act of piety. If he had thought that others would drop the hypothesis of the Divine and run with those "laws," he might have had second thoughts. (When Napoleon asked La Place where God was in his cosmic scheme, the mathematician replied that he no longer needed that hypothesis). That presently high school physics classes employ theses and concepts that transcend Newton's imaginal scheme in no way obviates his aesthetic vision of an ordered universe; it simply means we have better instruments, better questions today, and can imagine more.

Today the depth psychological enterprise is to track the movement of the invisible as it manifests in the venues of mind, body, patterns, neurology, dreams and the like. That so few psychologists address the interaction with the unconscious is a failure of nerve to take on the really difficult dialogue. Even so, the task for behaviorist, cognitive therapist, psychiatrist or psychoanalyst is the same: to track the movement of the invisible, swirling energies by attending the image which is currently animated by their ostensible presence.

The ineluctable passages of the gods, their rise, immanence, relocation elsewhere, the investments in the body of repressed affect, or the dreams which trouble sleep—all are the traces which the depth psychologist must track in order to discern their infections, blockages, misdirected vectors, and ultimate intentions. It is the sum of these movements, these passages, arrivals and departures, which constitute our personal biographies and collectively add chips to history's mosaic. The more we are able to follow these bread crumbs through the forests of the soul, the more we enhance consciousness, that fragile atoll in a raging, sometimes engulfing, sea.

Our branch of the evolutionary tree has survived because of its capacity to track these invisible energies, or at least to speculate upon them until better pictures emerge. While we have often fallen captive to our own constructions, thinking them the phenomena themselves, we are led by their autonomous transformations sooner or later to more evolved pictures of the pictures nature presents us. The German word for "imagination," *Einbildungskraft*, the "power of creating an image" illustrates; said image, then possesses the power to educate or inform consciousness. *Bildung*, sometimes loosely translated as "education," means the expectation that a person may acquire knowledge and capacity for choice, a range of cultural perspectives, and that he or she is adept in multiple disciplines including the sciences and the arts. Originally, *Bild,* or "picture, image" intimated that this capacity for forming a picture manifested a human reflection of the mind and powers of Divinity. As a more recent example, nineteenth century poet and critic Samuel Taylor Coleridge differentiated *Primary Imagination, Secondary Imagination*, and *Fancy* to illustrate this trope of Divine mimesis. Fancy is what today we would call fashion, taste, aesthetics—what color the rug should be, given that couch and coffee table over there. Secondary Imagination is the echoing of the Divine act through the overt powers we exhibit in creating art, music, literature, architecture, theory, models, and so forth. The Primary Imagination lies in our elemental constitutive powers which Kant, among others, identified as number, spatiality, sequence, and the like (*cf.* Kant, Critique of Pure Reason).

Additionally in the nineteenth century, both P. B. Shelley and Arthur Schopenhauer speculated that it was the imagination, not reason, that made morality possible, even empathy, sympathy, compassion. While reason can differentiate, and divide, and categorize, imagination can intimate the oneness beneath the disparity of things. I am not wholly separate from you, an alien planet apart from yours, if I can imagine your feelings, your pain, your suffering, and experience them myself. Thus, *Mitleid*, the capacity to "suffer with" arises from the imaginal power, not the rational power. So, too, quantum physics arises from alternative realities, even those alternative to the dictates of standard reason: neutrons can occupy multiple loci in an atom at the same time, and without traversing the distance between orbits. Newtonian mechanics, for all its utility, is a description without imagination, with all variables. e. e. cummings titled a book of his poetry *is 5* because he wanted to remind us that there are universes where two plus two is 5. When Einstein was asked if he believed in "God," he replied, "Spinoza's God," suggesting that he was, like Newton, interested in reading the nature of things without necessarily positing a personality to it as well. And who more than cummings reminded us of the fictive nature of natural limits, their relativity, than Einstein, Bohr, and others who imagined a picture that could do justice to phenomena that simply refused to fit into the pictures which had worked rather well for centuries? It is to the credit of science that it seems more willing to let go of its previous picture, more willing than most theologs, when a better picture is required.

A little over a century ago, C. G. Jung published an epochal book that almost nobody reads today except my students. Originally titled *Wandlungen und Symbole der Libido, Transformations and Symbols of Libido*, it is better known today in its subsequent editions as *Symbols of Transformation*. Jung used the term *libido* because it was the currency of the hour, a term he quickly redefines and by so doing splits himself off from Freud forever. While Freud had taken this old Latin word *libido* and used it to provide an energetic schema of the psyche in its many functions, he limited its use to the biological drives, frustrations, and secondary elaborations which this vast river coursing through the body took in seeking solace and satiety. Adler, Jung noted, had usefully reminded us that we are also social animals, and that a good deal of daily dynamics arise from the dramas of family life and social setting. To this, Jung added that his understanding of libido as the elemental life force is of course biologically driven, socially shaped, and yet, even more, reflects a central yet epiphenomenal curiosity that this particular animal craves, longs for, suffers the loss of, and is driven by the search for meaning. We are, Jung reminded us, symbol-making animals and through the tools of metaphor, symbol, and picture-making we seek to stand in some sort of conscious relationship to the Mysterium which our universe embodies for us. These tools do their work through analogue. Knowing that we cannot know the things in themselves, we approach them through things more commonly experienced. We understand Robert Burns immediately when he says his Beloved is like a red, red rose, and we do not think he is infatuated with a plant in his front yard. We know, through the relatively more knowable plant--however mysterious it is as well— enough to know that its image summoned forth is but an analog to the greater mysterium of the Beloved.

And so we stand before the infinite universe, the unfolding mystery, still: *black holes, quarks*, and *ablation* to *albedo* (also an alchemical term) to *Big Bang*, and *Blue Shift*, even to *Blue Moon* ("you found me standing alone..."), through *Dark Matter* to *Parahelion* and *Photon* (not to be confused with *Phobos*: Fear), to *Red Shift* and *Super Nova Remnant* to *Trojan* (Troy or the pharmacy?), to *Virgo Cluster* to *Yellow Dwarf*. What a pandemonia of god-terms, what a mass of metaphora, what an amphitheater of analogs!

In *Symbols of Transformation*, Jung studies the active imagination, or sustained reverie of an American woman living in Geneva whose real name was Frank Miller (cf. Shamdasani, 1990, "A Woman Called Frank.") In studying with psychologist Theodore Flournoy, Ms. Miller provides an example of a phantasy narrative which has apparently arisen spontaneously from her inner life and dramatizes her emotional isolation, desire for a hero partner, and yet fear of the serpent of sleep that could dash such consummate hopes.

While there are certain allusions to images from her conscious life, she further unfolds a mythopoetic, dynamic summons of the hero energy to rise out of the lethargic, telluric powers of the unconscious, only for that regressive serpent to bite the heel of her animus-carrier Chiwantopel, an Aztec chieftain. Jung diagnoses this toxification of the hero energy as a fatal dissociation which threatens her ego stability. Years later, in his 1925 seminars, he further recognizes that he was projecting his own semi-morbid anima state onto the text of Ms. Miller's narrative. As he was able to track how Ms. Miller's unconscious autonomously tracked those elements which urgently sought expression from deep within her, so he was able later to track his own autonomous processes in his mid-life passage in a work we now know of as *The Red Book*. In his work first on Ms. Miller, and then upon himself, he discovered for all of us the usefulness of finding the particular images behind our emotions, and thereby begin that most difficult of conversations: the *Auseinandersetzung*, or dialogical exchange between ego consciousness and the unconscious.

Additionally, Jung defined that energy which produced images as deriving from "the transcendent function." Jung posits that the self-regulating system we call our psyche, seeks its own healing and wholeness; thus image formations which carry transforma-tive energies in bodily states, affective expressions, dream images or symptoms, participate in both the conscious and unconscious fields and are apprehensible to both. When consciousness can align its hierarchy of choices with the seeming guidance from the unconscious, the person will experience healing, energy flow, and a general feel of the rightness of one's life at that moment. Most of the time we experience, and over-ride, the promptings from the uncon-scious, but to be able to ally with them is to serve a developmental, healing agenda. To be able to stand on the bridge traversing these two energy streams, without slipping from one side to the other, is to experience an enlargement in our relationship to soul.

In still another substantive way, we observe the power of creativity working through all of us. The power of constructing an image (*Einbildungskraft*) is native to each. Perhaps we may even say that the survival of our frangible branch of the perduring evolutionary tree is tied to this imaginal power. Whenever we experience something, it is a phenomenal event; what follows are the epiphenomenal exfoliations. So, warned or not warned, every infant will touch the hot iron or the dazzling flame. The quick shot of distress which rushes through its system is rapidly connected to an imaginal rendering, perhaps summarized as "that category of experience is painful; proximity to that object/situation seemingly caused that event, and therefore avoidance will serve to protect from future painful experience." That micro-story, spun forth in milli-seconds, will join thousands which enable, empower, protect, inhibit and rechannel the movement of libido in the context around it.

The moment an event of moment occurs, the human psyche begins to spin a narrative thread around that phenomena. The larger, or more sustained, the event, the more embroidered the narrative becomes. So, we become an assemblage of narrative fragments, some more developed than others, some more fragmentary than others. It is for this reason, for example, that one is forever examining, unconsciously serving, trying to get away from, or trying to heal the parent-child narratives. Generally speaking, what is more powerful in our formative lives than our first, primal, sustained experiences of self and Other, and the traffic in between? While other experiences may allow us to reposition, or even surpass the power of these imaginal constructions, they remain at the heart of our core narrative when self engages other.

One way of describing much depth psychological work is to make these imaginal narratives to which one is in service more conscious, and if possible to reframe them. The philosophical and argumentative fallacy known as the *post-hoc, propter hoc* says that just because A preceded B, A did not necessarily cause B. But it takes a lot of work to separate the received narrative, especially since it has been reinforced so many, many times in one's life. We hear, "well, that is just the way I am," or "it is always that way," or "I am really screwed up from the beginning," and so on. Separating one's journey from the narrative that adaptive imagination has woven for it is often the work of a life time, given how powerful these primal stories are, how much they have been reinforced through repetition, and how institutionalized in our lives they have become.

These fractal stories arise out of our archetypal need to understand, at least to stand in some relationship to the mystery in which we swim at all times. Just as the ancients stared at the heavens and wove narratives to explain their sidereal tangents, so we interpret the world around us on a daily basis. We cannot attribute to normal ego powers the narratives that show up in our dreams every night. In other studies I have, for example, recounted stunningly profound, imaginative dreams which confronted the ego consciousness of the dream with all the magic, terror, and wonder of our encounters with raw nature.

Of the thousands of dreams with which I have worked as an analyst, just let me summarize two to provide illustrations. In one, a 70-year-old man, about to undertake a rescue mission for his forty-some year-old daughter in another city, dreams he is with a magician in tuxedo and top hat, which he associated with his analyst. Together they are called upon to perform an autopsy on dreamer's long dead Mother. As they reluctantly near the casket the corpse arises to reveal it is instead his deceased wife who announces that she is back, and that "she rules here." She ascends from the casket, kisses the dreamer a bitter, acidic kiss on the lips and floats away, leaving him shaken.

First of all, who would consciously make up something like this dream? Throughout his life he had been conditioned to take care of a wounded woman, beginning with his Mother, electing to marry a troubled woman who died earlier of chronic alcoholism, and here he was about to embark on another mission of rescue. While one would not, in the abstract, criticize a Father offering help to a daughter, the dream arose to tell him that this was one more chapter in a long history of his captivation by a story. In that story, he had no choice but to associate with, and take care of, the wounded other. Two of the specific personages were now dead, but the narrative they formed was alive and still compelling him.

In this dream we see the Faulknerian adage that the past is not dead, and that it is not even past. The recognition of patterns in our lives, especially those which undermine our own legitimate self-interest, is ample testimony to the living presence of affect-laden, imaginal threads with the power to compel ego assent, provide ready rationalizations to legitimize the complex, and enact the script to which that image is attached. Such images ripple through our lives, steer the course of empires, and constitute the fate of nations as well.

The problem with a complex is that it has no imagination. Given that its "narrative" may have been a profound epiphenomenal mis-reading of primal events, and that the individual is quite capable of other courses of action, the monothematic character of a complex dictates the imprisoning cycle of Ixion's wheel, condemned to repetition until countered by a still larger imaginal possibility. The gift of dreams, symptoms, encounters with wisdom literature, and other modes of insight and inspiration are specifically counter to the iron wheel of complex and its grim repetition. The magnificence, the imaginal ingenuity of this dream, the emotional charge, impressed both dreamer and analyst with the recognition of, and the power of, both the determinisms of history playing out unto the third generation, and the presence of some larger force field that wishes his healing, and his release from the iron grip of the goddess Ananke, the terrible deity of Necessity.

Let one more example suffice for now. The most memorable dream I got while still in training in Zurich many decades ago came from a German woman who had lost both of her parents during and after WWII. She had known only a harsh step-mother in her developing years. At puberty she became severely bulimic and nearly died. Her life was saved during a stay in a clinic in Zurich. But now, in mid-life, she lived alone, had a rigid, severely astringent life-style, controlled eating and relational behaviors, and made her living as a translator and language tutor. While gifted intellectually, she had not gotten higher education, and lived a very modest life in virtually agoraphobic isolation.

One day she brought a dream whose power had shaken her. She is holding a doll, which she also knows in the dream is the simulacrum of her own childhood, when a witch enters the room and steals the doll. She pursues the witch in panic to retrieve this important doll. The witch refuses money but says she will only return the doll/child if the dreamer performs three tasks (as was so common in the Maerchen of medieval tradition): make love with a fat man, give a lecture at Universitat-Zurich, and return to Germany to have a meal with her still living Step-Mother. When the dreamer told her dream she was well aware of the symbolic tasks the witch's agenda asked. To make love with the fat man would be to come to terms with her body, which had always seemed alien to her, to sexuality, and to intimacy in general when that field of energy had always been painful for her. To give the public lecture would be to embrace her fine mind and her intellective gifts. Most challenging of all, to willingly return to the "evil Step-Mother," and to break bread with her, would be to break the iron grip of her understandable "story" prejudiced by the dark side of Great Mother, the archetype of life, an encounter which had mostly brought her hurt, denigration, and abandonment.

Again, we see the power of the primal imagination to weave a counter-image to the imaginative embroideries only possible to the child. The ego-imaginal limitations which constrict us in our "readings" of the phenomenal world, are ultimately countered, corrected, compensated by the larger "reading" which can arise from the soul. When we are able to separate the earlier readings from our identification with them, to see them as "readings," not reality, then we can open to the larger realm which wishes to be expressed in the world through us. In other words, each of us has to learn we are not what happened to us, attached as we are to our epiphenomenal stories. We are what wants to enter the world through us.

The imaginative range of complexes is severely limiting. The powers of conscious life, ideologies, and cultural forces are also limiting. But encounters with the soul, with the reality of the psyche, summon one to a larger life, a larger risk, a larger imagination than the limiting purview of ego consciousness. As Christopher Fry observed, affairs then become soul-sized. In the end, as noted through Rilke in the epigraph, and Plato before him in *The Meno*, such knowledge is the re-membrance of the soul, which has its locus in a realm much larger than consciousness.

References

Coleridge, S. T. (2014). *Biographia Literaria*. Edinburgh: Edinburgh University Press.

Hollis, J. (2002). *The Archetypal Imagination*. College Station: Texas A. and M. University Press.

Jung, C. (1967). *Symbols of Transformation. Collected Works, Vol. 5*. Princeton: Princeton University Press.

_____. *The Red Book*. (2009). S. Shamdasani, ed. New York: Norton and Norton Inc.

Schopenhauer, A. (1995). *The World as Will and Representation*. New York: Everyman Press.

Chapter 2

Painting and Being Painted: A Portrait

by Ann Ulanov

An experience of painting and being painted locates itself in a specific context, how this comes about and with what intent. Next, a process unfolds as the path of this event. But right away the painter and the painted are in the thick of it, being prompted into surprising directions, then interrupted, even subverted, full of excitement and unease. The unconscious walks in like an animal, adding its own processes to the invitation from the President of Union Theological Seminary to sit for my portrait, to be hung in the public Social Hall of the school along with pictures of illustrious ancestral faculty already hanging there. This venture is sponsored by the Institute of Art, Religion & Social Justice with the aim of stimulating fresh conversation between the artist and faculty member about their respective fields of study through the lens of social justice, an abiding focus of the seminary.

I had to be persuaded of the necessity of live sittings, instead of also painting from photographs. The time required for the space of the painting to come into being—how could we find it with both of us working and involved in our separate creative endeavors, for TM Davy, the artist, his own paintings, and teaching and later another commission that overlapped with ours, and for me my work with patients, writing, public lecturing, and lingering work with three PhD students and their dissertations, subsequent to my retiring my professorship the previous June 2014.

In TM's firmness about live sittings, I could feel a force of creative urge that had its own insistence to be honored. I consented, indeed, surrendered inhibitions and hesitations and came to see TM was absolutely right. An alive painting needs a living process. The finished portrait whom I knew to be of me, had an uncanny assertion of her own presence, a subject in her own right for whom TM and I were objects, but, even more so, subjects in relation to her subject-ness[1]. In other words, our interchange with each other, in the context of art, religion, and concerns of social justice, in the surround of my apartment and the stuff of paint, authored the true subject of the portrait—she who appeared.

Materia

The materials of a portrait range from physical matter to a hidden vision yet to emerge. We began with location. After photographing me many times in many places, and saying "no" to my request for copies of the pictures, and then drawing pastel sketches of my head, TM finally settled on one corner of my new apartment which was still unsettled, as I had recently moved upon my retirement from the Seminary[2].

---

1   Martin Gayford says of his sitting for Lucien Freud, "The portrait...has developed in Western art...since the age of the pyramids. Its subject is the individuality of a particular person: the sitter...It is also an expression of the mind, sensibility and skills of its creator: the artist...Out of the sittings comes, with luck, a new entity: a picture...that lives on in human memory or disappears—according to its power as a work of art." (Gayford, 2012, p. 20)

2   Union Theological Seminary wants its teachers to live on campus to contribute to community among students, staff, faculty. Hence, when retiring one is changing one's home as well as job, and must scram, as the apartment will be needed for another professor. This unsettling I found to be a great upheaval, both stressful and exciting.

Significantly, only the portrait would preside in the apartment; none of my paintings were hung on the walls during the entire months of our work. TM chose this corner because of the abundant light through the windows, bringing first paper for pastel sketches of my head and then setting up his wooden easel for the canvas. I felt exposed in my new yet to be created home; it was in process as the portrait was going to be. Recalling Rilke's notion that air is the materiality of space, even the air seemed part of the physical stuff we needed to embark on in the portrait (Gass, 199, p.140).

Painting demands the artist love the physical matters of painting, if not always the mathematics of its composition (*cf.* Alberti, 1956; *cf.* Bazzi, 1960). The artist loves the smell and texture of paint, turpentine, soft and bristly brushes bunched in the hand, special paper for each session's palette on which glow blobs of scarlet, white, brown, green, black, yellow, vermillion, fuscia, violet, deep red. Loving color, I was so taken by these lustrous daubs that I photographed them at the beginning of a session and then photographed the palette at the end of that session. Neat rows of gorgeous color ended in smears of conjunctions and separations, imbued with sunlight through the window, appearing as wonderful bits of abstract painting, which I urged TM to add to his repertoire[3].

Still more unsettling than being in the unfinished space of my apartment with boxes and unshelved books all around, was going through my closet to see what I would wear! One's closet is revealing; I submitted. I did not want to be painted in academic gown and hood, seated at the desk before bookcases, as did most of my soon to be colleagues on the wall at the Seminary. So we hunted, finally choosing a navy silk suit with trousers and a violet cashmere throw at the shoulders. Blues, especially darker ones, are my favorites, and when I saw the iris color displayed for sale, I knew absolutely that would be in the portrait. I simply showed it to TM, saying nothing and he, too, saw this iris/violet wool with its iridescent warmth as the necessary complement to the deep navy.

3　See figures 1 and 2.

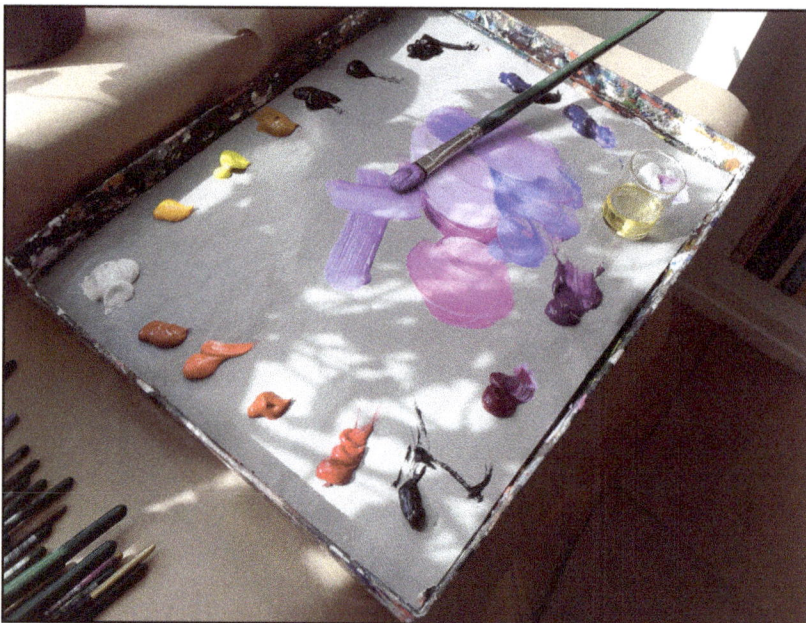

FIGURE 1. *THE PALLET OF T.M. DAVY 1* PHOTO BY A.B. ULANOV

FIGURE 2. *THE PALLET OF T.M. DAVY 2* PHOTO BY A.B. ULANOV

We both felt a certainty, yes, these are the colors. Matisse's words came to mind: "Colours win you over more and more. A certain blue enters your soul....I would simply say that colour exists only through relationships" (Matisse 1952 in Flamm 1978, p.143). Often I posed in this outfit though sometimes remaining in jeans from my earlier morning's writing work, as TM was blocking spaces that day, not painting raiments. We decided on my standing and with some motion in the figure, not like a statue.

TM dressed in black trousers and sweater, sometimes a snug black hat, as it was an exceptionally cold winter and a long one. We worked for three hours every Tuesday for fourteen weeks from January until early May with a few breaks, either because of illness or TM's necessity to paint angels for his other commission. Eventually, the portrait remained in my apartment with its easel but put away, not seen. We never ate, but had water to drink.

TM shows exceptional stamina and poise, standing with his arm elevated to paint, close to the canvas, and at each session's end looking at the painting from a far distance. He is composed physically, and I learned stillness in my standing, glad for a break each morning. It took tremendous aggression to subdue self-conscious nervousness and be still, to focus and relax, to look at the painter and simultaneously to let be, do nothing, drift between postures, glances, aversion of the eyes.

I discovered with surprise that this creative task we dared required conscious work, not only unconscious roots of inspiration. We had to be willing to be in readiness for each session. Again, Matisse's words came to mind, "One gets into a state of creativity by conscious work. To prepare one's work is first to nourish one's feelings by studies which have a certain analogy with the picture" (Matisse 1933, in Flamm 1978, p. 66). For me readings and even work on my own writing in the hours before our three hour session gathered elements in me pertaining to painting—its colors, my postures, even thoughts or sources to discuss with TM or he with me—this was a readiness for whatever might happen. Matisse describes such a happening as "the harmony of all the elements...imposes a spontaneous translation on the mind" (ibid.). The sessions were a workout. Conscious readiness, thoughts that would just appear like unconscious associations to be followed, silences, new possibilities for pose or glance or hand gesture, assembled into feeling for the task.

The materia of painting is also the body with its limits and its presence, both of us drawing on energy for our separate parts of the work. TM's physical resilience evoked my admiration. In contrast, I was ready to lie down after each three-hour session.

The Space in Between

My exhaustion stemmed from my discovery that I was raw material for the painting—consciously in what I brought to our conversations—and in that readiness. In addition, as an introvert to be talking for three hours, even punctuated by silences, wore me out. And, I was stirred, interrupted, by unconscious processes appearing in strange fantasies.

The space opening between TM and me amazed us both. There we were, doing justice work of subverting binary distinctions that exclude if followed as hierarchical prescriptions—he male, I female, he married, I widowed. We conjoined in deep love for our spouses, he for his husband, I for mine though dead very much alive, thus letting loose and surmounting the gap of death. TM younger, I older, yet an intensity of perception between us crossing the gap of age, both of us keen observers of the other's psyche, its unique life. Yet wild parts of each self kept appearing, letting in this untamed part of the world (Hirshfield 1997, p. 159). Trading secrets of religion through a psychological lens, and of psyche through a religious lens, we saw the subject emerging on the canvas, reflecting the specific world of this school that sponsored her becoming.

The woman emerging in the portrait revealed what it meant to work in the Seminary's specific environment--the suffering of its own periods of savage injustice woven into its ardent commitment to justice for each and all; the happiness of its extravagant learning, students coming alive to their vocation to put goodness into the world; the theological breakthroughs of faculty and students bringing the ungraspable God into view[4].

We pushed back obligations to create space in time to be painted and to paint: for the very first time a woman faculty member to display feminine presence in a room full of pictures of men. The fluidity of gender circulated between TM and me. I the male asserting my views and needs, sticking them out, showing him, and he receiving, gestating, creating; he putting forth in painting a seminal creation and I yielding, receiving his power as artist.

A quality of risk existed between us that sprung from what Jung calls the vision of art. This primordial experience is "as if it had emerged from the abyss...some tremendous process that in every way transcends our human feeling and understanding...Is it...of the darknesses of the spirit?" (Jung, 1950/1966, para 141). This "innate drive" in art "that seizes a human being and makes him its instrument...arises from the unconscious depths...from the realm of the Mothers" (ibid. paras. 157, 159).

The portrait thus exerted its own force from an originating point different from our conscious purposes. Both TM and I felt a bit pushed around by the portrait, even at times as if we were objects of its subject. The space between the three of us—TM, the portrait, me--spoke of Mother not as container (a dominant view in current analytic discussions), but as interpenetrating. This underlying matrix "an undifferentiated chaos of magical mentality" (Jung 1931/1966, para 99), penetrated our personal task of doing the portrait replete

---

4   TM caught through me, I believe, something of the rich life of the Seminary in which I had taught for nearly half a century and showed what Jung said: "the artist is the unwitting mouthpiece of the psychic secrets of his time" (Jung, 1934/1966, para. 184). And Erich Neumann catches that ungraspable God hidden in the ordinary, emblematic of the Seminary: "Because in our time the creative principle hides in anonymity and discloses its origin by no divine sign, no visible radiance, no demonstrable legitimacy, we have entered upon the spiritual poverty...the Messiah in the guise of a beggar...What is he waiting for? He is waiting for you. This means that creative redemption...is disguised as an Everyman" (Neumann, 1959, p. 168).

with our hopes, fears, limits and potentials, with an infusion of the unfathomable impersonal abyss, "like a deeply graven river-bed in the psyche, in which the waters of life...suddenly swell into a mighty river" (ibid., para. 127). This impersonal abyss permeated personal aims with autonomous, instinctive, overwhelming, strange, crude, beautiful, generative, "things yet to be" (Jung, 1950/1966, para 141).

The collective history of the school with generations of all male faculty ancestors already hung in its hall, intermingled in our singular project of portrait painting with the collective matrix of the unconscious whose "creative process has a feminine quality." Mixtures occurred of tradition and contemporary focus, male and female subjects, unconscious and conscious processes that led to expressing "something profoundly alive in the soul" (ibid., para. 159; cf. also Deri 1984, 245).

Destructiveness

This mixture of individual and collective brings me back to the appearance of unconscious fantasies--of betrayal in the task of portrayal a portrait demands. The unconscious made itself known through my fear of looking at the portrait as it was being constructed. I laughed at the ease with which Sandra, who took care of my apartment each week, left off vacuuming to walk right up to see the sketches and then oils and give her opinions, which TM took in good stride. I finally got the blunt words of unconscious language to express my obdurate hesitation to look, see. I feared I would not like what I saw and my reaction would interfere with TM's work: I would destroy his creative process. I feared not liking how he saw me and his interpretation would destroy me; I would be destroyed. Destructiveness all around, which dragged with it, a presumption of omnipotence—that to feel or to think is to do, that my feelings could destroy (*cf.* Milner, 1957/1979, chapter 6)[5].

---

5 "Omnipotence of thought: acting as if mere wishes or thoughts were realities, or as if they must have results in the external world" (English, H. B. and English, A. C. 1958, p. 356). Such unconscious forces surface in creativity as Rollo May says,

Destructiveness looms in different guises and moves one to renounce, to encounter, to bear, to mourn. One must give up the aim of a perfect picture and accept the gap between the ideal and the actual. One must confront that painting a face also means deface-ment (Stokes, 1965, p. 24). One must bear being subjected to processes outside one's control. One must take on the work of mourning. We suffer loss--of a perfect match--of an absolute equivalence of what is seen and what is created in the portrait. I cited to TM Giacom-etti's repeated distress in painting James Lord's portrait: "It's going very badly. It's too late. We can't stop now;" "It's impossible to paint a portrait;" "I simply can't seem to reproduce what I see." (Lord, 1965, pp. 9, 10, 23; *cf.* also Kalus and Wilson, (2015 lecture); *cf.* also Ricoeur, 2004/2012, pp. 10, 24).

We can only be faithful to the task at hand, accepting that a portrait can be painted many different ways, that there is no perma-nent image, no stabile, unchanging identity. Fantasies of perfection always bring fantasies of persecution and of revenge for failing to meet the ideal. Aims of self-sufficiency along with the flawless image get destroyed in acknowledging that the life of the subject persists in diversity, and that multiple interpretations exist of how to conceive a portrait. A creative venture offers opportunity to discover others within the self and between the self and the other.

The portrait of one person by one painter, this scrap of partic-ularity, reflects traces of relations with other human beings in life, and in the history of portraiture. Included as well are all the twists and turns of the body, of unconscious processes, even of signs of transcendence untranslatable at the core of existence, safeguarding the secret mystery of an individual while trying to reveal it (Ricoeur, 2004/2012, p. 28).

"Creativity occurs in an act of encounter;" symbols bring "into awareness...archaic, unconscious, longings, dreads...also bring out new meaning, new forms, disclose reality which is literally not present before...a road to universals beyond concrete experience;" "experience of encounter brings with it anxiety...rootlessness, disori-entation...anxiety of nothingness." "The creative person...can live with this anxiety, even though he may pay a high price in terms of insecurity, sensitivity, defenselessness" (Ruitenbeek, 1975, pp.284, 290, 291).

Shock struck me speechless when I did finally look at the beginning oil stage of the portrait. TM had painted there a part of me usually unguessed by others in my daily life. The figure in the portrait was looking into the abyss. That is familiar to me but unknown about me to most others in perceiving me. How did TM see this? Get this? And paint it so believably, convincingly? The portrait figure is standing, the background, blank--simply dark inhabited by a quality of light. She is looking into that dark that also holds a shimmer of light. She is not looking out at the viewer. Having told TM my fantasies of destructiveness, I could tell him my shock that he had perceived me so truly. I felt very pleased to be recognized and said so.

I also felt recognition of something present in or to myself that TM had now made visible in the portrait. That "something" drew me to Jung's notion of archetypal force or form-making, something I had always known was present in the raw material of life itself that will mold a symbol which expresses a truth, not an exactitude nor a replica, as Jung says, "not derived or secondary...not symptomatic of something else...it is an expression of something real but unknown" (Jung 1950/1966, para. 148)[6]. Perception and articulation of that symbolic reality is what makes Jung distinctive and is also what he sees as the arational creative urge in art (Jung, 1950/1966, paras. 135, 139, 141, 147, 159).

I was also able to say to TM that the part of me full of gladness in life's sheer givenness, and attuned to the seriously funny in life, did not seem apparent in the painting and was true of me too. Could we add it, as both parts belonged to me?

---

6   William Meredith-Owen describes such a moment of recognition as "an archetypal intimation" and Joseph Cambray, whom Meredith-Owen also references, describes archetype as emergent meaning (Meredith–Owen (2008,) p.460); Cambray, J, (2006, passim). Matisse declares, "L'exactitude n'est pas la verite" in reference to drawing his own portrait. "There is an inherent truth which must be disengaged from the outward appearance of the object to be represented. This is the only truth that matters" (Matisse, 1947, in Flamm 1978, pp. 119, 117).

Legacy Toward Death

To be a Professor Emerita, from *emereri*, means "to earn one's discharge, to earn out" (Weekley, 1952). My time in this graduate school of religion is done. I have earned my way out and am now gone. Hours posing for this portrait show a willingness to be in life in the world, and yet to mark a period of history, now over, in this institution when you no longer are there but stepping across a threshold into space, new, not yet known. The shimmer of light in the dark background shows this life along with death.

Your legacy is identified by your portrait hanging there in the school's Social Hall long after your death. You bear the burden of history for service given. For me such service of teaching was greatly enjoyed. I feel gratitude to this school and especially to Mrs. Ann Johnson and family to be the first "sitter" of their endowed chair for the Christiane Brooks Johnson Memorial Professor in Psychiatry and Religion. This gift secures the reality of psyche and especially its unconscious processes in theological curriculum, a mark unique to Union.

In the background of our work TM and I are aware of being intensely alive while mindful of death as indicated by this commemorating portrait. Our sense of existence, his painting and my legacy, extends to join others on a wall removed from life while we are here just at this moment in my living room painting and being painted. Our personal labor of the portrait becomes part of a collective—the history of an institution and of a scholarly discipline of psyche and soul, of psychic reality and religion. In this job of painting and being painted, we no longer belong to ourselves, but to unconscious forces of creativity that make such a picture possible and to the collective spirit of the school that sponsors it.

An odd thing happened to both TM and me in the weeks after I asked if the lighter aspects of me might be included in the woman in the portrait. TM agreed, seeing this buoyant joyous side of me as well. But she was not having any of it. The woman in the portrait emerged as a third presence. We had to reckon time and again with her point of view (so to speak). Of course, I saw this was a picture of me, but to my surprise she took on a life of her own, like a definite other conjoining the partnership between TM and me. "She," as I came to call her, pushed us both around and TM even said at the end he had never been so bossed by a painting. We wanted to do certain things, and she would not let us. TM would say, yes, I've got it, but at the end of the session when he gazed at the painting from a long distance, he saw, no, it did not happen; in fact it made it worse. I would ask myself, is this my defense to see her as Other, or is this my recognition of otherness in one's very own self?

FIGURE 3. PORTRAIT OF ANN BELFORD ULANOV
BY T.M. DAVY, 38" X 50", OIL ON LINEN, 2015

The whole project made me laugh and seemed one of those seriously funny things in life—we so diligent and dedicated and then upended by our new cohort with a mind of her own. We moved to follow this insistence from some deep creative root in all three of us. TM changed her viewpoint from away, toward the abyss, to near, looking directly to the viewer. That, and a slight upturn at the corner of the mouth, and the different looking in each of the eyes completed a whole portrait.

She belongs to the viewers now, in the school—to see what happens between her and them.

Jung says, "We let a work of art act upon us as it acted upon the artist. To grasp its meaning, we must allow it to shape us as it shaped him. Then we also understand the nature of his primordial experience...the healing and redeeming depths of the collective psyche, where man is not lost in the isolation of consciousness and its errors and sufferings, but where all men are caught in the common rhythm which allows the individual to communicate his feelings and strivings to mankind as a whole" (Jung, 1950/1966, para 161)[7]. Already in the reception for the unveiling of the portrait viewers caught two sides of the painting, some objecting, saying, where is the light that is in you that I see in you? Others arrested by the light there mixed with the gravity of seeing into the dark, were deeply moved.

I will miss our Tuesdays, and I will miss her.

Aperture and Beyond

Moments happen in painting as in any creative work where an opening occurs in the present to the beyond with an intense vital sense of connectedness between them. Painters agree on the necessity of a childlike consciousness in order to see without impediment of overwhelming projections, prior ideas of what should be there,

---

7   Kris comments, "The reaction of the public repeats in reverse order and in infinite variations some of the processes which the artist experienced...from the fringe to the center" (Kris 1965, 36).

or dominating cultural stereotypes. All those interferences obstruct what happens between the painter and the object. The artist must behold the object, "by continual observation...learn the secrets of embryonic life, of quiverings...One must know how to maintain childhood's freshness of contact with objects...be a child all one's life even while a man, take one's strength from the existence of objects—and not have imagination cut off by the existence of objects" (Matisse, 1952, in Flamm 1978, p. 145). Giacometti insists, "What's essential is to work without preconception, without knowing in a trance what the picture is going to look like...It's very, very important to avoid all preconception, to try to see only what exists....You can't do it. But one must try all the same...to translate one's sensation. It's the only thing I'm interested in." (Lord, 1965/1980, p. 79). He continued, "I should say that now is my childhood, because I'm just learning how to do what I want to do....not at all to see as others have already seen...There's an opening...a real opening. It's the first time in my life that I've had an opening like this" (ibid., p. 110).

That opening is what childlike consciousness begins with, and that we may be lucky enough to return to in creativity. As adults this childlike consciousness without predetermined results imposed on what reality should be is joined by a grownup capacity to reflect, choose, judge, experiment, analyze and unite (synthesize). The creative man, Neumann remarked, stays open to the unconscious (Neumann, 1959, p. 182). For saints, like Marguerite of Porete of the 13th century, that openness occurs even for a "simple soul" in responding to God. The soul opens to an immediacy with God, without mediators of sacraments or priest, and for that she burned. For Marguerite the aperture went one further step: in opening to what is, to unite with the author of all that is. The opening is a fleeting experience of soul to an infusion of divine radiance. This "simple soul" thus makes a space for Love to work in the world (Porete, 1993; Hollywood, 1955, pp. 99, 115).

To the image of aperture and what is beyond, Jung brings a symbol of a portal looked through from the *other* side, from the world of beyond to this world of familiar and daily: "What if there were a living agency beyond our everyday human world...a door that opens upon the human world from a world beyond, allowing unknown and mysterious powers to act upon man and carry him... to a more than personal destiny? "(Jung, 1950/1966, para 148).

We have only this life to live, take the chance.

References

Alberti, L. B. (1970). *Leon Battista Alberti, On Painting*. Trans. J. R. Spenser. New Haven, Ct.: Yale University Press.

Bazzi, M. (1960). *The Artist's Methods and Materials*. Trans. Francesca Priuli. London: John Murray Fifty Albemarle Street.

Cambray, J. (2006). "Towards the feeling of emergence" *Journal of Analytical Psychology* 5, 1, 1-20.

Deri, S. K. (1984). *Symbolization and Creativity*. New York: International Universities Press.

English, H. B. and English, A. C. 1958. *A Comprehensive Dictionary of Psychological and Psychoanalytical Terms*. New York: Longmans, Green and Co.

Gass, W. H. (1999). *Reading Rilke, Reflections on the Problems of Translation*. New York: Knopf.

Gayford, M. (2012). *Man with a Blue Scarf, On Sitting for a Portrait by Lucien Freud*. London: Thames & Hudson.

Hirschfield, J. (1997). *Nine Gates, Entering the Mind of Poetry*. New York: Harper Perennial.

Hollywood, A. (1995). *The Soul as Virgin Wife, Mechtild of Magdeburg, Marguerite of Porete, and Meister Eckhart*. Notre Dame: University of Notre Dame Press.

Jung, C. G. (1931/1966). "On the Relation of Analytical Psychology to Poetry," Collected *Works*, vol. 15. Trans R. F. C. Hull. New York: Pantheon paras. 97-132.

____. (1934/1966). "Ulysses: A Monologue," *CW* 15, paras. 109-203.

____. (1950/1966). "Psychology and Literature," *CW* 15, paras. 133-162.

Kalus, O. and Wilson, L. (2015). "Giacometti's Genius: Understanding the Artist's Creative Process." New York: Lecture to The Association for Psychoanalytic Medicine, February 3.

Kris, E. (1965). "Psychoanalysis and the Study of Creative Imagination," Ed. Hendrik M. Ruitenbeck, *The Creative Imagination*. Chicago: Quadrangle Books, pp. 23-45.

Lord, J. (1965). *A Giacometti Portrait*. New York: Farrar, Straus and Giroux.

Matisse, H. Statement to Teriade, 1933 [On Creativity] in Flamm, J. D. 1978. *Matisse on Art*. New York: E. P. Dutton, p. 66.

_____.1947. *Exactitude is not Truth*, 1947. In Flamm, pp. 117-119.

_____. 1952. *Interview with Verdet*, 1952. In Flamm, pp.142-147.

May, R. (1965). "Creativity and Encounter," Ed. Hendrik M. Ruitenbeck, *The Creative Imagination*. Chicago: Quadrangle Books, pp. 283-293.

Meredith-Owen, W. (2008). "'Go! Sterilize the fertile with thy rage' Envy as embittered desire," *Journal of Analytical Psychology* 53, 4, 459-481.

Milner, M. (1979). *On Not Being Able to Paint*. New York: International Universities Press.

Neumann, E. (1959). *Art and the Creative Unconscious*. Trans. Ralph Manheim. New York: Chilmark Press.

Porete, M. (1993). *The Mirror of Simple Souls*. Trans. Ellen Babinsky. Mahwah, N. J.: Paulist Press.

Ricoeur, P. (2004/2012). *On Translation*. Trans. Eileen Brennan. New York: Routledge.

Stokes, A. (1965). *The Invitation in Art*. New York: Chilmark Press.

Weekley, E. (1952). *Concise Etymological Dictionary of Modern English*. New York: E. P. Dutton.

Chapter 3

Of Creative Powers and Personalities:
Erich Neumann's Theory of the Origins and Nature of Psyche's Creativity

by Murray Stein

A client of many years in analysis recalled a dream that he had several days earlier, which had stayed with him ever since and retained a remarkable degree of vividness. This is the dream as he told it to me:

I am in a group of people from the medical profession. These are outstanding scientists and inventors of new medical technologies. One of them signals me over to the side to show me a new creation. He holds out to me a device with two metal handles that are attached to a basket-like structure which is holding a beating heart. He tells me that this heart has been created purely with stem cells, and this represents a major breakthrough in medicine. I am astonished as I look at this miracle of laboratory creation. It is a real heart made of cells and tissues, and it is beating steadily. I reflect on the incredible recent history of medical technology, beginning with open-heart surgery in the 1950's and continuing in a rapidly accelerating pace through the recent decades with inventions like pacemakers and stents until now this breakthrough. It is as though we had climbed a high mountain and now are looking into the far distance at even higher mountains to climb. I cannot take my eyes off the beating heart. The creator hands it over to me, and I take the handles and carry the beating heart over to my young daughter to show her this miracle of science. I realize that it will be only in her generation and her children's generation that the full impact of this creation will be recognized and fully integrated into medical practice.

As he tells me of this experience in the night, I sense his deep emotion. He continues to visualize the image of the beating heart, he says, and he has been meditating on it. He cannot remember a more impressive dream, and he has been recording dreams for decades by now. To me, this symbol seems to sum up a long span of personal development and inner creativity, which I will not interpret in this context. The image at the center of the dream is numinous, in a strong sense of that loaded word: it is awesome and inspiring. It signals a new creation.

This account strikes me as exactly to the point of what Erich Neumann describes in his essay, "Creative Man and Transformation": "This is our situation. We stand before the creative principle. Wherever we find the creative principle... we venerate it as the hidden treasure that in humble form conceals a fragment of the godhead" (Neumann, 1954/1959, p. 168). In this dream, the subject stands in awe of *human* creativity. It is Promethean. But there is recognition, too, that this new creation is the result of the mysterious creativity in nature, in the stem cells; it is not a purely human creation, although humans participate in it. The new creation—this beating heart—is a result of an interaction between human and nature's creativity. It is this combination that produces the stimulus for wonder and admiration. It is miraculous and, as Neumann says, "conceals a fragment of the godhead." For Neumann, creativity and divinity are, let's say, synonymous, and somehow the godhead has come to reside also in the human psyche as its creativity.

Neumann was obviously fascinated by what he calls in his mature writings, "the vital principle" and sometimes "the creative principle." Considering his *oeuvre* as a whole, which began haltingly in the 1930's and then accelerated rapidly after the Second World

War to achieve full authority by the time of his early death at the age of 55 in 1960, one cannot miss how much of it is dedicated to the theme of creativity. The works that focus explicitly on creativity and its expression in art and literature are: "Kafka's 'The Trial.' An Interpretation through Depth Psychology" (1933/1958); "Art and Time" (1951); "Leonardo da Vinci and the Mother Archetype" (1954); "Creative Man and Transformation" (1955); "Creative Man and the 'Great Experience'" (1956); "Chagall and the Bible" (1958); "A Note on Marc Chagall" (1954); "Georg Trakl: The Person and the Myth" (1959); *The Archetypal World of Henry Moore* (1959); and "Psyche as the Place of Creation" (1960). However, it must also be said that all of his works are in one way or another concerned with the topic of creativity and "the new." (As an aside, his name translates from German to English as New-man.) Creativity was a fundamental theme in all of Neumann's writings and is perhaps even the main trunk of his considerable body of work. He was deeply gripped by a sense of a new future coming into being in modern cultures and by new "forms" (Gr. *Gestaltungen*), inner and outer, arising out of a seemingly inexhaustible Source. His high respect for this Source is of a religious caliber. To say that Neumann is referring implicitly to *Ein Sof*, the Kabbalistic term for the wellspring of creation, would not be off the mark. (He was after all a student of Kabbalah and Jewish mysticism.) His fascination with creativity and creative power was as evident with respect to his outer life as a young Zionist in Palestine participating in the birth of a new nation as it was to his inner life as an individuating personality and in his brilliant contributions to analytical psychology.

Neumann was a theoretical thinker par excellence and did not hesitate to build immense metapsychological constructions of cathedral-like proportions. In this respect, he differed from his teacher, Jung, who as an "empiricist" was much more cautious in setting out his hypotheses and mostly would only cast hints and suggest possible directions for more speculative thinking and further research. Neumann took him up on this, and in turn Jung recognized and admired Neumann's bold contributions, looking upon them as significant additions to his pioneer work. I think we would be well advised to follow Jung in his estimation of Neumann's contributions.

Sadly, much of Neumann's work has been overlooked or undervalued by the field of analytical psychology as it has grown and evolved since Jung's death. One hopes that this neglect will be rectified now with the publication of the extensive and revealing correspondence between Neumann and Jung, *Analytical Psychology in Exile*. Jung writes a sharp letter of rebuke to Jolande Jacobi, who was venomously critical of Neumann's early essay, "Mystical Man": "I think that Neumann's work is excellent. It is not a dogmatic system, but a structured account, thought through in minute detail... One needs to think with him, otherwise one is lost. I even recommend a careful reading of his lecture ["Mystical Man"]" (Jung and Neumann, 2015, p. xli). Thus Neumann came to be known as the "thinking Jungian." Jung supported and defended the work of Neumann consistently and throughout his high profile career as a lecturer at Eranos (1948-1960) and as an author of such classics as *Depth Psychology and the New Ethic, The Origins and History of Consciousness, Amor and Psyche,* and *The Great Mother.* Indeed, there is evidence that he regarded him as his most promising student and successor. At the Eranos Conferences, Neumann came to be recognized as Jung's stand-in as spiritual center and intellectual leader after Jung retired from regular attendance following his lecture on synchronicity in 1951. In fact, Olga Fröbe-Kapteyn, the founder of Eranos and owner of its beautiful grounds on Lago Magiore in Switzerland, intended to leave the estate to Neumann upon her death for his lifetime (Bernadini). Unfortunately, he died before she did.

What I would like to do in this essay is to give an account of Neumann's theory of creativity as expressed primarily in two essays, "Creative Man and Transformation" and "The Place of Creation" and with brief reference to a number of his other works. These two essays were originally lectures given at the Eranos Conferences in 1954 and 1960 respectively. I will not try to explain why the subject of creativity was so important to Neumann, since I have no documented sources or evidence for that and choose not to speculate. Without question, however, the topic of creativity fascinated him and gripped him throughout his life with a kind of religious passion.

Creative Powers in Nature and Human Beings ("The Place of Creation," Eranos Lecture, 1960)

I will begin by reading Neumann backward, from the high perspective of his very late work, "The Place of Creation." This was his last lecture at Eranos, presented in August 1960, only a few months before his death in December. At the time, he did not know that he was seriously ill, so his demise came as a surprise to all, including his family. Even he was not aware that he was dying to the very end (Neumann, J.).

In this densely packed essay, which summarizes much of his previous writing on creativity and brings it to a culminating metapsychological summit, he gives expression to a theory that is all-embracing, extending from the most primitive manifestations of created order in the mineral and plant worlds to the most sublime level, the psychological. Looking back from this vantage point, one can recognize how the earlier works fall into a consistent pattern. One of Neumann's intellectual guides in this endeavor of creating a general theory of creativity was Adolf Portmann, the marine zoologist and fellow star Eranos lecturer; the other was, of course, C.G. Jung, his friend and most important mentor.

I will summarize the argument briefly. In this late essay, Neumann delineates three aspects of this creative power. In his vision, it can clearly be said, all manifestations of creativity, whether purely natural, human or transpersonal (archetypal), are fundamentally expressions of what he calls the Vital Principle (VP), or sometimes alternatively the Creative Principle. This is the driving force behind all of creation, a sort of God-factor, which is why I choose to capitalize it. Within or closely alongside the Vital Principle, there is a mysterious center that is responsible for order and form. This is the Ordering Agency (OA), a second aspect of the God-factor. By itself, the VP would create an excess of multiplicity. Its rampant profligacy is delimited and shaped by the OA. This dual process is exemplified in the creation of "species" in the animal world, for example: Each individual animal belongs to a species, which contains the plentitude of living beings in that order. Without the effective operation of the OA and its form-creating potency, chaotic multiplicity would prevail and spill out of all boundaries beyond measure. With the establishment of species, the animal world becomes ordered.

The combined action of the Vital Principle and the Ordering Agency is responsible for "creation" (in German, *Gestaltung*—Neumann, 1960/1989, p. 32). However, Neumann adds a third factor, the Directing Agency (DA), thus setting up a Trinity of powers for creation. This factor "arises out of the unitary 'field,' in which 'outside space with centers' and unicellular organisms distributed in the field are brought together in an orderly arrangement under unitary direction" (Neumann, 1960/1989, p. 333-4). The DA is teleologically oriented and gives the processes of creativity evolutionary direction, ultimately meaning and a sense of destiny.

This interplay of factors—dynamic (VP), shaping (OA), goal-oriented (DA)—results in ceaseless creative activities that take place from the most basic levels of existence—Neumann uses the example of the slime mold to illustrate this process at the unicellular level (Neumann, 1960/1989, p. 332)—to the most exalted plane in the human personality. At the human level, thanks to the presence of sufficient and adequate sensory and neurological networks, this Trinity implants itself in the human psyche, which will now give the creative powers specifically human, i.e., cultural, expression.

This stage of evolutionary development, where the Trinity is humanized, was long in preparation. In the course of cosmic and planetary evolution, ever more complex and refined orders have come into being through the activities of the extraneous (to the human psyche) Trinity of creative forces. This resulted, on our planet, in the formation of species within the animal kingdom. For animals in general, behavior is species-controlled. In-born instinctive reaction-patterns strictly rule behavior. Neumann describes this as a step in the "migration-into-the-interior of knowledge" (Neumann, 1960/1989, p. 341), replacing the purely "extraneous knowledge" of the "field" that had previously ruled creation. This migration was made possible by developments in the sensory organs and nervous systems of members of the animal kingdom. When humans appear on the scene, the physical and anatomical advances in the species result in the strict rules of species behavior to be loosened in favor of more conscious choice and freedom. There is now a distinctively human personality. In the human being (*Homo sapiens*), an organism has been created with the necessary means to take up and extend the project of ordering, of adapting to environments, and indeed of creating new forms. In this, Neumann concurs, whether deliberately or unconsciously, with the Biblical view that humankind is the highpoint (so far) of creation and indeed has received the gift of the imago Dei, if one considers the three factors mentioned (VP, OA and DA) as a representation of the Godhead, the Creator.

In short, this Trinity of previously extraneous creative powers enters into the human personality and is now housed there. This is the source of human creativity.

Having laid down the basic principles for creation and creative power, Neumann turns in his essay to taking a closer look at the development of human culture. How does this Trinity of creative powers develop on the human level? Neumann is a "stages of development" thinker, and here he draws on his earlier work, *The Origins and History of Consciousness*, to outline the major stages of humankind's cultural evolution. He describes three main stages of cultural development and a fourth one presently in progress.

1. The Primordial Stage. This stage in humanity's history (corresponding more or less to the existence of *Homo Neanderthalensis*) endured over countless millennia—some three hundred thousand years, according to Neumann (Neumann, 1960/1989, p. 343)—without significant cultural advance or change. It was a kind of slow incubation stage for culture. No creativity, or only the most basic sort in crude tool making, is in evidence in this long period of (pre- or proto-) human culture. The individuals are still largely dominated by strict species-guided adaptations as expressed at the small group (or family) level. This is not far removed from the tightly controlled collectivity that is found in the previous animal ancestors. In the Primordial period, there is no sign of the human psyche "characterized by 'continuous creative formation,' which we regard as characteristic of the human species" (Neumann, 1960/1989, p. 344). The Trinity of creative powers operates largely outside of the individual and has not yet entered into the individual psyche because there is no suitable home for it; human "personality" is not yet in place to receive it.

2. The Matriarchal Stage. In this stage, which began inexplicably about forty thousand years ago, there is a major breakthrough. (This corresponds to the appearance of Cro-Magnon culture, or "European early modern humans.") Here, a type of human consciousness begins to emerge quite dramatically. Humans show evidence of a personality on a collective level and are beginning to express creative powers in an entirely unprecedented fashion. Now we find evidence of symbolic expression and archetypal images in the form of clay figurines, cave paintings and other art works, and more advanced technologies. But individual consciousness, in the form of the individual ego, remains relatively unknown throughout this stage. Furthermore, no consistent cultural traditions are established on the collective level. Human experience remains "confined to an inspirational and mantic psychic activity... though this activity was already fully capable of forging morality and producing rituals" (Neumann, 1960/1989, p. 345). Humans in this stage live in a symbolic world and have a "biopsyche," while the nascent ego is passive and observant, according to Neumann, and not active. Elsewhere he calls this a "moon ego" (Neumann, 1950/1994). The archetypal images are received (whether from within or without makes no difference because all is symbolic) and recorded but not worked over and developed by an active, engaged, individual ego-consciousness. The Vital Principle and the Ordering Agency are emerging within the human psyche on a collective level, but conscious intervention and intentionality are minimal. At this stage, humans are symbol-receivers, not symbol-makers.

3. The Patriarchal Stage. This stage inaugurates "the increasingly independent ego and the self-organizing and systematizing conscious mind... man has reached the phase of the actively creative and formative psyche, which involves a completely new kind of takeover of the process of creation from the biopsyche into the psyche of man" (Neumann, 1960/1989, p. 347). It is a leap forward to a new kind of creativity on the part of humankind. Beside this, a creative inwardness appears with "a tendency towards individualization, spearheaded by its outstanding exponent in evolution, the ego-consciousness of man" (Neumann, 1960/1989, p. 347). We now begin to find "Great Individuals" as represented in culture by the King and the Priest. The notion of the individual gradually takes hold, which will generalize from the few to the many over time. Traditions begin to take shape in the form of distinct myths and priesthoods, and there is a deliberate preservation of symbolic material in the form of tablets, temples, and ritual action.

At this stage of development, the human psyche divides. A gap opens, or widens significantly, between ego-consciousness and unconscious processes. The modern psyche, capable of neurotic conflict, begins to emerge. The tension that results between ego and unconscious also sets the stage for a special form of creativity unknown previously in the history of the planet, which draws on the unconscious processes on the one hand and is shaped and carried further by the ego on the other. The freedom and independence of the ego to shape and execute, in tension with the unconscious (vital) processes that actively impinge on ego-consciousness in various ways (visions, intuitions, fantasies, dreams), makes possible the unique form of creativity that we see in this stage and continuing into our own modern times.

The Trinity of creation is also somewhat divided in this process, however, in accordance with the division of the psyche into conscious and unconscious components. The aspects of the Trinity are distributed into different parts of the personality. The Vital Principle is housed basically in the unconscious, while the Ordering Agency takes up its home quite strongly, though not exclusively, in the ego. The Directing Agency continues to do its work in the depths of the collective unconscious, guiding the large-scale evolutionary prospective developments in the history of humankind.

As we see in this section of the essay, Neumann grants tremendous significance to the role of the active (Patriarchal) ego for human creativity. Its emergence plays a decisive role in how creativity is expressed in the human world, in culture and its evolution. However, he is a Jungian and so does not want to attribute too much value and power to the ego. The development of a strong ego is the contribution of Patriarchy, but it is also only a step on the way to a further psychological development.

4. The Individuation Stage. The strong ego-development in the Patriarchal stage is superseded by the intensification of "inwardness," which discovers the ego's source of creative power in the self. (The term self is used here in the Jungian sense of being the center and totality of the personality, unconscious and conscious included.) In this stage, humans come to recognize the self as the center of creative processes and powers in the psyche, and the ego as agent of the self. This is the modern era, and depth psychology enters the picture to radically change consciousness. In this essay and elsewhere, Neumann speaks of this development as the realization of the "ego-self axis" (his term). This development surpasses the contribution of Patriarchy and takes the evolution of human consciousness a step further. The emergence of the ego-self axis into consciousness brings with it the awareness of the "self field," which overcomes the division between ego-consciousness and the unconscious on a new level. This is not a regression to the earlier stage of minimal differentiation in the psyche, i.e., the matriarchal; it is a new stage of self-realization on a conscious level. Now, from the vantage point of the ego-self axis, the creative process can be apprehended as a product of concerted action between both aspects of the personality.

While Neumann does not spell out the details of this fourth and post-patriarchal stage of cultural evolution in this late essay, he strongly suggests its basic outlines. (This development is brilliantly put forward in his earlier essay, "The Psyche and the Transformation of the Reality Planes: A Metapsychological Essay.") Much of his late work pertains to overcoming the one-sidedness of patriarchy and the retrieval of the feminine principle, to be integrated into the cultural canon as established by patriarchy. His conceptualization of the ego-self axis is his signature contribution to this vision of a possible cultural future.

Going beyond the patriarchal ego into the next stage of consciousness and personality development requires an intense intensification of what he calls inwardness. This is not an end in itself but only a tool for the discovery of the true nature of psychic reality. What the patriarchal ego will discover here is that its vaunted ability to utilize the Ordering Principle is not its own but depends on open access to the self. The Trinity of creative powers has set up a new dwelling place in the self. This is now separate from its original location in the "extraneous field"—equivalent for Neumann to the *unus mundus*, the unified field that underlies all of reality—but it of course remains connected to it, mirroring it in the human being. In the human personality, the self houses the Trinity of creation, and the developed and conscious ego recognizes that it is, as it were, an agent of the self, carrying out the function of the Ordering Principle. When the ego aligns with the self, forming the ego-self axis, it works alongside the Vital Principle of the self. Out of this combination arises human creativity in its supreme expression.

In Jung's theory, these two aspects in the self (the VP and the OA) could be conceived as anima and animus, the syzygy. Anima is the Vital Principle, the source of energy and imagination and fantasy; Animus is the Ordering Principle, executing its will through the ego function. The ego recognizing this and, working with the self, freeing itself of the one-sided commitment to the patriarchal canon and attitudes, gives equal place to the feminine principle. Without the anima, the Ordering Principle becomes sterile and empty of creative potential. Masculine and feminine working in tandem signals the next stage of evolution within human culture.

In the fourth stage, then, the ego is taken up into the Trinity of creation and becomes a participant in its creative activities as a fourth power. Thus the quaternity is completed. When the ego does this, it experiences individual life as destiny. This is the individualization of the Directing Agency, which when lifted into consciousness brings awareness of the meaning of existence, individual and collective, of humankind and nature as a whole. This is what Neumann calls the experience of "inner being," and this goes beyond inwardness, which is merely the means for getting to this level of consciousness. The experience of inner being is equivalent to the conscious experience of the ego-self axis as a unified quaternitarian totality.

Creative Personalities ("Creative Man and Transformation," Eranos lecture, 1954)

Looking back from Neumann's last lecture at Eranos in 1960 to an earlier one given in 1954 entitled "Creative Man and Transformation," I will discuss now his analysis of the creative individual. One clearly hears resonances in this earlier essay with the thinking laid out in 1960, as I will draw out. These ideas were already in the background of Neumann's mind as he considered those exceptional human beings that we regard as "creative personalities."

For the creative personality, Neumann writes, "[t]he creative principle is so deeply rooted in the deepest and darkest corner of his unconscious, and in what is best and highest in his consciousness, that we can comprehend it only as the fruit of his whole existence" (Neumann, 1954/1959, p. 169). Thus creative individuals in their whole being, conscious and unconscious, are given over to the creative process that takes hold of them in often overpowering ways. The Trinity of creation grips them and the ego-self axis takes over control of their lives, at least for a period of time. It is a kind of birth-giving process in which the entire personality is involved and seized by the effort.

What is being born in this type of creative process, writes Neumann, is an aspect of the "symbolic world." This invisible world of symbols is being transformed into a specific image or idea that will be brought into consciousness by the creative personality. Thus the creative person is a kind of medium or channel for symbols to come into the light in the world of consciousness. The creative principle, which takes hold of the creative personality like a daimon, is deeply linked to the symbol-making power of psyche, which in his later essay Neumann would call the "Ordering Principle." The creative personality, therefore, is an essential participant in transforming symbols from unconscious to conscious psychic reality. In this essay, Neumann places strong emphasis on the role of the creative personality as symbol-maker and on the great value this has for culture. He writes: "It cannot be stressed enough that the key to a fundamental understanding, not only of man, but of the world as well, is to be sought in the relation between creativity and symbolic reality. Only if we recognize that symbols reflect a more complete reality than can be encompassed in the rational concepts of consciousness can we appreciate the full value of man's power to create symbols. To regard symbolism as an early stage in the development of the rational, conceptual consciousness involves a dangerous underestimation of the makers of symbols and of their functions..." (Neumann, 1954/1959, p. 169). The symbol captures unitary reality prior to and beyond the split between "inner" and "outer," and the creative personality is the agent for making this symbolic reality visible.

The special thing about creative personalities is that they can perform this function for humankind because of the profound connection they maintain to the unitary world. Unlike normal personalities, they do not severely cut the link to the symbolic world as they develop into adults. Again, Neumann uses a developmental schema to explain this special gift, which does not come without a price.

For creative personalities, the stages of development when ego consciousness separates from the unconscious and engages strongly in the challenge to adapt to the cultural canon and its norms are different from that of so-called normal personalities. In the creative personality, the link to the archetypes remains much more intact and does not, as it does in the normal case, transfer fully over to the personal complexes and the reality principle, the ego complex.

This line of development sets up a particular challenge and tension of its own, different from that of the normal personality: "...the difference between the creative and the normal man... resides in an intensified psychic tension that is present in the creative man from the very start. In him a special animation of the unconscious and an equally strong emphasis on the ego and its development are demonstrable at an early stage" (Neumann, 1954/1959, p. 180). It is not that in the creative personality psychological development is necessarily retarded or arrested in the matriarchal stage with its weak ego and its close or even embedded connection to the unconscious. In the creative personality, there is a dual development: ego development may be similar to that of the patriarchal stage, but it is accompanied by an intensification of the presence of the unconscious rather than a distancing and reduction. This dual development will create problems in adaptation to the cultural canon, but at the same time it allows for creativity powerfully to take place within this personality.

Neumann marvels at this extraordinary development evident already in childhood: "In this state of alertness the child is open to a world, to an overwhelming unitary reality that surpasses and overpowers him on all sides... this waking sleep... is the unforgettable possession of the creative man... and we... marvel that the creative man should remain fixated in this stage and its experiences... From childhood onward the creative individual is captivated by his experience of the unitary reality of childhood; he returns over and over again to the great hieroglyphic images of archetypal existence. They were mirrored for the first time in the well of childhood and there they remain until, recollecting, we bend over the rim of the well and rediscover them, forever unchanged" (Neumann, 1954/1959, p. 80-1).

He wonders how this development can be possible because it seems to defy the normal sequence from the matriarchal stage of embeddedness in the unconscious world to the patriarchal stage of separation from the unconscious and consequent ego independence. If the conscious personality remains so deeply connected to the invisible unitary world—the "mother"—there must be a lacuna where the "father" should step in and draw the personality out of the maternal background. Certainly a danger lies here. With father weak or absent, the developing creative personality risks being arrested or even swallowed up and devoured by the mother. In such a case, the archetypal world would rule and insufficient ego strength would be present to function resourcefully in the world. A state of possession, even psychosis, could be the net result. Madness surely lies there. Neumann writes: "In the perpetual tension between an animated and menacing archetypal world and an ego reinforced by purposes of compensation, but possessing no support in the conventional father archetype, the ego can lean only upon the self, the center of individual wholeness, which, however, is always infinitely more than individual" (Neumann, 1954/1959, p. 187). This is the challenge handed out to the creative personality. A way to lean on the self and draw support from it must be found and utilized.

In fact, many creative personalities have not survived the onslaught of the "menacing archetypal world," and Neumann writes about such an individual in his essay on the young genius poet, Georg Trakl, who died in 1914 at the age of twenty-seven from an overdose of cocaine, evidently a suicide, after suffering severe trauma in the early stages of WWI. In the story of Trakl's early life, Neumann finds a powerful activation of the archetypal world combined with childhood trauma and a passive-to-absent father, so minimal ego structure came into play and certainly not enough to survive the brutalities of severe conditions. Under mild circumstances, Trakl could manage, with assistance from friends (Ludwig Wittgenstein, for example, supported him financially for a time), and in this phase of his life he was able to write his magnificent verse, which was heavily loaded with symbolic imagery. One does not know what might have become of him had he come through the war years and lived a longer life. The question is: could he have found a way to "lean upon the self," as Neumann writes? And would this have supplied him with the needed stability to survive subsequent strong activations of the unconscious, to which he was so closely bound? As Neumann analyzes his life and poetry, he finds in Trakl what he calls, quoting his work, "The Moon and Matriarchal Consciousness," a "moon ego"—"It is a 'lunatic' in every sense of the term and its fate is a lunar fate. It is bound to the realm of the nocturnal" (Neumann, 1959/1979, p. 226). This is creative personality with great vulnerability in patriarchal culture. But it is also vulnerable from within when the creative powers of the unconscious become strongly activated.

The now aged doyen of literary criticism in America, Harold Bloom, touchingly admits the fear of engaging directly with such creative powers in his most recent book, *The Daimon Knows*. There he writes: "I have been rereading *Moby-Dick* since I fell in love with the book in 1940, a boy of ten enthralled with Hart Crane, Whitman, William Blake, Shakespeare... a visionary company that transformed a changeling child into an exegetical enthusiast adept at appreciation rather than into a poet. A superstitious soul, then and now, I feared being devoured by ravenous daemons if I crossed the line into creation" (Bloom, 2015, p. 122). Instead of engaging the daimons directly, Bloom perhaps wisely decided to study the works of the daimon-possessed in the universe of imaginative literature. His all-time favorite poet (perhaps next to Shakespeare, for he is a self-proclaimed Bardolator) is the American Hart Crane, who like Georg Trakl wrote magnificently symbolic works and died early (age thirty-two) by suicide. Perhaps Bloom sensed in Hart Crane's tragic fate a cautionary tale.

The creative personality, writes Neumann, remains receptive and observant, like the ego state of the matriarchal stage of development, but must have the resilience and stamina of an ego grounded in the ego-self axis in order to participate in the creative process unleashed by the activated unconscious, and survive. One thinks here of Jung in his crisis at midlife being severely tested as he decides to follow the "spirit of the depths" in search of his soul and enter into the tumultuous journey to the interior that he recorded in the Red Book. In the powerful creative process that ensues, he struggles to maintain his identity as he relates to "ravenous daemons" that appear in his imagination and confront him with challenges of all kinds. Jung was a creative personality who survived the onslaught and lived to transform the experiences into symbols and into the thought forms of depth psychology. *The Red Book* is his epic poem interwoven with magnificent paintings, and all the clinical, theoretical and hermeneutical works that followed (CW 6-18) are further products that flowed from the torrent of creativity opened up by his confrontation with the unconscious. Close to the end of his life he writes movingly of his daimon-driven creative life: "There was a daimon in me, and in the end its presence proved decisive. It overpowered me, and if I was at times ruthless it was because I was in the grip of the Daimon. I could never stop at anything once attained. I had to hasten on, to catch up with my vision" (Jung, 1961, p. 356).

"The creative process is synthetic," writes Neumann, "precisely in that the transpersonal, i.e., the eternal, and the personal, i.e., the ephemeral, merge, and something utterly unique happens: the enduring and eternally creative is actualized in the ephemeral creation" (Neumann, 1954/1959, p. 189). In one of his (to me) most moving essays, written sometime in the late 1950's, entitled "A Note on Marc Chagall," Neumann illustrates this union of the temporal and the eternal. Chagall had all the marks of the creative personality—a kind of "moon ego" but a stabile one, an immediate and intense connection to childhood and the mysteries of the symbolic world, a profound dedication to love and the divine feminine—and his paintings reveal "symbolic centers" that are "unquestionably spontaneous products of his unconscious..." (Neumann, 1954/1959, p. 136). Chagall paints out of his childhood—the village of Vitebsk, the animals, the violin player, the bridal couple—but "[i]n this childhood there is as yet no separation between personal and suprapersonal, near and far, inward soul and outward world; the life stream flows undivided, joining godhead and man, animal and world, in the glow and color of the nearby... this is the reality of Chagall's childhood, and the eternal presence of the primordial images lives in his memory of Vitebsk" (Neumann, 195?/1959, p. 138). Chagall was a creative personality who, like Jung, survived the turbulence of youth and an unusual dual psychological development and continued to create into old age. Neumann would attribute this to the constellation and stability of an ego-self axis in the personalities of both men.

Conclusion

I began by recounting the numinous dream of a client in which he witnesses an astonishing creation. The beating heart, which is held at the center of the containing basket, is a totally new and novel being, but neither purely a creation of nature, like our bodies are when they emerge from the maternal womb, nor purely a creation of humans, of the scientists who brought it into reality and put it on display. It is the product of a synthesis of creative forces, natural and human. I believe this is a symbol of what Neumann is expressing in his magnificent metapsychological accounts of the creative process within the human world.

Human creation is an extension of the Trinity of creation at work in all of nature, which has lately (in evolutionary terms) migrated into the psyche of humankind. Human expressions of the creative forces, whether in science, art, philosophy, business, politics or in any other endeavor, are not purely the products of human intelligence and intention—the patriarchal ego's ingenuity and craft—although these are surely also a part of the story. Genuine human creations are a product of ego-self cooperative and coordinated activities, which draw on both conscious and unconscious agencies, and these agencies have roots in nature and draw sustenance from the world Source in the *unus mundus*. The source of human creative energy lies in the unconscious, and ultimately in the Trinity of creation that is active everywhere in nature and has now taken its home in the human psyche. The "shaper" that designs this energy and gives it form (Gr. *Gestaltung*), and which keeps it from dissipating or spilling out into excessive and chaotic proliferations of exuberance, is the "Ordering Principle." This too is fundamentally rooted in the unconscious (and ultimately in the cosmic world), whence it forms archetypal images in the psyche from the energies emanating from the Vital Principle.

The creative personality, which is by no means an unproblematic psychological construction and frequently falls into serious states of disintegration and suffering, is situated in relation to the unconscious and the world of consciousness and culture in such a way that it can bring forth the emergent creations of the unconscious and make them available to culture in a particular time and place, using language or artistic methods available and concordant with the culture or scientific techniques and theories of the times. In extroverted types of human activity, such as business or politics, the creative personality also plays the role of midwife, bringing new possibilities into the light and offering them to the relevant culture. Often creative personalities suffer from this birthing drama, either because they are far ahead of their times, or because of cultural misinterpretations and misunderstandings, or because of fatal flaws and vulnerabilities in their psychological make-up such as seen in the gifted geniuses who die young.

In all of creation as we know it, there is nothing else that participates so fully in the creative process as does humankind. This may beget dangerous hubris and inflation, narcissistic self-importance, and thus tragedy as in the fate of Icarus. Were it not for the Directing Principle, there would be little meaning in all the froth generated by the creativity in nature and humanity. Neumann shows an astonishing degree of faith for such a modern man, as he undoubtedly was, that in the deep and dim recesses of the collective unconscious there is a goal-directed agency moving toward a meaningful destination. We can only look backward, not ahead. If we regard with a kind and forgiving eye the millions of years of evolutionary history that have brought humankind to its present state of consciousness and creative potential, we may retain hope that the future will not be altogether catastrophic.

References

Bernadini, R. (in press). Neumann at Eranos. In *Turbulent Times, Creative Minds: Erich Neumann and C.G. Jung in Relationship (1933-1960)*. (Eds.) E. Shalit and M. Stein. Asheville, N.C.: Chiron Publications.

Bloom, H. (2015). *The Daemon Knows*. New York: Spiegel and Grau.

Jung, C.G. and Neumann, E. (2015). *Analytical Psychology in Exile: The Correspondence of C.G. Jung and Erich Neumann*. Edited and introduced by M. Liebscher. Princeton: Princeton University Press.

Jung, C.G. (1961). *Memories, Dreams, Reflections*. New York: Vintage Books.

Jung, C.G. (2009). *The Red Book*. New York: Norton.

Neumann, E. (1950/1994). "The Moon and Matriarchal Consciousness." In *The Fear of the Feminine*. Princeton: Princeton University Press, pp. 64-118.

Neumann, E. (1952/1989). The Psyche and the Transformation of the Reality Planes: A Metapsychological Essay. *In The Place of Creation*. Princeton: Princeton University Press, pp. 3-62.

Neumann, E. (1954/1959). Creative Man and Transformation. *In Art and the Creative Unconscious*. Princeton: Princeton University Press, pp. 149-206.

Neumann, E. (1954). A Note on Marc Chagall. *In Art and the Creative Unconscious*. Princeton: Princeton University Press, pp. 135-148.

Neumann, E. (1959/1979). Georg Trakl: The Person and the Myth. *In Creative Man*. (Princeton: Princeton University Press, pp. 138-231

Neumann, E. (1960/1989). The Psyche as the Place of Creation. *In The Place of Creation*. Princeton: Princeton University Press, pp. 3-62.

Neumann, J. (In press). Letter to Olga Fröbe-Kapteyn, December 1960. In *Turbulent Times, Creative Minds: Erich Neumann and C.G. Jung in Relationship (1933-1960)*. (Eds.) E. Shalit and M. Stein. Asheville, N.C.: Chiron Publications.

Chapter 4

Jung's "Living Mystery" of Creativity, Symbols and the Unconscious in Writing

by Susan Rowland

> *We have to break down life and events, which are self-contained processes, into meanings, images, concepts, well knowing that in doing so we are getting further away from the living mystery.* (Jung, CW 15 para. 121)

> *Every creative man knows that spontaneity is the very essence of creative thought.* (Jung, CW 7, para. 292)

> *The symbol... Its meaning resides in the fact that it is an attempt to elucidate, by a more or less apt analogy, something that is still entirely unknown or still in the process of formation.* (ibid., para. 492)

Two factors structure C. G. Jung's understanding of creativity in relation to the unknown or unconscious psyche. They are that creativity's ability to bring forth something "new," is dependent upon the unknown psyche's intrinsically *productive* nature, and secondly, that it is in figuring "wholeness" or completeness of psychic being that creativity exercises its spontaneous powers. Put another way. The psyche generates images of its own "living mystery," in the cause of psychic completion. These images, Jung termed "symbols."

My paper will explore how symbols in writing are both matter and spirit: they are creativity materialized.

I will then also consider how James Hillman mobilized the soul as intrinsically creative in his condemnation of ego-centered psychotherapy in *We've had a Hundred Years of Psychotherapy and the World is Getting Worse* (1992). How might such a polemic add or subtract to the possibilities of the Jungian symbol as the manifestation of the unconscious roots of creativity?

Introduction: Symbols as Immanence Connected to Transcendence

C.G. Jung defined a symbol as an image that pointed to the unknown, not yet known or unknowable (Jung, *CW*15: para. 100). The symbol is therefore a gateway to the unconscious. Not all images are symbols for some refer to a perfectly known and coherent content: these are called signs. So Jung's images come in one of his typical pairs of differences. Just as we have conscious and unconscious aspects of the psyche, so our images in dreams, art and mythology, are either signs (fully comprehensible) or symbols: ways of encountering the unknown and mysterious.

Symbols to Jung specifically include images in words. Jung habitually discussed symbols as possessing a quality that conveyed, or even incarnated, a depth of psychic reality. He called symbols "living" when they manifested something not accessible to consciousness *except* by means of this "pregnant" expression (Jung 1971, p. 145). Symbols are also remarkably pervasive.

> Since every scientific theory contains an hypothesis, and is therefore an anticipatory description of something still essentially unknown, it is a symbol. Furthermore every psychological expression is a symbol if we assume that it states or signifies something more and other than itself which eludes our present knowledge. (Jung 1971, p. 146)

Here Jung suggests that science is largely, or at least directed to, symbolic writing. Furthermore, "psychology," by association a science, is also symbolic.

Put another way, the symbol is where matter and energy meet. It is a way of experiencing and holding the tensions between immanence and transcendence. In immanence we are embodied, *grounded*, in a specific place/time with a particular history. The symbol comes to us in this somatic immanence and joins us to the unconscious in its fullest possibilities of collective, *transcendent*, spiritual energy. Expressed mythically, the symbol conjoins immanence figured by the divine earth, "Mother Nature," to a sky father, a monotheistic god who created everything as separate from himself; a god *transcendent* of his world. Symbols expand psychic being, connecting body to spirit.

Evidently, such a powerful psychic engine as a symbol has implications for creativity. The first part of my paper will carefully examine what Jung actually offers us by way of the symbol, in connection with creativity, art and therapy. The final part will take Jung's embodied symbol into new research in complexity theory and emergence. The symbol can be creative in a way that addresses one of the greatest wounds of our age: the split between human and non-human nature. I will argue that the symbol is a reciprocal portal to nature and a means of necessary psychic evolution.

So let me begin with a symbol that does not seem to be at all generative except as in creating by *figuring,* being a figure for new thinking about the efficacy of therapy. In *We've had a Hundred Years of Psychotherapy and the World is Getting Worse* (Hillman and Ventura 1992), James Hillman says:

> ...the ship of death is the world soul sinking like an overloaded garbage barge. That's why I say therapy–even the best deep therapy–contributes to the world's destruction. 100 years. (p. 51)

I am using such a provocative statement here for two reasons, neither of which is a simple agreement with it. First of all, I want in this paper to question some of the assumptions surrounding the topic of "creativity and the symbol" in Jungian psychology. Secondly this quote provides an example of issues *within* the straightforward definition of images as signs or symbols. "The ship of death" appears to be a symbol in that it evokes a lot more than the basic meaning of its words. Yet when the writer compares it to an overloaded garbage barge, is he not turning it into a sign? Suppose that symbols and signs are not intrinsically different sorts of images but rather a field of shifting possibilities that depend upon context and the will of the reader?

In taking the topic of creativity and the symbol I hope to place these in the context of revisioning Jung's teaching. In effect, I want to take on Hillman's challenge to psychotherapy and direct it toward testing out some of the assumptions about symbols and creativity. My paper will show firstly, just how radical and underappreciated is the work of C.G. Jung is in this area, and secondly how his work might be extended.

One aspect of creativity is revivifying, bringing to life, making new. By the end of this paper I will show how revisioning Jung renews not only our sense of the unconscious and creativity but also the whole world with symbols as the portals into re-imagining the cosmos. It is this ability to embody immanence and yet participate in transcendence that characterizes Jung's symbols. So this paper is about renewing symbols and creativity through questioning current implications. To begin, we need to look at where Jung is hopelessly lost.

Jung Discovers the Need for Creativity as Therapy: *"Ulysses": A Monologue* (Jung, CW15)

In this extraordinary comic excursion, Jung reads an impossible novel and it becomes a revolutionary mediation of how the creativity of the psyche may be frozen by a corrupt civilization. Being Jung, of course he finds a creative path to spiritual personal and collective renewal. He finds that the unconscious roots of creativity may be both trapped and unlocked by verbal symbols.

James Joyce's *Ulysses* (1922) takes the plot of the *Odyssey* and transposes it to the Dublin of 1904 on one particular day, June 16th. His Odysseus is a man wandering the modern city streets, where he is not entirely at home as a Jew in Catholic Ireland. In addition, Leopold Bloom is reluctant to return to his house because he knows is wife is unfaithful. Such is the mundane condition of the epic depicted by Homer. *Ulysses* shocked its first readers because of its explicit and extensive rendering of bodily functions, including sex. More challenging to today's readers is the dismaying variety of writing styles and perspectives that go to produce this multifaceted narrative.

It is also a long book, demanding a certain type of heroism by the reader. Jung says:

> Thus I read to page 135 with despair in my heart
> falling asleep twice on the way. Arrived at page 135,
> after making several heroic efforts to get at the book,
> to "do it justice" as the phrase goes, I fall at last into
> a profound slumber (*CW*15: para 165).

For much of the *Ulysses* essay, Jung's problem is his inability to inhabit the symbolic mode. He is stuck in the immanence of his own body with nothing in the book able to motivate the creativity latent in his psyche. He is literally unable to digest *Ulysses* and release his own spirit into a connection with transcendence. Reading is here the reverse of creation: it is degeneration! On the other hand, Jung's stuckness in an abyss of the psyche as uncreative, stony, frozen proves highly fortunate in ultimately providing a new way to foster creativity and symbols, as I will show.

Jung sees the novel as structured around a consciousness that is skewed to physical sensation and omitting thinking and feeling.

This is a consciousness stuck in immanence and looking in vain for symbolic connection to spirit. Jung is right about the focus of the novel; however, wrong that it is a figuration of the trickster-like hero, Odysseus. Symptomatic is a certain humorous participation mystique in his falling asleep, twice!

It has long been my contention that the humor in Jung's writing has been consistently undervalued, and is a key ingredient in his ideas. At least he takes his own jokes seriously, for he concludes that falling asleep is telling him something significant about the book: it radically and deliberately fails to engage the transcending tendency of the intellect, and that this somatic challenge requires further attention. What he does is what he often advocates when the psyche is stuck: he finds an image for what he calls "visceral thinking" (para.166).

> This singular and uncanny characteristic of the Joycean mind shows that his work pertains to the class of cold blooded animals and specifically to the worm family (para. 166).

Activated complexes are diagnosed first by the irritation that Jung confesses (para.167). This irritation is sufficient to provoke him to try reading the book another way. He says, "[a] therapist like myself is always practicing therapy – even on himself" (para. 168). Jung is here resorting to therapy to cope with intolerable disturbances produced by a work of art on his psyche. This is far from *using* a work of art to promote therapy. You could say that this is almost the reverse of art psychotherapy: using therapy to save us from art!

The complex provoked in Jung from reading *Ulysses* could be named a tapeworm complex, for this is how the book at first reveals itself to him. Suffering, rather than comprehending the book, Jung is in the underworld: "[f]rom this stony underworld there rises up the vision of the tapeworm..." (para. 169). Made visible by his annoyance, this tapeworm complex of images is also the *matter* of his participation in it, since it is both in the novel and in the reader's psyche. Jung is suggesting that reading this challenging book is to gain a most unpleasant parasite! Yet now Jung has shifting his perspective from reader to therapist of the reader, himself. He is not finished with complexes. Finding no authorial persona amongst the many lively characters, he suggests that Joyce himself is a complex of *Ulysses*; that the author is merely a complex of the narrative focus of the whole book.

To investigate this startling notion, it is necessary to return to symbols. At first this is straightforward; Jung finds no symbols in the novel. A work that "strives to attain the utmost objectivity of consciousness" has no hidden depths; it cannot conjoin immanent and transcendent modes of psyche (para. 185). Hence, perhaps Jung's rather brutal mention of nature. In its intensity of "visceral thinking," the book's detachment from conventional feeling makes it unsentimental to be "natural" in a naked sense of "the boredom of nature" (para. 169). Put another way, Jung begins by regarding the book as "desouled" (ibid.), a body at the psychoid level of intermingling with psyche, analogous to nature without anima. Put yet another way, to be stuck in the material body as pure immanence is to be cut off from making meaning that an experience of transcendence requires.

However, Jung the therapist is not as stuck as he was previously. In producing his own image for his "stuckness," the tapeworm, therapy conducted upon himself, Jung employs what is surely a version of active imagination (not named as such) to psychically mobilize himself in the underworld. If symbols are not found, they can be, with the right attitude to the matter as *matter*. Jung as therapist has a singular position on the role of beauty in art. Visceral *Ulysses* destroys conventions of politeness, respectable ways of depicting human social and bodily functions and accepted forms of representation. To Jung this has real value as social and cultural revolution.

Joyce has created "an art in reverse, a backside of art" that constitutes an "anti-world" that reveals by its destructive nature the sentimentality of the modern age. Moreover, the cultural criticism is substantiated by the novel evoking the era destroyed by modern industrial society. *Ulysses* in its tapeworm cosmos harks back to medieval Catholic Ireland. This does not make the book Irish, exclusively addressed to those citizens.

Rather, Jung makes clear that the novel succeeds in showing medieval Catholic Ireland to be a psychic component of the modern person. That is, the book's destruction of conventional assumptions about beauty in art do not refer to Ireland as a literal nation state, but rather *symbolize* those different cultures that provide an "underworld" to modern Western persons in all their diversity.

Jung could not find symbols in characters and motifs in Joyce's *Ulysses*. What he did find, as a therapist, was the symbolic nature of its refusal of conventional beauty. Such an achievement makes it easier to work with Jung's assertions about Joyce as a complex of the narrative voices of the book. The emphasis on the body as organ rather than ensouled leads to Jung concluding that there is no ego in the book – no single complex of consciousness with its characteristic modern structuring of detachment from the body.

The heterogeneity in the narrative approaches of *Ulysses*, together with its determination to render the material world into writing, including what has often been excluded in the excremental body, makes the book a kind of image of totality for modern materialism. Put another way, Jung finds a "oneness" in all the impossibly diverse matter of Dublin in the course of one day. Since he identifies the narrative perspectives of the book with Odysseus, this figuration of the Wanderer becomes the symbol in/of the novel.

> Try to imagine a being who is not a mere colorless conglomerate soul composed of an indefinite number of ill-assorted and antagonistic and individual souls, but consists also of houses, street-processions, churches, the Liffey, several brothels and a crumpled note ... yet possesses a perceiving and registering consciousness (para. 198).

Jung perceives a symbol in the artistic *creativity in the form* of the work of art rather than in its content. By working therapeutically,

Jung realizes, *makes real*, how the books horrifying immanence in the unlovely aspects of embodiment is actually a road to a transcendent renewal of a whole culture. By provoking the symbol function, *Ulysses* invokes creative to re-make an entire world. I will say more about this point later in the context of James Hillman.

> Considered causally Joyce is a victim of Catholic "authoritarianism" yet Jung prefers to regard *Ulysses* as future-driven. From the standpoint of the novel written for the future, teleologically, Joyce is a reformer in the stage of clearing the ground of dead matter (para. 183).

It is in this context that Jung offers *Ulysses*, the whole novel, as a symbol. If it is a symbol of creativity however, it is notably collective rather than individual. In a wonderfully vivid phrase, Jung sums up what the novel is trying to destroy: "[s]entimentality is the superstructure erected upon brutality" (para. 184). Those outworn conventions of beauty are not simply within the domain of something called "art" that is isolated from other personal and social aspects of living. Rather, aesthetics as a deadening of psychic creativity plays a role in legitimizing the dark corners of modernity in exploitation, treating nature as *in*-animate, and war.

The true symbol in art is part of a creative act that involves more than the individual psyche. The symbol that is the Odysseus figure/narrative voices in Joyce's *Ulysses*, opens a door to the underworld of Western culture by means of destroying its canons of aesthetics and beauty. Jung puts it this way: "O *Ulysses* you are truly a devotional book for the object-besotted, object-ridden white man! You are a spiritual exercise, an ascetic discipline, an agonizing ritual, an arcane procedure..." (para. 201). I interpret "white man" here as a surprisingly acute indictment of Western materialism as connoting colonial conquests. Here the book as symbol unites immanence and transcendence to tear down the complacency that it discerns in modernity.

A world has passed away and is made new (Para. 202).

Jung's symbol of art and its creativity is suprapersonal, ambitious and collective. It calls into question whether the Jungian symbol can be properly confined to creativity as understood in a personal sense. In this way, Jung's article on *Ulysses* paves the way for Hillman and Ventura's assault, in *We've Had a Hundred Years of Psychotherapy and the World is Getting Worse*, on psychotherapy as an institution.

At one point in Hillman and Ventura's daring and provocative book Ventura discusses three styles of acting. There is a soft kind of acting for popular culture he calls "shtick," a "concrete or outer acting" and "abstract or inner acting" (HV 1992, p. 109). In the latter two lies a profound cultural change that began in the 1940s when the precise skilled fixity of concrete acting began to encounter something experimentally fluid.

> Olivier or Hepburn will play the moment where its most itself, where it's *that* moment and no other. Clift or Rowlands will play that moment at the border, where its begun to change into something else. (ibid., p. 110)

In a book structured as conversation and letters between figures who are described by Ventura as "instigators, goaders, conceptual adventurers," we have an attempt at psychology writing on the edge of becoming something else. As the book does not quite say, for reasons I will come to, it itself is a transforming act of psychelogos, or psychology, into performance art. The book enacts Hillman's major arc in the dialogues, the re-framing of psychotherapy as an art oriented toward performing for the collective, rather than a private practice "disciplined" in several senses by medicine and science. Before looking at Hillman and Ventura's improvisationary movement toward therapy as art as spontaneous creativity, it is helpful to consider its objections to psychotherapy as conventionally practiced.

The fundamental style of *We've Had a Hundred Years* is addressing its subject in challenging the notion of psyche as bounded into one person. Psyche is not just "inside;" it is also "outside" insists Hillman in ways that ought to do away with that distinction (ibid., p.3). What is fundamentally wrong with psychotherapy is that it has served to institutionalize the psyche as interiority. What has been left out of psychotherapy is the growing crisis of a world rife with toxicity, and is sick. Does not a world manifesting symptoms suggest psychic damage? By us denying the animation of the world, is the world not responding to our materialism's poisoned matter? (ibid. p.4)

The problem with psychotherapy is not that it is simply ignoring the planet's crisis. Rather it is significantly contributing to that crisis by building up a narrative of human psyche that has become a drive within individualist consumer ideology. Psychotherapy is *making* the world worse, insists this book. For whatever depth psychology has bred the practice of psychotherapy infantilizes by insisting upon contacting an "inner child." (6). Therapy is not just un-creative, it is anti-creativity because it is dedicated to removing the possibility of "something new" coming into the world.

"Psychotherapy converts pain into self-importance in confusing the significance of events with the significance of the individual" (ibid. p. 27). Thus, we are taught to "consume" our own psyche in a monetary relationship. Trauma, however brutal, does not have to be "processed" into creating victims and scapegoats that convert suffering into self-pity. Other cultures, says Hillman bracingly, might define child abuse as initiation into some powerful collective role (ibid., p. 26).

Above all, psychotherapy as conventionally conducted is against creativity because it drastically limits the stories by which we define ourselves. By instituting a foreshortened origin story in traumatized infancy and limiting the psyche to the interior of the individual, psychotherapy is a great engine of de-souling the world.

At this point Hillman is revolutionary in two senses. He wants a revolutionary psychotherapy that turns around conventional attitudes toward matter and self. He also wants an epistemological revolution that departs from the Cartesian model of a separate self. Hillman is determined to redefine self as *"the interiorization of community"* (italics in original ibid. p. 40). Psyche is in the world, and the world is in the psyche. Self is not something separate but exists "among" others that are human and nonhuman (p. 43). We are not single or separate. The many are within and speak to, interact with, the many outside our bodies. This interior community is dead unless it is mobilized *through and as creativity.*

Here, it is Ventura who begins to speculate about how psyche is collective, and *of* the world, acting in response to collective movements or waves. Artists begin to be useful models for where this potent conversation is going, for artists are tuned to the collective in their openness to news from the universe. Suggestively, C.G. Jung may be in the company of artists in tuning in to collective movements.

> The genius of a [Charley] Parker or a [Jackson]
> Pollock or a Jung is not what they originate but what
> they're susceptible to. (MV pp. 59-60)

In turn, Hillman brings in the *form* of matter as an essential ingredient of the creative and animate psyche-world. Perhaps toxicity is more than just chemical, but also pertains to aesthetic quality (Hillman, 1972, p. 125). Referring to Aristotle, who attributed a *formal cause* as well as a material cause to things, Hillman suggests that ecology, caring for the earth as home, means aesthetic justice in countering toxic forms (ibid., p. 126). Good therapy would therefore empower the imagination in participation with aesthetic form as a dimension of animate matter. Good therapy here means creatively trans-*forming* the world.

However, Hillman stops short of equating therapy with "good design" in the world (ibid., p. 127). It appears that he is reluctant to entirely embrace art as the new psychotherapy; a reluctance stored in his fundamental hesitation over the animate qualities of different academic disciplines, as I shall show later. Hillman says that to truly liberate the imagination design and therapy involves encountering the demonic (ibid., p. 127). Good design, he says, is concerned with embodying beauty in form and cannot deal with the demonic aspects of the human psyche. It is time to look more closely at the model of art as the new psychotherapy dashingly proposed by *We've Had a Hundred Years of Psychotherapy and the World is Getting Worse.*

Can Practicing Art or Codifying Creativity Model Practicing Therapy for *We've Had a Hundred Years*?

Hillman claims not to be literal about citing the artist as model for the therapist (Hillman and Ventura, p. 30). He sees artists as examples of questers into the imagination. They seek other modes of consciousness, are creators, open to trying the new, the risky, the outrageous. *We've Had a Hundred Years* has a fully Romantic notion of the artist as the seeker of form and rules by which to define the work as art. As a result, the future artist-therapist will not *subject* a person to therapy as a set of assumptions derived from the institutions of psychotherapy and the conventions of society. Rather, the artist-therapist will seek imagination in *otherness* to habitual, received thought. Hillman's artist-therapist is creative as her defining feature.

As Ventura has insisted, the artist proper is not merely a more colorful version of modernity's typical creation: the autonomous individual. Artists make themselves permeable to influences or waves from the collective. Figures like the painter Pablo Picasso and the novelist Doris Lessing are pioneering versions of Hillman's "self among," in seeking to capture intimations from a deep collective and not wholly human psyche.

Hillman concludes that his call for a new kind of art-inspired psychotherapy rests on three indigenous aspects of art: the notion of forming something "new" out of chaos, the evocation of social justice and, in its fidelity to the imagination, the rejection of mediocrity (ibid.). Above all, psychotherapy as a creative art will need to be sublime; meaning that it must express the inexpressible, and always be open to the indigenous strangeness of the psyche.

This is a characterization of therapy as a wholly Romantic art, not least in its violation of boundaries between different types of cultural production. In fact, Hillman's sublime creative psychotherapy has potential to break down all sorts of cultural divisions. Even the pervasive sense of historical melancholy in the book is subject to creative revision. If we are, as both men agree, in an era of decline and crisis, then the apocalyptic story itself will survive. Modern society may not survive its current excesses, but its story will not be "shipwrecked" (HV 228).

To these authors, story exceeds and has more staying power than the culture generating it. In both form and content, *We've Had a Hundred Years* challenges many assumptions about psychotherapy and creativity, using the post-Romantic condition of art to propose a new paradigm. The two writers counterpoint, contrast and blend their voices and ideas until, in much of the text, while individual speakers are identified, the generation of ideas cannot be precisely attributed. Here, of course, the book does what art does: form and content are inextricably linked.

What seems as the essential ethos of *We've Had a Hundred Years* is the denial of the autonomous modern self whose psyche is skin-bound, leaving the world without soul. Hillman finds a relief from what is to him a nightmare vision in the artist's need to en-vision beyond their own egos. In so doing, *We've Had a Hundred Years* sets up important echoes and resonances with Jung on James Joyce's *Ulysses*. Jung ends his humorous and provocative essay:

> "O *Ulysses* you are truly a devotional book for the object-besotted, object-ridden white man! You are a spiritual exercise, an ascetic discipline, an agonizing ritual, an arcane procedure..." (para. 201).

Jung finds reading the book at first a cauterizing exercise in conventional notions of meaning and artistic representation. The book's sheer resistance ultimately opens his psyche up to creativity. *Ulysses* is a hideous tapeworm that invades his psyche and paralyses his body in sleep. Yet through these drastic initiatory processes, Jung is forced first into his therapist role and then into revisioning it as co-creator, with the book, of a new consciousness. Again we have an example of the "story" being more robust than the culture that purports to generate it. Odysseus from Homer is re-framed in Ireland then misread or re-envisioned by Jung, finally providing a quest motif for the modern person as reader of art.

The autonomous self is quickly abolished by the book's resistance and parasitical properties of creatively seeding psyche in the world. For when Jung discovers that medieval Catholic Ireland extends to contemporary Zurich, he becomes a citizen of Hillman's ensouled world. The book's creativity is revolutionary; its symbols incarnate a re-creation myth, and after him, his reader, as we follow the epistemological struggles of this quest. This is an advance example of the kind of psychotherapy advocated by *We've Had a Hundred Years*.

Above all, revisioning the Jungian symbol makes relationships between therapy art. It is time to scrutinize the new possibilities for the symbol that Jung, in *Ulysses*, and *We've Had a Hundred Years*, are seeking. For in new evolutionary science is *matter* that offers the reality of reciprocity, of conjoined and mutual being between self and other, including non-human other. Finally, this paper will look at Hillman's reading of Jung on Dionysus, to situate art, creativity and symbols in the dismembered divinity of our ways of knowing called academic disciplines.

The Creative Symbol That Joins Us to the Wildness of the Cosmos

Without using the term "symbol," Hillman and Ventura in *We've Had a Hundred Years* wanted a therapeutic practice that took account of the inevitable wildness of the universe (Hillman and Ventura. p. 167). On the other hand, the entire book is a not entirely hopeful call to attend to the pain of the world soul that includes suffering human societies as well as the polluted planet.

Adding Jung's "therapeutic" work on *Ulysses* offers an intimation of an expanded sense of the Jungian symbol as possessing properties beyond constructing the psyche as merely individual. At this point it is worth recalling that symbols are archetypal images; they possess energy from the embodied, inherited capacity of archetypes to structure certain sorts of images and meaning. As embodied, archetypes have roots in instinct, in the psychoid unconscious where psyche and body are liminal.

This means that the images generated by archetypes are not entirely controlled by them. Archetypal images or symbols have content deeply affected by the culture into which they emerge. The Jungian symbol is both body and history: it therefore knits the individual psyche into the fabric of the world.

In the twentieth century, ideas of evolution began a major revision that arguably begins to show a profound convergence between it and Jungian psychology. As I proposed in an earlier work, *The Ecocritical Psyche* (2012), "complexity evolution" or "emergence" shows the Jungian symbol as capable of creativity or making whole a great wound of modernity: the split between human psyche and non-human nature. Art that invoked symbols would therefore become a *reciprocal* dialogue between humans and nature.

Complexity theory or "emergence" is a significant development of evolution after Darwin. Evolved nature is not so much a competition between competing species as Darwin originally envisaged, but is more like successive, ever more complexly interpenetrating environments. These Complex Adaptive Systems (or CAS) interact in ways that cannot be mapped nor considered with notions of linear cause and effect.

Rather, the interpenetration of CAS stimulates evolutionary change by the emergence of new "wholes" that are more than the sum of their parts. Such evolution has to be called "creative," in suggesting a kind of innate creativity or animation in non-human nature itself. Nature possesses creativity in the "intelligent" emergent properties of Complex Adaptive Systems, of which the human body and psyche are one. Human beings participate in complexity evolution on an unconscious embodied level with non-human complex adaptive environments. Indeed, Jung had a name for these kinds of unconscious creative processes: synchronicity.

Jungians such as Helene Schulman and Joseph Cambray have researched Jung's identification of synchronicity and the collective unconscious in connection to the new science of complexity, or emergence. My own contribution in *The Ecocritical Psyche* is to propose that complexity evolution occurs in the making and appreciation of art by means of the synchronous Jungian symbol as an evolutionary portal to psyche, offering the return of an animistic sense of non-human nature.

The symbol is in this way creatively healing the great split from nature that came about first of all in the transition between pre-Christian animism and monotheism. As Anne Baring and Jules Cashford have argued in *The Myth of the Goddess* (1990), the construction of modern Western consciousness is witness to an incomplete conversion from an ancient Earth Mother creation myth that was manifested as animism to a Sky Father myth of a masculine god creating nature, matter and body discrete from himself. Earth Mother fostered immanence, embodiment, nature as sacred and articulate and was almost, but not entirely, eclipsed by an aggressive form of the Sky Father. In the dominant mode of Christianity, this is the drive to transcendence, disembodied rationalism and discrimination.

I have argued in several books, following Baring and Cashford, that Jung's entire project was driven by a possibly barely conscious awareness of the desperate need to revive Earth Mother embodied "feminine" consciousness, because the dominance of Sky Father separation has made modernity sick (Rowland 2005, 2010, 2012). Earth Mother figures in Jung's work in Eros consciousness of connectedness and feeling, in the trickster as embodied and multiple, and of course in synchronicity, as creativity that is not causal in a Sky Father structure of rationality.

Earth mother also resurfaces in modernity in various theories of evolution, James Lovelock's Gaia hypothesis, and in depth psychology as the pre-Oedipal mother. This latter is an important clue to "her" nature as potentially containing both genders. "She" is not exclusively female, for "she is prior to the division into two genders." It is her unequal partner, Sky Father Monotheism, who instates dualism and two genders by creating an "other" than himself.

It is here that the Jungian symbol is the crux for the potential creativity of the modern psyche. For the symbol, that image pointing toward the unknown and generated by embodied archetype, unites immanent experience in time to possibilities of transcendent consciousness and spirit. The symbol is the means of rapport between Earth Mother and Sky Father. The lessons of complexity evolution and biosemiosis are gifts of the return to the Earth Mother creation myth in evolution, giving us back our immanent, earthen, animal bodies. Biosemiosis and emergence invoke animism as the multiple communicative spirits in nature. James Hillman invoked animism in the symptomatic cries of polluted nature, and the de-formed distress evoked by a harshly built environment.

The Jungian symbol is a form of animism indigenous to art and culture. It incarnates many voices in its multiple potentials for meaning. My point now is that the symbol is indigenous to art *as a portal to nature, as a form of reciprocal unconscious, synchronous communication.* Therefore, the symbol in art joins the embodied psyche to the cosmos, in its linking of psyche and matter. It heals the split of nature and human nature. The Jungian symbol abolishes the separate human subject and does what Hillman wants: makes a self among other people, other nature, and other things. The symbol unites Earth Mother immanence to Sky Father transcendence; so that we possess some coherent autonomy, yet are intimately connected with the ensouled world.

When Jung's realizes, makes real in his psyche, the form of *Ulysses* as a symbol, he makes the world anew in his dialogical relationship with the work of art. He models not so much how we can use symbols, but how symbols are dynamic instances of the ensouled world invoking in us creativity and rebirth.

I want to end this paper by taking another look at a form of modern cultural division that continues to haunt this subject: the division into different academic departments disciplines such as psychology, art, medicine. Since we know from cross-cultural studies that there is nothing eternal about these ways of making and justifying knowledge or epistemologies, what myths might be revealed in or applied to, their condition? Will this affect our understanding of the symbol in its capacity to unite nature and psyche?

Revisioning Dionysus after Hillman and Jung

In "Dionysus in Jung's Writings," Hillman notes that scholars appreciate Dionysus according to their own biases. Jung's Dionysus, according to Hillman, is a god of dismemberment (1972, p. 26). Moreover, Jung offers a two stage dismemberment. After the transmutation into opposites comes a more plural dispersal of body parts, or something suggestive of the multiplicity of archetypes in the Jungian collective unconscious. What Hillman sees as particular to Jung is that this second dismemberment is a move to an instinctual life force requiring a body metaphor (ibid., p. 27). Jung says:

> The divine powers imprisoned in bodies are nothing
> other than *Dionysus dispersed in matter*. (*CW*9, ii, 158n,
> qu DW 26)

It is in the "visceral thinking" of Jung on Joyce's *Ulysses* that Hillman discerns the most overt presence of this dismembered god (*CW*15, para. 166). In a note, Jung links visceral thinking to a consciousness incarnate in the body's organs (ibid. n.8). Such "organ consciousness," insists Hillman, is not to be confused with a stage in a process of re-assembly into a unified "whole" (ibid. pp. 27-8). What is the determining factor of the dismembered Dionysus is rather a consciousness aware of the differences, of the organs or parts of the body as parts, not ingredients to be submerged into a uniform perspective (ibid.).

Indeed, the movement between the first dismemberment into opposites and the second into parts is a psychic revolution which results in consciousness becoming located *inside* the cosmos of Dionysus (ibid. p. 26). The old and overly transcendent senex is beheaded, the body dismembered so that visceral thinking may flow from psychoid Dionysus.

> Conceptual fantasies such as "visceral thinking" ... refer on another level to the psychoid Dionysus ... By attributing a god to zoe [the life force of the body], the life force is given psychic interiority and a specific kind of consciousness which might partly be characterized as an awareness of self-divisibility into many parts. (ibid., pp. 28-9)

So the movement achieved by Jung's Dionysian dismemberment is an authoritarian control via enantiodroma shifting into a Dionysian archetypal cosmos in which consciousness is aware of many parts, possibilities, perspectives. Dionysus in this way is the unconscious roots of archetypal creativity.

So where does this leave the creative power of the symbol in art? Let us take another look at the symbol quoted at the start of this paper.

> ...the ship of death is the world soul sinking like an overloaded garbage barge. That's why I say therapy—even the best deep therapy—contributes to the world's destruction. *100 years*, p. 51.

Symbols are to be found everywhere the unconscious uses images to activate our being in creativity. Here, "the ship of death" stands as a symbol and sign for Hillman and Ventura's book. *We've Had a Hundred Years* portrays modernity as heading for the rocks, and the single person is holed up in a cabin with a therapist, with the only hope being to start a mutiny, overthrow the captain and turn the boat around. While in the essay on *Ulysses*, the sign of Jung's discomfort, the tapeworm, becomes the symbol of the form of the book as a transforming power to make the world new. For the Jungian symbol is a Dionysian property.

The symbol belongs to dismembered Dionysus in finding our long lost *zoe*, or life force. It is not just that the symbol is soma and psyche rooted in the archetypal embodied unconscious. Rather, the symbol is the organ of *zoe* because it invokes that interiority of Dionysus of parts conscious of the life force in other parts as well. The symbol connects our material bodies to the ensouled world by invoking the dismembered bodies of knowledge, culture and history. Symbols do heal, but they heal *not* by re-assembling or re-integrating the old king who controls meaning. Control of meaning is the aim of totalitarian power in all its forms, and thus is the enemy of imagination and creativity.

Symbols heal *creatively* by re-enlivening the somatic body and the dismembered body of our knowing, and by extension the dismembered body of different ontologies by which humans live. In this sense the role of art is to house symbols as organs of the creative psyche. The role of psychotherapy is to make symbols that enliven the ensouled body of the single person in relationship to the dismembered body politic. Hillman did not like the word "symbol" because of its cultural appropriation by individualism. Jung did not explicitly explore the innate transpersonal power of *his* symbol, but he did enact it by his therapeutic treatment of the difficulties of reading *Ulysses*.

The context of complexity evolution and biosemiosis is yet another instance of *zoe* emerging from the beheading of the Western understanding of the Bible as *the* story of the cosmos. Evolution as interaction of complexity provides material to show how much the Jungian symbol *matters* in creatively healing the split from nature. In Dionysus we find a symbolic myth, a home to receive symbols to help make the world anew, a new creation myth that is the figuring of our creativity.

References

Baring, A. and J. Cashford (1991) *The Myth of the Goddess: Evolution of an Image*, New York and London: Vintage.

Cambray, J. (2012). *Synchronicity: Nature and psyche in an interconnected universe*. College Station: Texas A & M Press.

Hillman, J. (1972) 'Dionysus in Jung's Writings,' *Spring: A Journal of Archetype and Culture*, 1972, in *Mythic Figures: Uniform Edition of the Writings of James Hillman, volume 6.1* (Putnam, Connecticut: Spring Publications Inc., 2007), pp. 15-30.

Hillman, J. and M. Ventura. (1992) *We've had a Hundred Years of Psychotherapy and the World is Getting Worse*, New York: HarperCollins.

Jung, C. G. Except where a different publication is noted below, all references are, by volume and paragraph number, to the edition *of The Collected Works of C.G. Jung (CW)*, edited by Sir Herbert Read, Dr. Michael Fordham and Dr. Gerhard Adler, translated by R.F.C. Hull (1953-91), London: Routledge, Princeton N.J.: Princeton University Press.

Jung, C. G. (1971) *Dictionary of Analytical Psychology*, London and New York: Routledge, ARK paperbacks.

Rowland, S. (2005) *Jung as a Writer*, New York and London: Routledge.

Rowland, S. (2010) *C. G. Jung in the Humanities: Taking the Soul's Path*, New Orleans: Spring Journal and Books.

Rowland, S. (2012) *The Ecocritical Psyche: Literature, Complexity Evolution and Jung*, New York and London: Routledge.

Shulman, H. (1997) *Living at the Edge of Chaos: Complex Systems in Culture and Psyche*, Zurich: Daimon Verlag.

Wheeler, W. (2006) *The Whole Creature: Complexity, Biosemiotics and the Evolution of Culture*, London: Lawrence & Wishart.

Chapter 5

Fellowship of the Word:
On Complexes, Chaos, and Attractors

by Leonard Cruz, MD

FIGURE 1. *PUZZLE PIECES* BY DAWSON MIMS.

Between the blank page and a first draft, is a numinous portal where the *mysterium tremendum et fascinans* (blank wonder, awful terror, and the charm of attractiveness) is encountered (Otto, 1958). Writers traverse this portal equipped with all their accumulated experience, their artistic craft, and the unintegrated elements in their psyches. At times, the writer is compelled by something that demands to be expressed. I suspect that if every step in the writing process could be traced to its source, we would behold with awesome wonder that each word choice, each sentence, each paragraph is holographic—the fruit of the author's entire being. According to Jung, "it makes no difference whether the artist knows that his work is generated, grows and matures within him, or whether he imagines that it is his own invention. In reality, it grows out of him like a child its mother." Where the "creative force predominates, life is ruled by the unconscious" (Jung, 1971). Although the writer begins with a conscious intention to write, unconscious currents helplessly sweep her along.

These unconscious currents are the subject of this exploration. I use the feminine pronoun throughout this chapter for the sake of clarity and readability. I also choose the feminine pronoun out of deference to what I believe to be true of writing; writing has a feminine valance.

The blank page is like a *tabula rasa* onto which the writer inscribes words with a certain cadence, rhythm, and timbre that will evoke images and emotions in the reader. What does it mean to create a piece of prose or poetry? How does artistic creation differ from simple production of a piece of writing? Can a computer write poetry (Schwartz, 2015)? Machines can be trained to produce something that bears a striking resemblance to a writer's creation. If a reader is moved by such a piece of writing, was creativity involved? These philosophical questions provide a window into what we mean by the unconscious roots of creativity.

This chapter explores creativity from the perspective of the writer and the reader. It also explores the intersubjective realm that develops between them. By extending insights derived from the field of Chaos Theory, a model is proposed for how the unconscious roots of creativity coalesce into a completed piece of writing. These explorations are likely to apply to creativity in other arts though the focus is how unconscious material finds expression in consciously produced writing. It will be helpful to remember Alfred Korzybski's warning, "The map is not the territory."

Emergence

Writing is an emergent phenomenon. In Chaos Theory, emergence is a term used to describe a phenomenon in which small, simple elements interact in such a fashion as to produce larger entities or patterns. When the writer assembles words, sentences, and paragraphs, she brings order out of chaos. According to Calvin Schrag, "speaking is a creative act, at once a discovery of self and a self-constitution" and the same thing can be said of writing and reading (Schrag, 1997). Anaïs Nin wrote, "I believe one writes because one has to create a world in which one can live. (...) I had to create a world of my own, like a climate, a country, an atmosphere in which I could breathe, reign, and recreate myself when destroyed by living. That, I believe, is the reason for every work of art." (Webber, 1978). The reader also engages in an emergent phenomenon of her own. While there are distinct differences, writers and readers engage in creativity.

The written word is a bridge that connects two sentient beings who are unlikely to ever meet. They may be vastly separated in space and time. Nevertheless, a relationship exists between them. That relationship has an intersubjective dimension that resembles the intersubjective realm between therapist and patient, an interplay that is multilayered and unpredictable.

One year before I completed high school, I entered into dialogue with Joseph Conrad. That conversation continues to this day. Recently, I gave a copy of *Heart of Darkness* to a young man in his mid-twenties. I cannot predict the effect, if any, Conrad's novel will have on him. I know that he aspires to teach English overseas and that he learned Chinese in college. He intended to work for the United Nations and to travel after college. Did my familiarity with these details of his life shape my choice of novels for him? Was it my own pleasure from reading Conrad that influenced me? Perhaps it was the fact that Conrad was itinerant or polyglot that directed my choice. The confluence of forces that in all likelihood shaped my selection of *Heart of Darkness* is unfathomable. By sharing a beloved novel, I was extending an invitation to this young man to meet Conrad and possibly develop his own relationship. He and I may or may not talk about the book. Whatever unfolds, Conrad engaged two souls, at different times, in unique ways. There were three unconscious domains involved in this exchange, Conrad's, my young friend's, and mine. One of the great mysteries of the printed word is that it comes to life when the author creates and it is given a rebirth when the reader engages the text. As Anaïs Nin says, "We write to taste life twice, in the moment, and in retrospection" (Nin, 1971).

Mercurial Nature of Creativity

The act of creation is mercurial. Mercury, one of the pantheon of Roman gods, ruled eloquence, communication, and boundaries. He was a guide for the souls to the underworld. Mercury also delivered the dreams Morpheus furnished to sleeping humans (Littleton, 2007). The reader's experience with a text is just as Mercurial and unpredictable as the author's experience of creation. A taproot descends to the personal and collective unconscious that sustains the creativity of both writers and readers. The unconscious furnishes ideas, images, dialogue, and narrative themes that coalesce on the page. Unconscious undercurrents animate the experience and support the germination and gestation.

An intersubjective domain between artist and audience for the art is different for the written word than live performance and other arts. A live performance that is not recorded produces intersubjectivity between artists and their audiences. Visual arts do not rely on words that are inherently symbolic as intermediaries.

In his effort to develop a general theory of creativity, Arthur Koestler coined the phrase "bisociation" to denote the phenomenon whereby two previously unrelated matrices of thought coalesce into a new matrix of meaning. He noted that this occurs through processes involving abstraction, categorization, analogy, and the use of metaphor (Koestler, 1964).

Chaos Theory, Fractals, and Attractors

In all chaos there is a cosmos, in all disorder a secret order.

C. G. Jung

In 2005, I audited a class in Fractal Geometry at a local university. At the time, my reasons for leaving my clinical practice for 5 hours per week over a period of 4 months were unclear. Ostensibly, I had failed to understand certain concepts in Chaos Theory on my own. I believed there was a deep mystery waiting to be discovered by studying the mathematics underlying chaos. When preparing the first draft of this chapter, I drew from a deep cistern that had been filled more than a decade earlier. It furnished me the basic idea for how the unconscious shapes and informs the creative experience. It comingled with ideas about Einstein's theory of General Relativity that envisioned gravity as a deformation of the space-time continuum. This led to the overarching idea that there is an unconscious-conscious continuum.

"Jung assumes a complex structure for the entire psyche" (Dieckmann, 1999). Originally, Jung envisioned complexes as being associated with the personal unconscious. "Later, he modified this in the sense that, indeed the shell of the complex with its amplifications and associations often reside in the personal unconscious, but the actual core of the complex is native to the collective unconscious" (Dieckmann, 1999). Barbara Hannah noted, "Unless they are extraordinarily integrated, instincts are like dim luminosities that encompass and extend beyond the consciousness of our ego-complex, luminosities that can guide us in places where our ego-consciousness is not yet up to the situation" (Hannah, 2006). Analytical psychology might have been named Complex Psychology in deference to the central role of the complex.

Chaos Theory offers insights into the mystery of how regions of the unconscious exert strong influence over writing and reading. I propose that the unconscious-conscious continuum is deformed by anything that is highly charged with affect. This introduces a concept from Chaos Theory, *attractors*, to illustrate how memories and innate proclivities shape the unconscious roots of creativity. These attractors give each individual's unconscious-conscious continuum a unique topography. In most respects, the attractor is equivalent to a complex. Dieckmann observes, "The further removed from consciousness a complex becomes and the stronger the energy it contains, the more it tends to include mythological and archaic from the collective unconscious in its repertory of active imagery" (Dieckmann, 1996).

Chaos Theory is a field of study describing the behavior of dynamical systems (function involving time dependence of a point) that are highly sensitive to initial conditions. Fractal geometry is a branch of mathematics involving equations that are nonlinear and dynamical.

In fractal geometry, there are sets of solutions to certain systems of equations, known as Julia Sets, that reveal intriguing features when they are plotted on a graph. These sets (graphed points) are identical in appearance whether they are viewed from afar or if the view zooms in. Below is a figure of a particular sort of Julia Set that is seen to have a repeating pattern when we zoom in or zoom out. This feature is known as self-similarity. In a sense, these graphs depict the alchemical idea of *as above, so below.*

FIGURE 2. *JULIA SET.*
WIKIPEDIA IMAGE OBTAINED ON 8/8/16.

The branching of the bronchial tree of our respiratory system or the branching of roots and tree limbs of a tree provide examples of fractal patterns in nature.

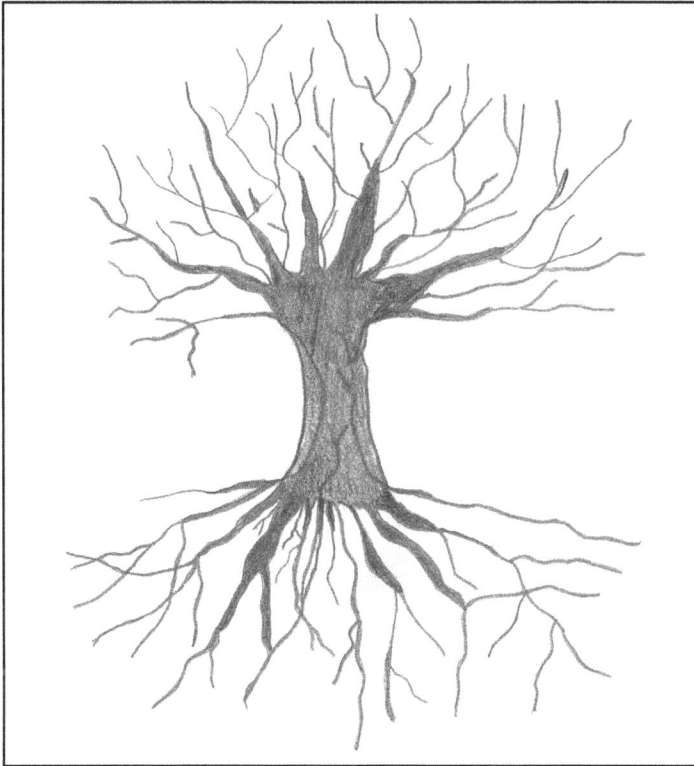

FIGURE 3. *Fractal Branching Tree and Roots.*

There are certain points or regions of graphs like the Julia Set that seem to draw other points in a particular direction.

Early weather models developed by Edward Lorenz, a pioneer of Chaos Theory, exhibited *chaotic* behavior when plotted on a time dependent graph. Lorenz developed a set of relatively simple equations to describe the behavior of an extremely simple model of a weather system. He imagined a solid, rectangular box with a heat source on the bottom of the box. Here are the equations he developed to describe his simple weather system.

- P represents the ratio of the fluid viscosity to its thermal conductivity,

- R represents the difference in temperature between the top and bottom of the box

- B is the ratio of the width to height of the box.

The values Lorenz used as initial conditions are P = 10, R = 28, B = 8/3.

When the results are plotted in three dimensions, the Lorenz Attractor pictured below, is obtained.

In order to generate elegant graphs with these sorts of fractal patterns, a set of initial inputs are chosen and the system of equations is solved for specific outputs. These solutions (outputs) become the inputs for the system of equations to be run again. Each time the equations are solved a point with specific coordinates is plotted on a graph. After the equation is run hundreds or even thousands of times, elegant, ethereal looking pattern can appear.

Some sets of equations produce results that display regions on the graph around which the points seem to orbit, as if the region of the graph "attracts" the graphed points. These regions are called attractors. These attractors provide an intriguing model of how ideas and words coalesce within the writer's unconscious. The attractors almost appear to bend the curve to its will. (This is an intentional

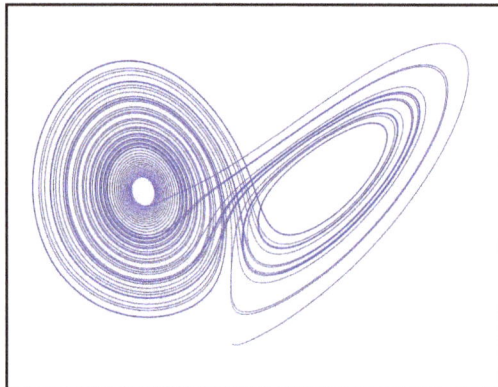

FIGURE 4. *LORENZ ATTRACTOR.*

anthropomorphism.) They define the topography of the curve that is plotted. Above all, these systems and the elegant patterns they produce are examples of an emergent phenomena.

Let us suppose that the unconscious possesses regions akin to an attractor. If unconscious attractors function like they do in a Julia Set, then a writer's choice of words, the length and cadence of a sentence, the brevity or lengthiness of a paragraph, as well as the completed work may well display features similar to self-similarity. In other words, if we could view the creative moment through the perspective of unconscious attractors we would notice something similar regardless of the scale at which we are observing word, sentence, paragraph or completed work. The writer's entire being is brought to bear in creating the text. What Jung said about astrology can be extended to writing, "We are born at a given place in a given time and like vintage years of wine we have the quality of the year and if the season in which we are born" (Jung, 1996). My choice to interweave fractals, chaos, and complexity is itself a testament to how the unconscious roots seek expression.

Attractors and the Writer

The way unconscious contents find expression in a piece of writing resembles the chaotic attractors. The unconscious acts with a force that pulls together words, ideas, images, emotions and fashion elegant patterns from them. Something akin to gravitational force exerts its effect upon the writer. This force draws everything in its vicinity toward certain regions of the unconscious. Larger patterns emerge from these elements to produce motifs, narrative arcs, and recurring themes. Like the complex in analytical psychology, unconscious attractors are the black holes of the mind. They draw together, coalesce, and assemble all manner of things in novel ways.

Mario Vargas Llosa says, "A writer is not always conscious of the influences he has received. (...) I have been reading Borges ever since I discovered him (...) this attention has left some kind of mark on what I have written, although I cannot say in what specific areas it is present." Reflecting on why some experiences encouraged him to write and others left no trace on his literary work, Vargas Llosa supposed that the "literarily fertile" experiences touched some essential aspect of his personality about which he was not conscious (Llosa, 1991).

Many things contribute to the formation of unconscious attractors in the writer. These include biological propensities, skills the writer intentionally cultivates, and personal/collective unconscious material. One of Jung's profound discoveries was that symbols, imagery, and motifs that appear in the stories, art, and myths across different cultures and during different epochs arise from a collective bedrock. The manifest stories Jung's patients recounted often reflected collective themes. These collective roots showed forth in art, symbols, myths, fairy tales, and more.

The personal unconscious exerts tremendous force on the writer. The material banished from consciousness includes traumatic memories and other personal history associated with intense affective charge. Other aspects of the Self may be relegated to the personal unconscious by things as commonplace as benign neglect of a child's gifts, talents, or natural affinities. At times a writer's *oeuvre* take on the appearance of a repetition-compulsion in the classical psychoanalytic sense. It is as if the writer's willful choices are bent in the direction of some original trauma or complex to which she returns again and again.

The person under the influence of an unconscious attractor originating in the personal unconscious re-enacts original traumas in symbolic fashion. John Van Eenwyk writes "The defense dynamic is fractal: Self-similar across scale and transcending categories (unconscious)" (Van Eenwyk, 2013). This means that from the level of the overall narrative arc down to the granular level of a word choice the writer is guided by something displaying repetitive pattern, self-similar patterns like the Julia Set pictured in Figure 1.

The unconscious attractors, like their mathematical counterparts, are extremely sensitive to initial conditions. Once the unconscious attractor forms, all sorts of things can initiate the convergence into the orbital region of that attractor. It is often the remembrance of things past, whether it be an original trauma or an original pleasure, that can kindle the influence of an attractor. Similarly, personal and collective unconscious will seek expression and often the most compelling prose blends individual and universal themes in novel fashion. The unconscious attractor helps explain how complex, elegant forms of writing emerge from small, simpler elements. In this respect, writing qualifies as an emergent phenomenon.

Quite possibly the regions surrounding an unconscious attractor are simply a modern restating of how the Muses guide and direct the writer and artist. The writer in search of the next idea, scene, or even just a word draws from a sort of aquifer that has rich interconnections. It could be compared to the vast network of freshwater sinkholes spread out across the Yucatan Peninsula (cenotes) on which the Mayan people depended. A piece of writing is stitched together in complex ways. It is constellated around emotive tones (Freud, 1910). When unconscious attractors are at play, the manifest story is really a surrogate for a much deeper story. This deeper story often follows one of three patterns: repeating, remembering, or working-through.

Repressed material with high affective charge can of course produce symptoms, but it can also be a source of creativity. Writers endlessly draw from these regions and are drawn toward these regions where the unconscious attractors constellate. With perseverance, the writer strings together words to produce a completed piece of writing. When past experience or innate proclivities are activated, things converge and orbit around the unconscious attractors seeking expression.

Author Sketches

According to Wallace Stegner, "Any work of art is the product of a total human being" (Stegner, 2002). The writer brings order of her own making out of chaos. From whence do the ideas for a story arise? Often, the narrative arc of a story bears striking resemblances to the writer's biography. These resonances may be unacknowledged by the writer. Freud's essay, *Repeating, Remembering and Working-Through* provides clues about three categories of the narrative arc wherein the unconscious seeks expression in a manifest story (Freud, 2001). A great deal of fiction falls within one of these three categories that Freud used to describe the process of psychoanalytic treatment. Some authors appear to repeat the same themes again and again. Others strive to remember. And there are poignant stories that resound with the timbre of conflicts resolving. As Graham Greene observed in *Ways of Escape* "Writing is a form of therapy; sometimes I wonder how all those who do not write, compose or paint can manage to escape the madness, melancholia, the panic and fear which is inherent in a human situation" (Greene, 1980). Freud said that it "is very useful to designate a group of ideas which belong together and have a common emotive tone, according to the custom of the Zürich school (Bleuler, Jung and others), as a 'complex'" (Freud, 1910). A writer constructs a manifest story that is a "disguised surrogate" for the unconscious story. The unconscious story variously strives to repeat, remember and work-through. This same process unfolds for the reader engaging a text. Four authors are cited to illustrate how repeating, remembering, and working-through wafts through a writer's *oeuvre*. These writer's manifest stories move in tandem with elements of their life's stories and possibly unconscious themes having roots in these writer's unconscious attractors.

Joseph Conrad was a perennial immigrant, and his fiction often reflects the multidimensional, complex features of the immigrant experience. Although Franz Kafka's passion was writing, he resigned himself to working as an insurance agent where he distinguished himself with such things as inventing the first hard hat. Kafka's father disapproved of his son's literary gifts. That disapproval combined with a painfully introverted, self-conscious nature played out in stories of alienation like *The Metamorphosis*. Both

Kafka and Conrad seem to repeat the themes from their personal lives in their fiction.

Charlotte Perkins Gilman's short story, *The Yellow Wallpaper*, originally published in 1892, depicts a woman narrator whose physician husband has rented a house for the summer in which she is to recuperate from a nervous disorder. The story has a gothic tone that leads the reader to feel that the narrator is actually imprisoned in an upstairs room of the house that has barred windows. She writes despite the fact that her husband has discouraged her from doing so. In due course, the narrator perceives that there is a woman imprisoned in the yellow wallpaper that covers the room. The woman in the wallpaper desperately seeks to communicate her plight to the narrator. *The Yellow Wallpaper* that was published three years before *Studies on Hysteria* is an example of a story of remembering.

In a compilation of radio interviews with the author Pat Conroy, whose own father was the model for the brutal protagonist of *The Great Santini*, Conroy praised his father for what he described as great literary criticism. "Son, you will never be able to write the word father without my image coming up." Conroy went on to say, "And my father's right. You know, father is a damaged word with me" (Gross, 2016). Much of Conroy's work appears to be repeating; however, beginning with *Lords of Discipline* and culminating with his memoir, *My Losing Season*, his work reflects a writer working through unresolved conflicts with his father.

Analysis and Literature

Freud sought traces of unconscious conflicts and pathology in literature. He resorted to literary references (Oedipus) to capture symbolically a large swath of psychological terrain. Jung was apparently drawn to visionary literature where he saw elements of the unconscious showing forth—both personal and collective. Freud instead appeared to focus more of symbolism in literature that often allowed him to reduce things to a struggle with libidinal impulses. Jung appreciated symbols for their expansive qualities that often furthered the process of individuation. Together, Freud and Jung offer important insights about the topography of the unconscious where the author goes time and again to bring forth her prose.

Attractors and the Reader

The reader is also possessed of unconscious attractors in her psyche. These unconscious attractors arise in the same way they would for a writer. The reader's unconscious attractors result from a confluence of genetic, biological, temperamental, and archetypal factors. The notion of unconscious attractors resembles Jung's theory of the complex. They share the quality of luminosity that Jung ascribed to complexes. Unlike complexes, attractors do not rise to the threshold of part personalities.

The reader is no less subject to the influence of unconscious attractors than the writer. In the course of encountering the text, the reader's unconscious shapes the result she obtains. The reader creates from the material the writer provides and her own vast aquifer of unconscious material. The story grows out of a reader like a "child its mother" too. It is not necessary for the reader to recognize this process for it to be at work.

At first glance, it may appear that the careful crafting of a piece of writing, the countless revisions, the seemingly endless starts, stops, and dead ends is wholly different from the reader's passive experience. Reading sweeps us along, and we are at the mercy of the writer's intention. Anyone who reads an O'Henry short story understands how vulnerable to manipulations a reader can be. Good stories fashion entire worlds into which the reader enters and is quickly immersed and overtaken.

While visiting my sister a few years ago, I conducted an experiment after she asked me for my thoughts about a print of a farmhouse that hangs in her breakfast nook. She taught middle school English for 32 years and has sometimes edited my writing. I proposed to write her a story loosely based on the print. Every 500 to 700 words I paused and allowed her to read what I had produced. As I watched the effect my story produced, I intentionally turned the story in unexpected, sometimes disturbing directions. Where I had evoked feelings of disgust toward a character in one segment, I then warned her that in the next installment I would cause her to feel sympathy for the same character. Despite her protests, I even resolved the story with a deeply disturbing, ambiguous end. Even the title, *Angus Must Die*, was crafted to produce a particular effect. Never before had I witnessed first-hand and in real time the mysterious effect that writing exerts on the reader. Moreover, there was an interplay between my unconscious-conscious continuum and that of my sister's that left an indelible mark on me. I know words have power, but to see that power displayed at each plot point was unprecedented. For all I know, this entire experience was nothing more than reading her brother's story as if it had been serialized. However, her creativity was a vital ingredient in forming *Angus Must Die* and in bringing it to life ultimately. This raises the question of the intersubjective realm between writer and reader.

Intersubjectivity

The reader and the writer share words? Jung's early word association experiments demonstrated that certain words carry strong affective charge. Advertisers are known to choose words with ancient linguistic roots perhaps to evoke subliminal responses that derive from ancient languages or protolanguages. Prius is a hybrid vehicle that debuted in 1997 whose manufacturer relied on a word that means *that which comes before*. The founders of the Janus Fund chose as their moniker a Roman god with two faces, one facing into the future and the other the past. Words have power. Words provide a bridge connecting the writer and the reader. Words are also portals through which the unconscious communicates with consciousness.

Readers imagine characters, settings, and action and thereby participate in the creative experience. Although there is a passive dimension to reading, the reader still brings the entirety of herself to the text. Reading is more active than watching a movie. Occasionally, I have avoided viewing a movie adaptation of a beloved novel knowing that once I'd seen the film my own imagination becomes blighted. The writer shapes the reader's experience, but the reader is still left the task of conjuring and assembling the details for herself.

To some extent, a therapist and a patient engage in a similar pattern. The therapist attempts to maintain the therapeutic frame while the patient is still left with the responsibility of furnishing the material with which to work. The Jungian therapist remains alert for evidence of the Self leading this process. The therapist's unconscious interacts with the patient's unconscious. The intersubjective field resulting from this interplay shares a great deal in common with the interplay between writer and reader. Just as two patients experience very different processes with the same therapist, two distinct readers of the same text cannot be expected to have identical experiences. The experience of each reader is a unique creation. Heraclitus observed that "No man ever steps into the same river twice." Similarly, even the same person reading a story at different times does not have the same experience. To begin with, the novelty of the story is lost on the second encounter. Additionally, re-reading often reveals subtle, nuanced features that were missed the first time. This sometimes makes re-reading a story a very different experience than the first encounter. Life marches on and the reader changes. No person rereads the same story. The reader, like Heraclitus' river, is never the same.

Writer/Reader, Patient/Analyst

Let us turn now to intersubjectivity. The writer sees the words coalescing on the page, she becomes vaguely aware of the unconscious currents, the attractors making their demands. Likewise, the reader makes particular choices as she imagines the story. At least one unconscious attractor may be at play. Of course, several attractors may exert simultaneous effect. Susan Sontag wrote, "Needless to say, I lend bits of myself to all my characters" (Sontag, 2001).

Otto Fenichel discusses a form of screen memory he calls "the inner injunction to make a mental note." He tells of a patient who set out to test his memory by trying to remember a particular advertisement he'd seen for margarine. Margarine is a substitute for butter and this led to various associations that reminded him of a childhood song with the words "My mother always smeared the butter on the wall." These words struck the patient as being inconsistent with his "proper" mother. Fenichel reveals that the patient's mother had died when he was a child, and he had been raised by a stepmother. He was unaware of this until he was an adult. Presumably, "the antithesis butter-margarine signified mother-stepmother, and the patient's "stressing of his stepmother's 'genteel' nature helped him repudiate his unconscious knowledge." He chose to remember the fact that margarine is a substitute for butter instead of remembering the details related to his stepmother.

Something like this happens for the writer and the reader. For both of them, certain things percolate up from the substrata of the unconscious in search of expression that are symbolic substitutions. There is a latent level to a story for the writer and the reader. Except in rare instances like my story crafting with my sister and occasions when an editor or acquaintance reads a writer's work, intersubjectivity between writers and readers is unidirectional. It is unlikely that a writer will have direct interactions with a reader's unconscious. However, to the extent that the writer's source of creativity is the unconscious, the reader is interacting with the writer's unconscious at some level.

Literature and poetry offers an ability to experience life through the prism of other characters. I do not have to leave earth to be moved by Heinlein's rendering of a man raised by Martians who returns to earth in *Stranger in a Strange Land*. When I saw the way the humanoid creatures in James Cameron's *Avatar* lived in close sympathy with their world, I immediately recalled Heinlein's book. I might conjecture that Heinlein struggled with his own deep, visionary capacities that made him feel like a *Stranger in a Strange Land*. If nothing else, reading is among the most egalitarian form of creativity. It also requires something more than watching a story on a screen.

A psychoanalyst supervisor of mine once estimated that after a thorough analysis 98% of a person's choices are still governed by unconscious factors, down from 99.9% before the analysis. As dismal as those results seemed to me 35 years ago, I see that he was probably right that the vast amount of what shapes our choices and actions remains unconscious. That is not all bad, provided you have some form of creative expression that will let the unconscious speak. When it does speak, it is likely to have a distinctive voice. When it comes time to fill the blank page, the writer can take comfort in knowing that the voice of her unconscious will find a way to be heard. The contours of the unconscious voice, the authorial voice, will show the remnants of the unconscious attractors that drew it all together.

In the beginning was the Word...

References

Dieckmann, H. (1999). *Complexes: Diagnosis and therapy in analytical psychology*. Wilmette, IL: Chiron Publications. February 1954. *The Diary of Anaïs Nin*, Vol. 5 as quoted in (p. 38) J. L. Webber & J. Grumman (Authors), *Woman as writer* (1978) Boston: Houghton Mifflin.

Fenichel, O., & Fenichel, H. (1953). The Inner Injunction to "Make a Mental Note" In *The collected papers of Otto Fenichel* (pp. 153-154). New York: Norton. [Foreword]. (2002). In W. Stegner & L. Stegner (Authors), *On teaching and writing fiction* (p. xi). New York, NY: Penguin Books. [Foreword]. (2002). In W. Stegner & L. Stegner (Authors), *On teaching and writing fiction* (p. xi). New York, NY: Penguin Books.

Freud, S. (1910). The Origin and Development of Psychoanalysis. *The American Journal of Psychology*, 21(2), 181. Retrieved March 21, 2016, from https://dspace.mit.edu/bitstream/handle/1721.1/65347/sts-003-spring-2008/contents/readings/freud.pdf

Freud, S., Strachey, J., Freud, A., Strachey, A., & Tyson, A. (2001). Remembering, Repeating, and Working-Through. In *The standard edition of the complete psychological works of Sigmund Freud*. (1911-1913) (Vol. 12, pp. 366-376). London: Vintage.

Greene, G. (1980). *Ways of escape*. New York: Simon and Schuster.

Gross, T. (2016, March 11). Remembering 'Great Santini' Author Pat Conroy. Retrieved March 20, 2016, from http://www.npr.org/2016/03/11/469944762/remembering-great-santini-author-pat-conroy

Gross, T. (2016, March 11). Remembering 'Great Santini' Author Pat Conroy. Retrieved March 20, 2016, from http://www.npr.org/2016/03/11/469944762/remembering-great-santini-author-pat-conroy [Introduction]. (2006). In B. Hannah (Author), *The archetypal symbolism of animals: Lectures given at the C.G. Jung Institute* (p. 11). Willmette, IL: Chiron, Enfield.

Hannah, B. (2006). *The Archetypal Symbolism Animals* (p. 11). Wilmette, IL: Chiron Publications.

Jung, C. G., & Jaffe, A. (1989). *Memories, dreams, reflections*. New York: Vintage Books.

Jung, C. G., & Shamdasani, S. (1996). *The psychology of Kundalini yoga: Notes of the seminar given in 1932 by C.G. Jung*. Princeton, NJ: Princeton University Press.

Jung, C. G. (1971). *The spirit in man, art, and literature* (Vol. 15). Princeton, NJ: Princeton University Press. Para. 159.

Lacan, J. (1977). The Freudian thing. In *Éscritis A Selection* (p. 116). New York, NY: W.W. Norton.

Littleton, C. S. (2007). Mythology: *The illustrated anthology of world myth and storytelling*. New York: Barnes & Noble by arrangement with Duncan Baird.

Llosa, M. V., & Lichtblau, M. I. (1991). *A writer's reality*. Syracuse, NY: Syracuse University Press.

Otto, R., & Harvey, J. W. (1958). *The idea of the holy: An inquiry into the non-rational factor in the idea of the divine and its relation to the rational*. New York: Oxford University Press.

Schrag, C. O. (1997). The self in discourse. In *The self after postmodernity* (pp. 16-26). New Haven, CT: Yale University Press.

Schwartz, O. (2015, May). Can a computer write poetry? Retrieved April 03, 2016, from http://www.ted.com/talks/oscar_schwartz_can_a_computer_write_poetry

Sontag, S. (2001). Writing as reading. In *Where the stress falls: Essays* (p. 266). New York: Farrar, Straus, and Giroux.

Chapter 6

The Creative Encounter and the Theory of Formation

by Carol Thayer Cox

> *The creative process is the expression of...passion for form.*
> *It is the struggle against disintegration, the struggle to bring*
> *into existence new kinds of being that give harmony and*
> *integration.* (May, 1975, p. 146)

Creativity happens! It is just part of the human condition. The most recent evidence discovered in 1994 reveals that art was being made over 30,000 years ago on the walls of the Chauvet Cave in southern France (Nelson & Ciuffo, 2010). We can assume these ancient peoples likely engaged in other arts as well, such as sculpture, music, and dance. Ellen Dissanayake (1992) posits that there is a biological, evolutionary need for being creative in both the making and viewing of art. Countless studies examine the cultural, sociological, psychological, perceptual, or neurological components of art-making, which have resulted in a plethora of fascinating theories about creativity. Analyzing an artistic work as to its abstract or representational content, its color and formal elements, its harmonies and rhythms, its symbols and metaphors, its archetypal and mythological imagery, yields further insights into the enigma of the creative act.

Although I have deep respect for the diverse approaches to understanding creativity, my focus in this chapter is different. As an art therapist, I fervently believe in the inherently healing qualities of engaging in the act of creating, and therefore I have been and continue to be curious about why, where, when, and how it happens. But I am also interested in what gets in the way of its happening, when creativity gets stymied and people get stuck. If we investigate the variables of the creative process, perhaps we could begin to understand why, where, when, and how this process gets interrupted. In so doing, we can be in a better position to nurture and sustain it for ourselves as well as our clients. I propose an integrative approach for thinking about the creative encounter using the quadrated mandala as the blueprint and the Holistic Round of Formation as the lens for exploration.

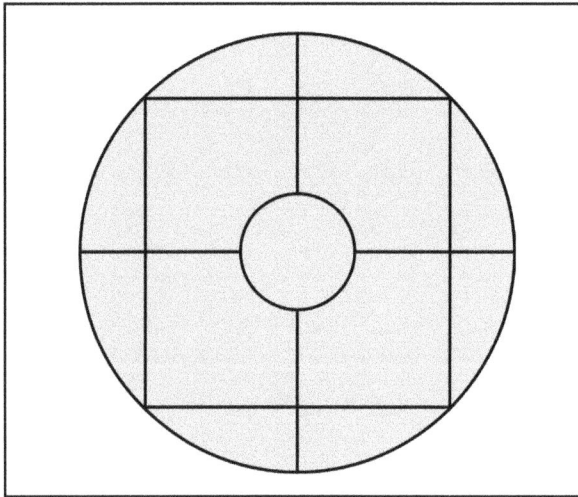

FIGURE I. *QUADRATED CIRCLE.*

The Quadrated Mandala

The quadrated circle (figure I) is configured in various ways, but always containing a circle combined with either a square or an equidistant cross or both of these shapes. Angeles Arrien (1992) has synthesized all the various meanings that have been ascribed to these three universal symbols. In summary, the circle represents "wholeness and the experience of unity" (p. 31); the square signifies "stability... security," and a sense of "responsibility" (p. 63); the equidistant cross is a sign of "relationship...integration and balanced connection" (p. 39).

Employing this structure of the quadrated mandala helps identify and honor the center, establish the four directions, and square the circle. When speaking of the symbolism of mandalas, Jung (1959/1973) states, "...as a rule the center contains the motif of the *rotundrum*, known to us from alchemy, or the four-fold emanation of the squaring of the circle" (para. 660). In another reference to the alchemical process, Jung (1953/1968) says that the symbol of the quadrated circle "breaks down the original, chaotic unity into the four elements and then brings them together into a higher unity. The unity is represented by the circle, the four elements by the square..." (para. 165). He explains that this distillation process can result in the production of the purest essence, the ultimate goal in alchemy. The quadrated mandala is an archetype that synthesizes opposites, making order out of disorder; it also provides a path to the center and a holistic way to make sense of the world, both above and below.

John Weir Perry (1953/1987) presents an extensive study of the etiology and symbolism of the quadrated mandala. He contends that "...the sun wheel can be shown to form the root symbol for all derivative symbols [in both western and eastern cultures] based on the quadrated circle" (p. 83). Paleolithic sun wheels are considered to be the earliest examples of mandala art. Many of these simple circles were quadrated. Primitive people found themselves in a circular and cyclical world, and to distinguish where they were in space they would need to establish directionality so as not to get lost and also to define their position. Within the circle the first straight lines got drawn from a central point probably symbolizing the sun, seen as the life-giving force.

Primitive humans saw the regularity and predictability of the movement of the universe in the rhythmic comings and goings of the sun, moon, stars, and seasons. *Karahundj* in Armenia and Stonehenge in England are two of the earliest examples of what are believed to be sacred stone circles built as ceremonial centers for solar and lunar calendars or for tracking astronomical happenings. *El Castilla* at Chichen Itza in Mexico was built as a temple by the Mayans and was also used as a solar calendar. All of these early structures were oriented according to the directions with the center as essential to the whole cosmic system.

The center point, or the axis mundi, symbolizes the connection between earth and sky and the path for communication between the upper and lower realms. It is like the *omphalos*, or umbilical of the world, the point of creation. Different cultures represent this holy center by various forms—sacred mountains (Mt Fuji), sacred trees (Bodhi tree), pyramids, maypoles, totem poles, stupas, pagodas, minarets, steeples, centers of domes, central altars, shrines—all symbolizing humans' desire for connection to the other world.

Balanced geometric designs in architecture reflect the harmony and perfection of the sacred. The combination of the circle symbolizing spirit or heaven and the square symbolizing matter or earth is a metaphor for balancing all opposites. The beautiful Byzantine *Hagia Sophia* and Gothic Chartres Cathedral are both fine examples of architecture that focused on the mandala form as a symbol of the perfection of God, incorporating both the equilateral cross and the dome with precise proportions. An excellent example of Islamic architecture, the Blue Mosque, also combines the square and circular shapes as an expression of divine unity.

There are some other architectural examples of the quadrated mandala in ancient structures in the East, such as the Buddhist temple *Borobudur* in Java, Indonesia. Circumambulating the five square levels and four circular terraces to the top is a sacred path to the center, symbolizing a journey to the source of creation. The concept of being on such a journey is also exemplified by walking the labyrinth, done as a substitute for the pilgrimage to Jerusalem. The classic labyrinth design at Chartres shows the four directions embedded in the circular design; each quadrant is experienced again and again on the journey to the center.

Some of the most beautiful quadrated mandalas that incorporate circles and squares as well as the four directional gates are Asian. Those used for Buddhist ritual prayer meditations, painted on silk cloth or made with colored sand, are considered a facilitator for integration of opposites and the ultimate path towards harmony and enlightenment. A tantric Hindu mandala, the *Sri Yantra*, is also used for sacred meditation. Inscribed with a seed mantra and created during complex rituals, it is believed to contain thought and sound energy patterns that enhance connection to the metaphysical realm.

Mandalas were also used as medicine. Some diagrams have been found from ancient China that were designated for medicine ceremonies and were believed to be used for meditation and healing rituals, similar to Navaho sand paintings of the American Southwest, still being used today. Both are based on the circular design with four directional gates. This motif of the quadrated circle is repeated over and over again in just about every culture to represent the world of humans and the world of gods, and how people tried to emulate here on earth the perfection of nature and the sacred order of things (Perry, 1953/1987).

In summary, these examples of quadrated mandala art and architecture spanning thousands of years and numerous cultures and religions provide us with insight into their various functions for humankind:

- An understanding of space, time, and movement in the world
- An honoring of the principle of order
- An expression of duality and a balancing of opposites
- A protected place for sacred ritual and ceremony
- A means to achieve healing, transformation, and rebirth
- A path, pilgrimage, or journey towards enlightenment
- A longing for wholeness or for a sense of unity

Though not often consciously acknowledged, the act of creating has the potential of fulfilling these various functions held by this archetypal symbol residing in the collective unconscious.

The Quadrated Mandala as Blueprint

My adoption of the quadrated mandala as a blueprint for states of consciousness is because of its universality. After decades of study, Perry (1953/1987) reasoned, "Symbols in the form of the squared or four-pointed circle can be said...to represent the self as the totality of the psyche, embracing both conscious and unconscious components" (p. 7). Carl Jung spent years researching the psyches of his patients as well as his own (which now, after a century, is finally available to us in *The Red Book*), and he concluded that the mandala is the quintessential archetype for the transcendent Self that is striving for wholeness through the process of individuation. This quest, Perry says, comes from "the unconscious...the very source of the creative impulse." He states, "The individuation process is the psyche's most impressive creative activity" (p. 135).

Unlike Freud, who thought human development was determined by the time a person became a young adult, Jung believed that people could continue to evolve throughout their life spans, through four stages of development: childhood, youth, middle age, and old age. Eric Erikson expanded upon Jung's concept by including eight (a multiple of four) stages of psychosocial development that start at infancy and end at old age, each with opportunities to further grow psychologically. Jung and Erikson believed in self-actualization that is possible through integration and balance and attention to the conscious and unconscious. Their developmental theories are holistic in nature and thus conceptually circular rather than linear. Jacobi (1942/1973) explains Jung's thoughts on the life span: "The cycle of human life closes meaningfully and harmoniously; beginning and end coincide, an event that has been symbolized since time immemorial by the Uroboros" (p. 149).

Art therapist Joan Kellogg studied the work of Carl Jung and, like him, became interested in mandalas and the multicultural myths and symbols in the collective unconscious. Involved in a seminal study of states of consciousness with Stanislof Grof and Helen Bonny, Kellogg (1978/2002) subsequently integrated prenatal and transpersonal theories of personality development with the traditional life cycle theories that just went from birth to death. She increased the developmental stages to twelve (also a multiple of four) and created a circular construct for the life cycle that she called the "Archetypal Stages of the Great Round of Mandala" (p. iii). Having read Jung's descriptions of the archetypal images in the drawn mandalas of his patients and then sorting through her own collection of drawn mandalas from patients and research participants, Kellogg designated specific archetypal imagery to each of the developmental stages of her Great Round. Using a circular format to present theory was not a new concept, but her ability to determine the placement of archetypal forms to represent stages of the life cycle was her genius.[1] Kellogg's theory has been the inspiration and springboard for my working hypotheses about creativity.

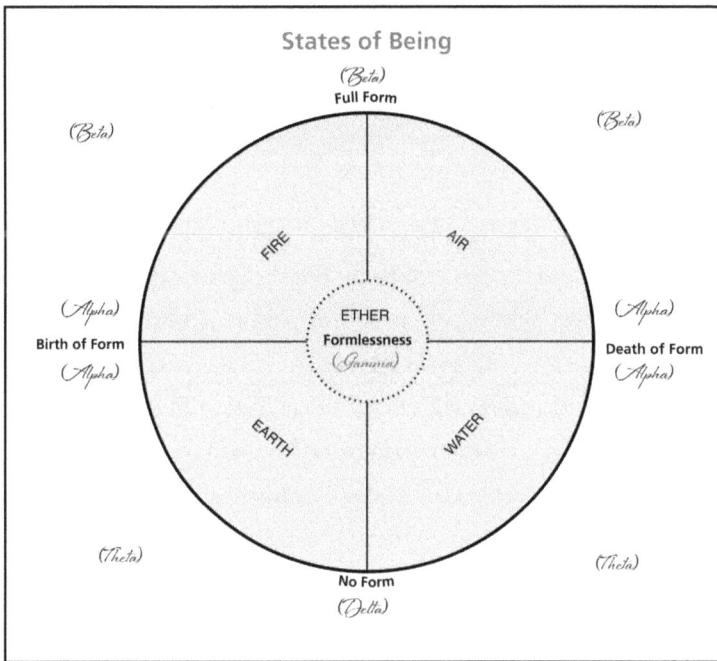

FIGURE 2. *HOLISTIC ROUND OF FORMATION #1.*

---

[1] For a biography of Kellogg, see Cox's article, *In Memoriam,* in reference list.

The Holistic Round of Formation

The Holistic Round of Formation (figure 2) is my synthesized and streamlined way of viewing states of being. I like to use the quadrated mandala for two reasons. First, the archetype carries with it a holistic view of life. Second, it affords a way to integrate various concepts I have been thinking about for many years. I have discovered that this model divided into four basic parts is applicable to most theoretical constructs, which I will illustrate after explaining the metaphorical geography of The Holistic Round.

When teaching about the Great Round, Kellogg divided her circle according to consciousness and the basic elements. The horizontal line that bisects the circle separates consciousness above (quadrants II and III) with unconsciousness below (quadrants I and IV). Kellogg believed that each of the four elements considered essential to life would be represented as follows: earth in quadrant I, fire in II, air in III, and water in IV. It would likely follow that a fifth element, ether, would reside in the center.

The energy field of this quadrated mandala can be described with brainwaves. At the very bottom, which is the deepest area of the unconscious, would be the slowest brainwave, Delta, which is deep, dreamless sleep. Moving upwards, still in the unconscious section, is Theta, which is a lighter form of sleep where dreams occur, or it can be a place of very deep relaxation in meditation. Then midway through the quadrated circle, at the transitional places from unconscious to conscious, is Alpha, which is a calm, relaxed, non-thinking, but very alert state that is ideal for mindfulness meditation. And at the top of the Round is high frequency Beta, the wide-awake, normal, thinking state in full consciousness. At the center would be Gamma, the highest frequency brainwaves of expanded consciousness.

The quadrants have specific functions. In ancient times, humans knew the essence of each season and the importance of the solstices and equinoxes in terms of understanding their own cycles (figure 3).[2]

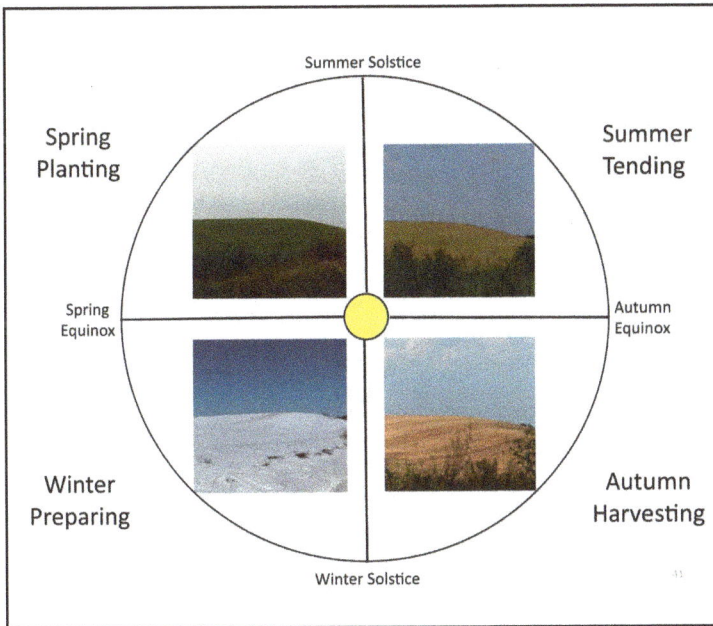

FIGURE 3. *THE SEASONS.*

The winter is a time of preparation. Snow gives the soil protection and nourishment, allowing it to rest. Roots or bulbs hibernate in the dark. Planning of the garden happens. New seeds are chosen. In springtime, plants break ground, seeking sunlight to grow. Seeds placed deep in the soil start to sprout. New seedlings are planted. They are tender and young but have energy to thrive and survive, even though unpredictable weather may present obstacles. The season of summer is for weeding and watering the garden, tending the plants into their full maturity in the sunlight. It is a time of ultimate harmony and acceptance. In autumn, there is a reaping of the harvest. What is left of the

2 Photos I have taken during the course of a year of a field near my home in Virginia.

plants' decayed forms returns to nurture the earth. It is the end of the life of these plants. It gets cold once again, and the cycle continues.

Notice the demarcation of the equinox and solstice. The equinox is the transitional place between the unconscious and conscious, not more of one than the other; lightness and darkness are equally divided—whereas the solstice points denote the extremes of lightness (the longest day) at the top of the mandala and the extremes of darkness (the shortest day) at the bottom.

The Holistic Round of Formation (figure 4) outlines the phases that are important in generating something into being from non-being, bringing it into full consciousness, and then letting that being return to its source. (The direction of the energy starts at the center, comes downward to the bottom, and then proceeds clockwise around the circle.)

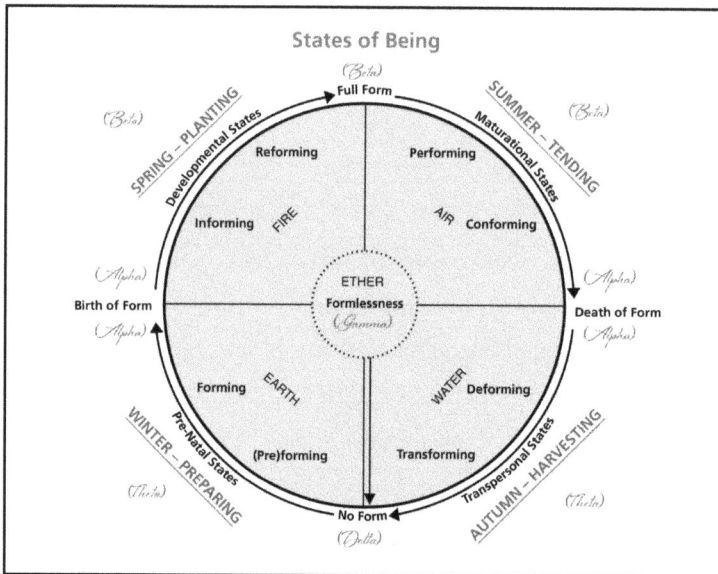

FIGURE 4. HOLISTIC ROUND OF FORMATION #2.

The center, the place of Formlessness, is the container for all potential form. Think of Form as something that comes into existence from the unconscious to consciousness. The idea of Form exists in our dream world where there are lots of possibilities and unconscious preparation. True Form doesn't happen until it is born at the liminal place at those Alpha levels between the unconscious and conscious realms. The highest point of consciousness, at the very top of the quadrated circle, is where Full Form exists in its most complete manifestation. And then eventually the Form must die and transition back into the unconscious once again, where it will go back to its beginning, the source.

Reviewing Kellogg's Archetypal Stages of the Great Round,[3] in which she conceptualized 13 stages (the 12 developmental stages and stage 0 in the center), will enhance our understanding of each quadrant's function in the life cycle. The winter quadrant of Preparing is equivalent to pre-natal states of being. The Spring Time of planting would parallel developmental states; the Summer Time of Tending corresponds with Maturational States, and the autumn quadrant of Harvesting relates to Transpersonal States.

I will refer to Kellogg's stages of the life cycle as states of being. I have chosen a different descriptive name than she has for each state (with the exception of the 4th state) and also a variation of the word FORM for each state.[4] Whereas Kellogg has selected three archetypal mandala images for each of her stages, I have instead chosen to expand upon the qualities of each state by using examples of art-based experiences to enrich meaning.

Think of each state as one that could exist in any cycle of creation. It could be within a person's life cycle or maybe it could reflect a time in a relationship. These cyclic journeys are metaphors for the creation of just about anything—a theory, a poem, a musical composition. The cycle could be as simple as a day in a person's life

---

3   I acknowledge the dedicated work of the other early teachers of Kellogg's Great Round. For years we discussed her ideas, some of us doing research. Together and individually we have developed and expanded upon her theories.
4   I am indebted to wordsmith Peggy Heller for suggesting that I play with the word FORM in its many variations.

or as complicated as the evolution of society. These archetypal states of being are familiar to us all on many levels.

0: Formlessness—Longing

The state of 0 is the *axis mundi*, the sacred center. In his first *Sermon to the Dead*, Jung says, "Nothingness is the same as fullness. In infinity full is as good as empty...We call this nothingness or fullness the *Pleroma*" (2009, p. 346). It is the Tao—or the energetic Source of everything, the provider of *Qi*. On the earth plane there is a longing for it. Formlessness in the center means there never has been nor ever will be anything likened to Form in this place of soul, the genesis of all being. Consider the minimalist *White Paintings* by Robert Rauschenberg or T.S. Eliot's "still point" when you think of dance.

Quadrant I: Winter—Preparing

This lower left quadrant of pre-natal states is the part of the life cycle that Stanislof Grof (1985) studied. He was a pioneer in the area of perinatal influences on personality. In the womb, the fetus is affected by all kinds of experiences. The last 20 years there has been much research in this area substantiating Grof's hypotheses.

1: Attaching—No Form

Energy descends from spirit to matter (from the sky realm to the earth plane) into the first state, at the bottom of the Round. No Form, as opposed to Formlessness, on the earth plane means there is form potential, but at this moment it is just at conception and is only a point or a dot in the confined darkness, totally unformed. Deeply unconscious, in the earth realm, the strands of attachment are precarious. Hear the beating of your heart in the middle of the night. Think of the primal drumbeat of the Shaman who knows this magical place well.

2: Incubating—(Pre) Forming

A place of unlimited possibilities, everything is in flux in the second state, seeking form; nothing is fixed. It reflects the time *in utero* when cells of the fetus are multiplying and dividing. Visualize snowflakes softly falling. How about lying in a bubbling hot tub at night beneath an infinite sky full of stars while listening to cosmic New Age music? It is a dissociative state of no boundaries where fragments of images or sounds can incubate.

3: Focusing—Forming

Towards the end of gestation, the third state is a time of rapid growth and differentiation. At this forming phase, the fetus is preparing to spiral through the birth canal and be born. There is a focused pull towards following the labyrinthine path with no clear awareness as to destination. Trust is paramount. See in your mind's eye a Whirling Dervish striving for an ecstatic state. Still in that hot tub, now imagine viewing the spiraling Milky Way taking form. From the former fragments, a storyline begins to take shape.

Quadrant II: Spring—Planting

This upper left quadrant of developmental states parallels the years of growth from birth to adolescence. Freud's, Jung's, and Erikson's life cycles all begin here.

4: Beginning—Birth of Form

The event of birth, at the transitional place between the unconscious and conscious realms, is the fourth state. It is the time of infancy, when basic needs and nurturance are necessary. The baby, held and protected, also demands attention to grow and survive. Think of little birds in a nest reaching up with open beaks to be fed by their parents. Picture the mother-child paintings by Mary Cassatt. Then rock back and forth in a rocking chair to the sound of a lullaby and you will experience this beginning state of being.

5: Struggling—Informing

The fifth state is a time of early childhood when rules are introduced. The toddler's family, surroundings, and environment are informing him so he can learn how to be in the world, how to do things. Power struggles ensue, and boundaries and defenses (represented by the repetition of lines) are formed. Rituals and routines are established to maintain order. Predictability, perfection, and protection are sought. Remember those childhood sayings not to step on that crack? Think of Kenneth Noland's carefully painted stripes.

6: Confronting—Reforming

Occurring first during childhood and renegotiated during adolescence, the sixth state is about confronting authority (as well as the shadow aspects of self), dealing with polarities, and holding the tension while in perceived battle. It is also a time of idealism, passion, heightened creativity, and sometimes rebellion. Adolescents may think of better ways of doing things, ways of reforming their world. Remember the hero's journey in *Star Wars*. Think of the divisiveness of black and white thinking, watch *West Side Story*, and then embrace the symbol of the yin-yang with the hope of finding harmony through balancing opposites.

Quadrant III: Summer—Tending

The upper right maturational quadrant correlates with adulthood and its many challenges. Erikson's and Jung's theories of the life span include the study of these states of consciousness as vital to understanding psychosocial health and potential. Geriatric psychiatrist Gene Cohen (2000) focused his research on older adults at a time when seeking meaning becomes significant as one "sums up" what one has done. He proposes "four developmental phases [that] shape the way our creative energy grows and the way we express it" from mid-life to elder years (pp. 78-79), encompassing the ninth and tenth states, bridging Quadrants III and IV.

7: Integrating—Full Form

At the very top of the Holistic Round of Formation is the seventh state, that of young adulthood. Here one is able to integrate previous dualities, is capable of abstract thinking, and is ready in this full, seemingly expansive, form to take on responsibility and a significant relationship. It captures the feeling of having arrived at last and that these moments in time will continue forever. The sun is at high noon. Read Walt Whitman's *Song of Myself*. While imagining a beautifully balanced quadrated mandala, listen to the melodic music of Vivaldi's *The Four Seasons*.

8: Committing—Performing

The eighth state is about establishing one's unique identity as a mature adult, being confident and competent in whatever career one has chosen. All the knowledge and training one assimilates gets applied. It is a time of performing, trying to do one's best in his or her line of work. Ideally one can function independently and continue to commit the energy and interest necessary to fulfill one's goals. Imagine walking through a portrait gallery and encountering artists' conceptions of each individual. Listen to Leontyne Price sing an aria, or watch Gene Kelly dance his famous solo in *Singing in the Rain*.

9: Completing—Conforming

During mid-adulthood, at the ninth state, it becomes necessary to conform to society's rules and expectations to complete goals. Collaboration with others takes place (family, colleagues, society) wherein homeostasis is attained. This state reflects the epitome of achievement and fulfillment, holding a sense of harmony and perfection. However grand, this state of being is ephemeral. Remember those beautiful symmetric images in a kaleidoscope. Think of how one feels at his or her graduation ceremony. Or imagine being a musician in a concert performance of Bach's harmonically sophisticated Brandenburg Concerto. This is a place of knowing the dance well, with the concomitant realization that it cannot last.

Quadrant IV: Autumn—Harvesting

Back in the unconscious, the lower right transpersonal quadrant is the place where therapists, such as Stanislof Grof, who work with altered states of consciousness and are interested in spiritual transcendence, do their best work. Carl Jung's enigmatic exploration of his own psyche in *The Red Book* emphasizes the qualities of the three states of being in this last quadrant.

10: Ending—Death of Form

Next comes old age when energy slows down, entropy sets in, and death of form happens at the tenth state, a place of transition into the unconscious once again. It is a time to acknowledge the end, along with feelings of separation and loss. A place of despair and sacrifice, it also offers opportunity for reassessment and hope for spiritual understanding and grace. Visualize descending imagery in paintings done in somber colors while listening to Rachmaninov's elegiac symphonies. Go see the promise portrayed in Georgia O'Keefe's skull paintings against light-filled desert skies.

11: Disintegrating—Deforming

In an actual life cycle, the eleventh and twelfth transpersonal states of consciousness theoretically manifest beyond death, but they are metaphorically accessed in life during times of profound transition and deep meditation. The eleventh state is when the previous form disintegrates, activating chaos, disorientation, and confusion. Nightmarish and surreal, the state of deforming is an irrational place that no longer makes sense. Its lack of order calls for surrendering and releasing what is no longer necessary, calling for creative spontaneity to establish a new kind of order. Think about "the center" Yeats speaks of that "cannot hold." Hear shattering, discordant sounds. Visualize Edvard Munch's famous painting, *The Scream*. Then realize that "revelation" is at hand.

12: Returning—Transforming

And finally, the twelfth state of being is the place of alchemical transformation. Energy moves upward and outward through a newly aligned center. *Kundalini* or peak experiences can happen along with a profound change of consciousness. It epitomizes epiphany, renewal, and rebirth, signifying a time to return to the Source once again. It is the place of inspiration and enlightenment, often with a feeling of connection to a higher power. This is the state of finding the true center of the transcendent Self, which can be accessed in a variety of ways. Visualize being in the most beautiful, serene, luminous place you can imagine. Or light a candle and listen to Wagner's peaceful Prelude to Act I of *Lohengrin*. You are lifted upward and you know intuitively that the cycle goes on and on.

To understand the broad potential for each state of consciousness outlined in the Holistic Round of Formation, think of experiencing each state somewhere on a continuum from the least to most optimum way, as each one provides challenges and insights. We encounter every state over and over again, as there are many cycles occurring simultaneously throughout our lives. Engaging with each state in one way or another is vital to our path towards wholeness.

The Holistic Round of Formation as Map for Integrating Ideas

> We have mentioned finding the progression of four in indigenous cultures, in other religions, in various psychological and philosophical writings, and in clinical Sandplay practice. ... In literature from worldwide cultures, the Hero's Journey invariably follows the same arc. As they developed, classic structures for opera, symphony, and theater all demonstrated this same pattern ... throughout our journey the underlying pattern persists, and for all of us, the rhythm beats in a measure of four. (Schaia, 2010, pp. 30 & 32)

The quadrated circle provides a useful structure for viewing theoretical constructs that often have four important components or steps. Each theory's four sections seem to parallel the archetypes of the quadrants of the round. Although I have correlated this model with many theories, I have chosen only several to illustrate my hypothesis. I apologize for what will seem like a simplification of some very complex theories. But my purpose is to use them as examples to further an understanding of how the Holistic Round of Formation can be an excellent aid for integrating various ideas (as might happen in the collective unconscious where this archetype lives).

Jung's theory of psychological types includes four fundamentally different ways that people experience the world. Jung considers two functions (thinking and feeling) to be rational and two (sensation and intuition) to be irrational. Although I realize that the placement of these functions in my diagram differs from the placement in circular diagrams drawn by other Jungians, I believe that each quadrant of the Holistic Round naturally carries the energy of the predominant function I have assigned to it. The two rational functions live in the conscious area and the two irrational ones in the unconscious area of the Holistic Round (figure 5).

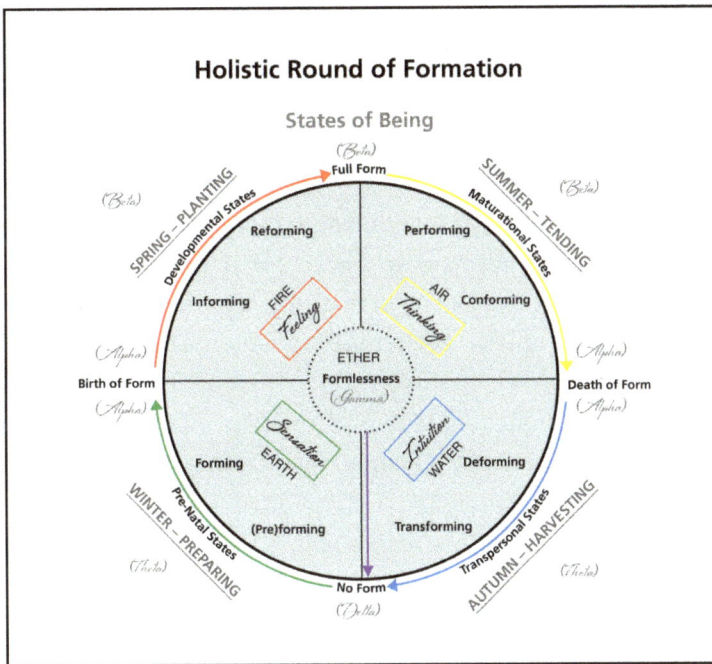

FIGURE 5. *HOLISTIC ROUND OF FORMATION #3.*

The winter quadrant of pre-natal states, where everything is in its preliminary state of being, is a place where the function of sensation would likely live best. Sensation has to do with direct experience of the senses, what is there is there, plain and simple. Sensation would be amplified in the non-rational first states of being and would be the predominant way of encountering the world.

Feeling is mostly subjective and involves what value an experience might have, good or bad, pleasant or unpleasant. The spring quadrant of developmental states, when everything exists in reaction to its environment, would easily engage the feeling function.

Thinking is conceptual and objective. The summer quadrant of maturational states, all highly conscious and therefore cognitive-driven, would logically employ thinking to determine the meaning of an experience and to distinguish it from other experiences.

Intuition incorporates the implications of an experience, what might be possible with this information and where it came from. The autumn quadrant of transpersonal states, where the world doesn't make rational sense anymore, is the place where the function of intuition would be paramount.

Gong Shu (2012), psychotherapist and integrator of both eastern and western approaches to medicine, created a treatment modality, which she calls "*Yi Shu*... The Art of Living with Change" (p. 57). Healing, in her method of combining meditative practices and spontaneous creativity, is all about the "process of balancing...the psychological, biological, social, and spiritual realms of the self"— so that there is union of opposites (the yin and the yang) and an ultimate sense of harmony (p. 57). The quadrated mandala, which symbolizes the entire psyche, can be the holistic container for these realms. The biological in the first quadrant of sensation is about what physically is. The psychological relates to the developmental quadrant of feeling, as the social must correspond to the maturational quadrant of thinking where group consciousness lives. Lastly, the spiritual parallels the transpersonal quadrant of intuition.

I believe these four areas that constitute the psyche along with the four functions are intricately involved during the creative process, but in varying degrees depending on where there might be blockages.

Jean Gebser, an important 20th century, Swiss-cultural philosopher, wrote brilliantly about multi-leveled structures of consciousness and the evolutionary ascent of the human psyche. Archaic consciousness relates to universal wisdom and is *in potentia* (much like all we have said about the place of the *axis mundi*, the state of 0). Magical consciousness is one-dimensional and works on the basis of instinct and ritual, which would be in the very deep unconscious of the first quadrant, where shamanism exists. Mythical consciousness is two-dimensional and relates to the psyche through imagination, which gets activated in the developmental years of the second quadrant when the hero sets out on his journey. Mental consciousness is three-dimensional and incorporates rationality, logically pairing with the third quadrant of the maturational years. Integral consciousness brings in the fourth dimension, with spiritual knowing and intuition, thus corresponding with the transpersonal fourth quadrant. "Gebser [said] in his own words: 'Every manifestation of our lives inevitably contains the sum of the past as well as what is to come'" (Feuerstein, 1987, p. 29).

James Hollis (2013), Jungian analyst and author of many books, formulates four essential questions from what he calls the "four great mysteries" of the collective archetypal myths that reside in our unconscious. These questions, he says, "never go away" (p. 106). Each of them has a natural home in a respective

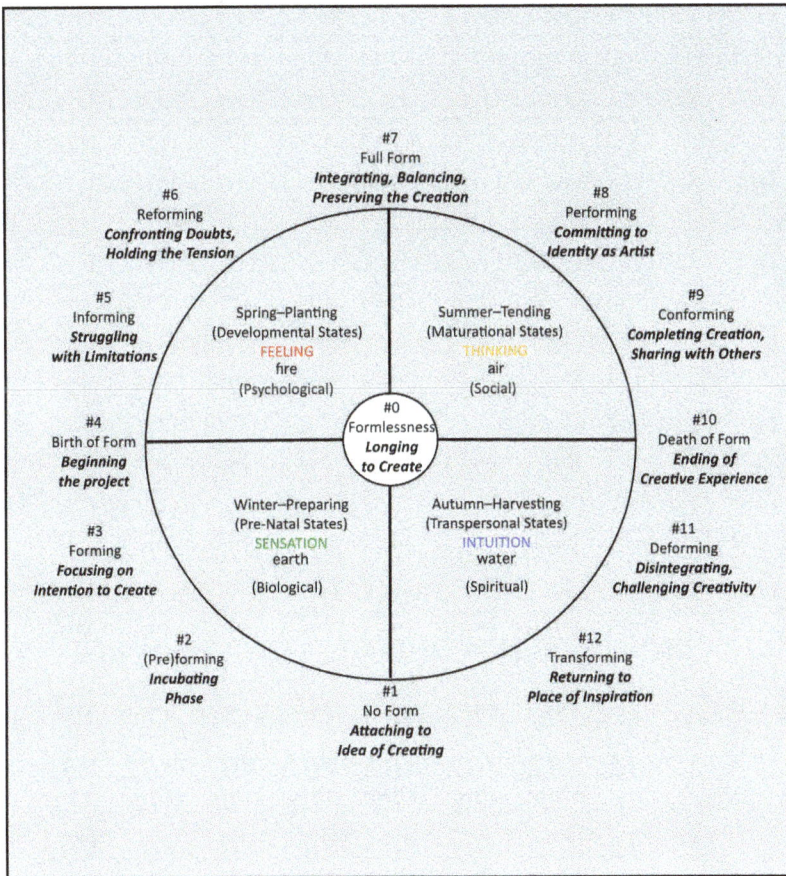

#7
Full Form
Integrating, Balancing,
Preserving the Creation

#6
Reforming
Confronting Doubts,
Holding the Tension

#8
Performing
Committing to
Identity as Artist

#5
Informing
Struggling
with Limitations

Spring–Planting
(Developmental States)
FEELING
fire
(Psychological)

Summer–Tending
(Maturational States)
THINKING
air
(Social)

#9
Conforming
Completing Creation,
Sharing with Others

#4
Birth of Form
Beginning
the project

#0
Formlessness
Longing
to Create

#10
Death of Form
Ending of
Creative Experience

Winter–Preparing
(Pre-Natal States)
SENSATION
earth
(Biological)

Autumn–Harvesting
(Transpersonal States)
INTUITION
water
(Spiritual)

#3
Forming
Focusing on
Intention to Create

#11
Deforming
Disintegrating,
Challenging Creativity

#2
(Pre)forming
Incubating
Phase

#1
No Form
Attaching to
Idea of Creating

#12
Transforming
Returning to
Place of Inspiration

FIGURE 6. *CYCLE OF CREATIVITY.*

quadrant of the Holistic Round; thus my presentation of Hollis's four questions will differ from the order in which he introduces them. The winter quadrant of the earth element, pre-natal states, and the function of sensation: "How are we as animal forms, empowered with spirit, to live in harmony with our natural environment? (*the ecological question*)" (p. 106). The spring quadrant of the fire element, developmental states, and the feeling function: "Who am I, how am I different from others, what is my life about, and how am I to find my way through the difficulties of life? (*the psychological question*)" (p. 106).

The summer quadrant of the air element, maturational states, and the thinking function: "Who are my people, what is my duty to others, and what are the rights, duties, privileges, and expectations of my tribe? (*the sociological question*)" (p. 106). The autumn quadrant of the water element, transpersonal states, and the intuitive function: "Why are we here, in service to what, and toward what end? (*the cosmological question*)" (p. 106).

The questions Hollis articulates are ones that have universal relevance and thus correlate with Gebser's structures of consciousness. I maintain that those who engage in acts of creativity are driven to do so by these very quests for meaning. I also suspect that the amount of energy invested in any particular quadrant may be due to the compelling question at hand.

The Holistic Round as Lens for Exploring Creativity

Rollo May (1975), an existential and humanistic psychologist, discusses the various qualities of encounter common to artists and scientists involved in the process of creating. I have selected some of these qualities to introduce each quadrant of The Holistic Round of Formation, which I use as a lens for understanding states of being (or form) coming into existence during the process of creation. In this example of a creative cycle (figure 6), I make reference to the perspective of a visual artist, but the steps are applicable to any process of creativity. Quotes from artists describing their creative process serve as illustrations.[5] Also, I include notes on each axis to glean further insight. (There are six axes—two states opposite one another on the round—and each one indicates complementary or paradoxical dynamics.)

0: Longing to create

This is the blank canvas, where there is paradoxically nothing and yet everything. The potential to create is fueled by trust and faith, an inner knowing. People gain closeness to the creative source in many ways, including dreams, mediation, prayer, and chanting.

Quadrant I (Sensation): Encounter as readiness and receptivity

> "Images appear to me, not quite formed, like chickens breaking out of eggs with only the cracks showing... the beginning of the creative process, already in flux as to its form and unpredictable as to its outcome" (Kelley, 2006, p. 88).

1: Attaching to the idea of creating

A deeply unconscious state, here a seed is planted, with a trusting that it can survive and not be lost. One can begin to make connection with this creative urge, but one has to remain attached to the idea, to nurse it, support it, keep it safe, lest it disappear. (Axis 1–7: One dreams of making something concrete and integrative.)

---

5   All of the quotes come from the book I edited with Peggy Heller called *Portrait of the Artist as Poet*. We requested essays from artists on their creative process.

2: Incubating phase

Moving into a Theta state of consciousness, the idea of creating something becomes more of a reality. The mind is flooded with possibilities; fleeting forms and colors emerge and recede. The senses are activated, and the memory of sights, sounds, and textures can filter into consciousness. (Axis 2–8: One might dream of being an artist.)

3: Focusing on intention to create something

Transitioning from Theta to Alpha consciousness, energy mobilizes towards engaging in the creative process. There now is an intention, born out of the previous place of inspiration. This is a strong place of arousal (sexual and/or spiritual) that gets activated by the anticipation of the birth of being from non-being. (Axis 3–9: One dreams of finishing a product, visioning the process with completion.)

Some people love to stay in this quadrant of possibilities and sensation without ever following through. There can be many plausible excuses, but the reality often is fear-based—fear of failure, or in some cases, fear of success. Blockages are easier to identify in the next quadrant, a tenuous time of development.

Quadrant II (Feeling): Encounter as absorption and engagement

"In painting, I enter mortal combat. I question my abilities, I struggle. If something new occurs that I have never processed before, I anguish between the familiar and the logic of a newer method" (Stenstrom, 2006, p. 145).

"My heart races as I choose brilliant colors and textures; this is an adrenaline filled activity. Totally involved and consumed by the creative process, I have an intimate and passionate affair with the art materials and my creative spirit" (Kunkle-Miller, 2006, p. 97).

4: Beginning the project

Wakening to Beta consciousness, but maintaining the ability to drift in and out of Alpha and Theta states, the artist starts the project, requiring resolute dedication. It is the birthing place of form. The artist must pay attention to it, nurse it along if it is going to survive. (Axis 4–10: Subliminally, the birth-death continuum underlies the threshold of creativity.)

5: Struggling with limitations

Boundaries and restrictions imposed by the art materials may not accommodate the artist's vision. Perfection cannot be attained. A power struggle can ensue. This is the place where projects may break down and get rejected. The clay can get thrown back into its bin. The paper may be balled up and trashed. (Axis 5–11: Order vs. disorder, there is danger of falling into chaos.)

6: Confronting doubts, holding the tension

Respecting the inherent limitations of the media is crucial to the survival of the art. Perhaps some rebellion takes place—a desire for something innovative. The artist as hero does battle with the shadow, passionately engaged towards a mission or goal, maintaining idealism. However, remaining in conflict, not able to bring the process to climax, will sacrifice the creation. (Axis 6–12: This is the creative axis, representing the *Kundalini* energy of the creative act where transformation can happen.)[6]

---

6   Phyllis Frame and I did research with visual artists and non-visual artists to

Potential blockages in this next quadrant occur when the process is not carefully tended or when it loses its Eros energy and becomes too cognitive.

Quadrant III (Thinking): Encounter as commitment and interrelating to the world

> "A painting remains a changing form until I determine that it is complete. I keep checking out line, texture, and composition, deciding when all parts are balanced and alive" (Hartenstein, 2006, p. 69).

> "The art form is my response to my urge to communicate" (Vertein, 2006, p. 151).

7: Integrating, balancing, and preserving the creation

At this point, the artist, with a new level of self-awareness, feels full of love for the artwork that is coming together. It is high noon for the artist, who can step back and honestly analyze what is working and what is not. Overconfidence in the success of the art that is not yet finished can cause it to crash. (Axis 7–1: Two extremes, full form at the highest point of consciousness contrasts with no form deep in the unconscious.)

8: Committing to identity as an artist

This is a place of confidence. Good choices have been made, and the process is going well. The artwork is looking fine. The artist is totally fulfilled by creating and may feel secure enough to mentor others in this process. (Axis 8–2: One can reflect on the place of possibilities and the potential for more creations.)

---

determine if there would be a difference in mandala card choices. With a significant level of difference, the axis choice for the artists was 6-12. See reference list for article.

9: Completing creation, sharing with others

With the finishing touches, the artwork is done. Everything has come to full fruition and might involve showing the artwork at a gallery. The artist can feel praise from others for work well done and also may feel connected to a community of artists. (Axis 9–3: There is danger of stagnation, a need to keep things moving, to start something new and different.)

Quadrant IV (Intuition): Encounter as unconscious inspiration and ecstasy

> "Engaging in the creative process allows me to release as well as receive" (Fibich, 2006, p. 54).

> "Making art means entering the domain of the sacred" (Barker, 2006, p. 7).

10: Ending of creative experience

There is distance from the creative process and the product that was created. Perhaps it was sold. The feelings previously experienced are difficult to remember. There is a sense of anxiety and possibly despair, sense of loss and separation, a going inward, a search for renewal. (Axis 10 - 4: When something dies, there's a knowing that something else will be reborn.)

11: Disintegrating, challenging creativity

Back in the unconscious realm, nothing makes sense anymore. This place of disorientation and confusion may bring surreal and bizarre nightmares. Often creating comes to a standstill, and one's identity as an artist might come into question. This state brings out the muse in some artists who strive to creatively organize the disorder into something meaningful. The trickster may be evident and transformation is possible. (Axis 11 - 5: Fear of being here may result in defensiveness and boundaries, but that is not the way to regain one's creative spirit.)

Creativity can become blocked in the tenth and eleventh states, because dealing with endings, letting go, and powerlessness can be overwhelming.

12: Returning to place of inspiration

Here there is complete integration of all the states, potential for renewal, and restoration of trust in the process. There may be awareness of a higher power in this place of intuitively knowing. Here is where the passion for form can result in transcendent experiences. It is the gateway back to the Source where there is hope for the creative process to be reawakened again. (Axis 12 - 6: From reforming to transforming, the creative axis is activated.)

Artists speak of being in touch with spirit, mystery, awe, vastness, the sacred, or an invisible force. At some point during the creative cycle, artists often connect with the center in their quest for meaning.

Inspiration to create can begin anywhere on this cycle. We just looked at artists who feel an internal sense of longing and start their process in the sensation quadrant. Some artists start in the feeling quadrant. They begin right away to work with the art materials, and the sensate qualities or meditative rhythms of working (or playing) with the media can take them into an altered state of consciousness in the first quadrant. Creations can emerge seemingly on their own, as if there were an inherent structure within.

Others start in the thinking quadrant. They have in mind exactly what form they want to produce, and they practice and practice until they have gotten it exactly the way they had intended. The process of repetition, such as in traditional Chinese painting, may evolve into a ritualized, mindfulness experience. Or maybe the art begun here is intended as a sociological statement and thus may be cognitive-driven. However, during their interaction with the media and their experience of achieving their goals, something else shifts inside that takes those who start in the thinking quadrant into the qualities of encounter in the other quadrants as well.

Then there are those who begin in the intuitive quadrant, finding inspiration from the irrational aspects of the unconscious, perhaps trying to create order from disorder. Some artists are truly inspired to create by the pathos of the tenth state or the chaos of the eleventh. The twelfth state is the place of transformation where a creative act can transcend the previous state of disorder. It also can be accessed from the sixth state of tension and passion. In either case, profound shifts in consciousness can happen in this integral place. Rollo May (1975) says, "Ecstasy...the intensity of consciousness that occurs in the creative act...involves the total person, with the subconscious and unconscious acting in unity with the conscious" (p. 43).

I believe that no matter where one starts, each of the states of being with their various qualities of encounter will be experienced during a successful creative process, some simultaneously. All are necessary in their own way, and ignoring any of the states might ultimately contribute to an interruption in one's ability to bring the creative act to a successful completion. The archetype of the quadrated mandala in the collective unconscious may just be the architecture that supports an integrated creative encounter.

People's creativity gets stymied for any number of reasons. Trauma, grief, and illness are just a few. But understanding where their creative cycles tend to start and where they break down during the process might offer us a clue as to how we can help them. I hope that viewing the cycle of creativity through the lens of this integrative method will stimulate ideas about how we might help nurture people's innate desire for expression and meaning and their longing for wholeness, unity, and transformation and, thus, how to capture well-being in their creative moments. This well-being, fostered through creative acts that seek to answer the ecological, psychological, sociological, or cosmological questions Hollis (2013) has delineated, can manifest as a shift in consciousness first in our communities, then our countries, and ultimately our world, where healing and harmony are essential to our survival.

References

Arrien, A. (1992). *Signs of life: The five universal shapes and how to use them.* Sonoma, CA: Arcus.

Barker, C. (2006). Cara Barker. In C. T. Cox, & P.O. Heller (Eds.). *Portrait of the artist as poet* (pp. 6 - 11). Chicago, IL: Magnolia Street Publishers.

Cohen, G. (2000). *The creative age: Awakening human potential in the second half of life.* New York, NY: Avon Books

Cox, C.T. & Frame, P. (1993), Profile of the artist: MARI® card test research results. *Art Therapy: Journal of the American Art Therapy Association,* 10(1).

Cox, C.T. (2004). In memoriam: Joan Kellogg (1922-2004). *Art Therapy: Journal of the American Art Therapy Association,* 21(2).

Dissanayake, E. (1992). Homo aestheticus: *Where art comes from and why.* New York, NY: The Free Press.

Fibich, M. (2006). Mary-Michola Fibich. In C. T. Cox, & P.O. Heller (Eds.). *Portrait of the artist as poet* (pp. 53 - 57). Chicago, IL: Magnolia Street Publishers.

Feuerstein, G. (1987). *Structures of consciousness: The genius of Jean Gebser.* Lower Lakes, CA: Integral Publishing.

Gong, S. (2012). Yi Shu: An integration of Chinese medicine and the creative arts. In D. K. Kalmanowitz, J. S. Potash, S. M. Chan (Eds.). *Art therapy in Asia: To the bone or wrapped in silk* (pp. 53 – 64). London, UK: Jessica Kingsley

Grof, S. (1985). *Beyond the brain: Birth, death, and transcendence in psychotherapy.* New York, NY: State University of New York Press.

Hartenstein, B. (2006). Bonnie Hartenstein. In C. T. Cox, & P.O. Heller (Eds.). *Portrait of the artist as poet* (pp. 68 - 72). Chicago, IL: Magnolia Street Publishers.

Hollis, J. (2013). *Hauntings: Dispelling the ghosts who run our lives.* Asheville, NC: Chiron Publications

Jacobi, J. (1973). *The psychology of C. G. Jung.* New Haven, CT: Yale University Press. (Original work published 1942)

Jung, C. G. (1968). *Psychology and alchemy*. Princeton, NJ: Bollingen Series. (Original work published 1953)

Jung, C. G. (1973). *Mandala symbolism*. Princeton, NJ: Bollingen Series. (Original work published 1959)

Jung, C. G. (2009). *The red book*. S. Shamdasani (Ed.) New York, NY: W.W. Norton.

Kelley, C. H. (2006). Carol Hunter-Kelley. In C. T. Cox, & P.O. Heller (Eds.). *Portrait of the artist as poet* (pp. 87 – 90). Chicago, IL: Magnolia Street Publishers.

Kellogg, J. (2002). *Mandala: Path of beauty*. Belleair, FL: ATMA, Inc. (Original work published 1978)

Kunkle-Miller, C. (2006). Carole Kunkle-Miller. In C. T. Cox, & P.O. Heller (Eds.). *Portrait of the artist as poet* (pp. 96 - 99). Chicago, IL: Magnolia Street Publishers.

May, R. (1975). *The courage to create*. New York, NY: W.W. Norton.

Nelson, E. & Ciuffo, A. (Producers), Herzog, W. (Director). (2011). *Cave of forgotten dreams* (Motion Picture). USA: MPI Media Group.

Perry, J. W. (1987). *The self in psychotic process*. Dallas, TX: Spring Publications. (Original work published 1953)

Schaia, A. (2010). *Hidden power of the gospels: Four questions, four paths, one journey*. New York, NY: Harper Collins.

Stenstrom, R. (2006). Ruth Stenstrom. In C. T. Cox, & P.O. Heller (Eds.). *Portrait of the artist as poet* (pp. 144 - 149). Chicago, IL: Magnolia Street Publishers.

Vertein, C. (2006). Christine Vertein. In C. T. Cox, & P.O. Heller (Eds.). *Portrait of the artist as poet* (pp. 150 - 153). Chicago, IL: Magnolia Street Publishers.

Chapter 7

The Pillar of Isis

By Robin van Löben Sels, PhD

Place with a capital "P" meant a lot to Carl Jung. Think of the lovely home he shared with Emma on the shore of Lake Zurich. Or picture Jung in his beloved Library, or in Küsnacht at Bollingen—a place Jung built by hand, stone by stone, for his own individuation. Jung's Bollingen became sacred to his personal renewal and vision. Though he was to travel widely in his later years—India, Africa, America—most of Jung's time in Bollingen was spent alone.

Jung's instinctive connection of place with individuation interests me. When we grow up with a sense of place the world feels secure and full of promise. For Jung, as for all of us, an insecure sense of self portends a less than promising world. Describing in his late life memoir how for all kinds of reasons he lacked the sense of security he would later find in individuation, Jung tells us a little of how his idea of individuation developed. Sometime in his mid-forties he carved two little figures out of wood, thinking of them as "spirits of place," or genius loci: the earth must have "a spirit of her own;" he mused, but then the unconscious supplied a name for one of them: "It called the figure Atmavictu," Jung writes, "meaning 'breath of life'" (Jung, 1989). Early in mid-life, then, Jung equated his experience of a creative earth spirit with a "breath of life" that needed and nourished unconscious individuality. Later, as he gathered stones for building Bollingen, Jung carved a larger version of Atmavictu to place in his Küsnacht garden.

Details from his personal story clarify why creating Bollingen literally meant "the world" to Jung. They tell us where and how he found the right place, at the right time for an experience that felt like "coming home"—an experience he later referred to as "becoming whole." Looking back over forty years of clinical work and writing (my own meaningful experience of Jung's "breath of life,") I can see that my ideas about dream gathering and dream tending took root in reading about Jung's connection of experience of place to individuation, so that my following pages are inspired as much by Jung's late life musings as they are by my own.

Concepts like Place and Individuation refer to big areas of human experience. To me the concept of Place is many-layered: it begins within a single body—"the place where my body is"—an exterior place and interior space of what I experience as "being in the world," no matter size or age. Within a slowly growing personal history, the meaning of place widens, morphing through early experience of mother-womb, emerging through a specific birth experience that unfolds into personal infancy. There in infancy we are "placed" among dense webs of social and cultural interactions as we become what conservationist and biologist Carl Safina calls a "who" animal. To be "who" animals, says Safina, means that who we are and who we become—our personalities—matter to others of our kind within a shared social sensibility (Safina, 2015, 346.) We are "placed" within our social group.

For "who" animals, mother-child bonding is biologically given. Human bonding employs human senses: touch, taste, smell, vision, hearing (all *sensate progenitors* of consciousness and soul) and all the affects, attachments, and emotions that communicate feelings and behavior among us. Cohesive social groupings indicate how we matter to each other: we've begun to care about issues like right and wrong, good and bad, and "us" and "them." As we affect and influence each other in increasingly complicated social and cultural interactions, other "who" animals miss us if we are lost, or when we die.

As Jungians, we assume that we feel, intuit, sense, perceive and communicate (consciously and unconsciously) by way of the psyche. Perhaps it is when we care and matter to each other that we also begin to dream—another biological phenomenon that we share with other creatures: elephants, wolves, dolphins, dogs and cats, some birds, even octopuses and electric eels (Montgomery, 2015). An evolutionary differentiation of "who" animals who matter to each other from creatures more or less indifferent to individuality undergirds all our efforts towards developing a self-reflective consciousness and it is to this emergent struggle that Jung's idea of individuation applies. So when, in Jung's idea, we begin to sense "who" we are to others, we have begun to individuate and sense "who" we are meant to be. And perhaps it is when we feel that "who" we are meant to be matters to someone else, that we feel "placed" in a world for the very first time.

For the past decade, at various conferences around the world, I've been collecting and sharing gathered dream imagery woven into a dream-tapestry to present to participants at a final panel, an experiment that indulged my personal preoccupation with individuation (especially in terms of dreams), my curiosity about the importance of "place" in the psyche, and my sense of what it means to lead a meaningful and symbolic life. I assumed that a personal experience of psyche has to emanate out of a personal experience of landscape and place, and so, I wondered, what feeling temporarily dis-placed at an international conference might evoke from the unconscious material of the attendees: might personal imagery of "home" be prominent in dreams dreamt in far-away places like India, Ireland, Switzerland, or Greece, for example? Or might elements of the earth's spirit of place—genius loci, as Jung and the Romans called them—appear alongside personal material? Over years of these experiments, I've organized my thinking with the help of an emerging, five-level model of the dreaming psyche that I've come to call The Pillar of Isis, and I will refer to this model in its final form (Figure 1) as an organizing image throughout the following pages.

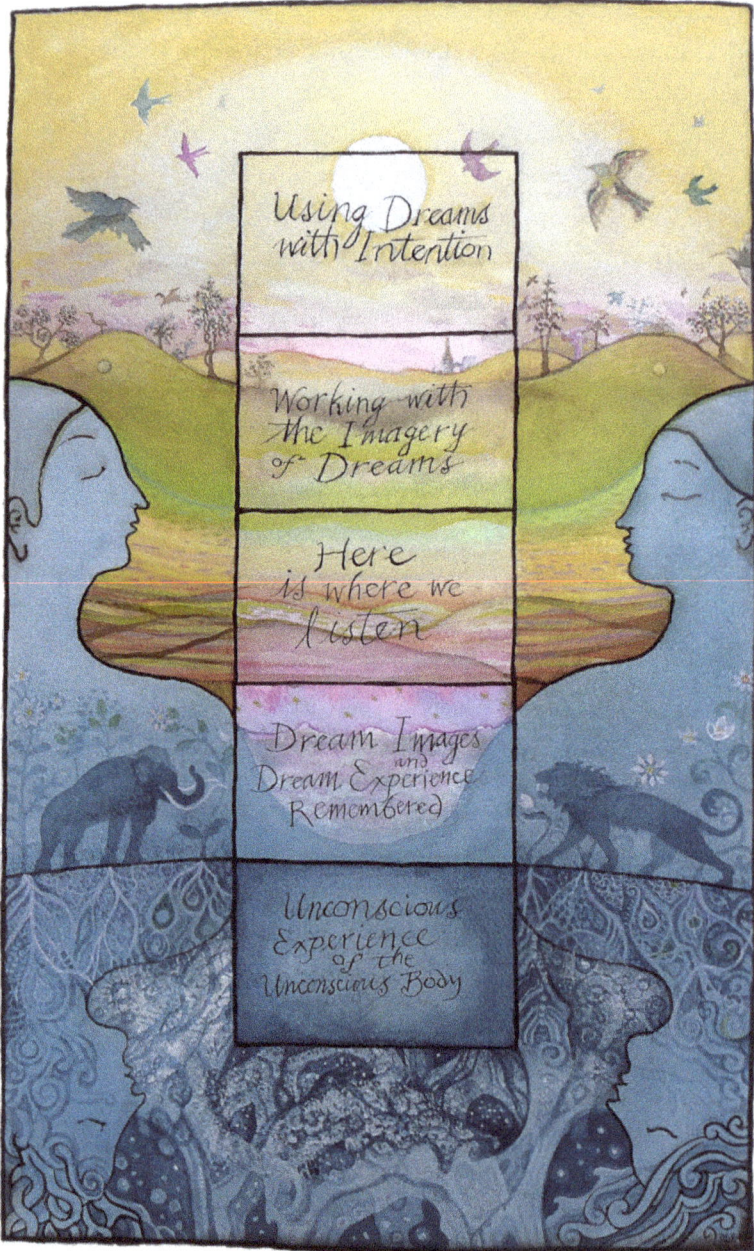

FIGURE 1. *THE PILLAR OF ISIS. ILLUSTRATION BY MARK RICHARDSON.*

My conclusions, anecdotal and impressionistic, reflect primarily on the unconscious roots of creativity as they relate to dreams, psyche, soul, dreaming in place, and individuation. Poets are precise in finding words to name inner experience, so I quote poetry, but I also reflect on ideas offered by biologists, scientists, and ecologists. Take ideas about place and individuation: we know that place—ranging from feelings about home to the country of one's birth, say—affects us deeply. We can feel faithful to a place to the point of disaster, and/or we can seek a new home out of need. These are aspects of belonging to a species that, overall, tends to be so on the move that at this point we inhabit all the continents of the earth. Yet journalist and science writer Elizabeth Kolbert suggests that little has been more damaging to our home, earth, than persistent habits of movement and migration (Kolbert, 2014). Can we correlate our ideas of the necessity for psychological individuation and Place with our ideas of "being on the move?" Poet Alicia Ostriker under-scores this *not-only-human trait*, suggesting that beneath the frantic moving about that we do, we—like many other creatures—seek an experience of being

"in the right spot somehow, like a breath

Entering a singer's chest, that shapes itself

For the song that is to follow." (Ostriker, 1989, 83)

Describing an experience of feeling in just the right place at just the right time for something that feels to be of great signif-icance, Ostriker articulates a sense of instinct that is as old and inarticulate as time. Approaching his idea of individuation with the passion of a scientist rather than a poet, Jung glimpsed psycho-logical evidence of a similar evolutionary instinct and called it individuation. He described individuation as a process to which we either consciously accede or into which we are unconsciously dragged, and he ascribed a "fated feeling" to the experience, which clearly places it in the realm of the species-specific song described by Ostriker. Perhaps because it is hard to name what cannot be seen, Jung called on his dreams to guide his individuation, and felt that they pulled him toward "light" (and possible conscious naming?) whether he consciously affirmed and accompanied the unconscious process of dreaming them or not. Jung's personal reflections reflect the experience of many of us. Drawn to ponder the big arcs of life, we, too, find ourselves mysteriously drawn on by longings that may find clearest expression in poetry or dreams.

Thinking as a scientist about the mystery of his longings, Jung felt that a religious instinct formed the basis of his own "song" of individuation. Other scientists sought more rational/material explanations for such a "homing" instinct, like the incredible migrations of fish. Some found otoliths (ear-bones) in the skulls of salmon and grains of magnetic matter in salmon brains: others posited capacities for magnetic resonance with the earth in the bones of birds—or, like Konrad Lorenz and Joseph Campbell, they posited the existence of innate releasing mechanisms. Amidst all kinds of speculations about the unconscious psyche, fascination with the mysteries of unfolding instinct led Jung to posit "archetypal" patterns of behavior and experience hidden in the foundations of the conscious mind, as if the roots of psyche were so sunken into earth and world that links and connections between its chthonic nature and the world became tangible. He felt that an instinct toward individuation (a "religious" instinct) was what led him by way of archetypal experience and patterned behavior to a sense of innate destiny that felt as "fated" as the instinct he observed in a Baltimore Oriole, fatedly led to build species-specific teardrop shaped nests, or the way White Ants (termites) seemed fatedly led to build their magnificent mound-like structures without apparent coordination by any external organizing principle.

Whatever archetypes are, and however we may think about them, Jung found dreams to be primary among other unerring factors that connect us to magnetized elements in the psyche, elements that point like lodestones to a North Star of individual life. He seems to have known about the power of dreams from the very beginning—how they lead us on, one after another—and eventually he claimed that he could clearly see how all his professional work had been presaged by and through his dreams.

Clinically speaking, I'm sure many of us can recall times when only dreams seemed to point toward something meaningful. Especially after trauma, dreams seem to stand sentinel, solitary markers that somehow embrace unreachable knowledge not only of who we someday might become but, more poignantly, a lost knowledge of who we were before. Dreams are so foundational to the healing aspects of individuation that when we align ourselves with them correctly we glimpse in their slow, inevitable-seeming sequence a remarkable, unfolding process that re-members broken life. Somehow a dream becomes an inner "other," a psyche-shaman who can re-mind, re-connect, and re-align us with something greater than the self we imagine at the moment and certainly greater than any self we knew of before.

Jung's conviction about the big part dreams played in his early discoveries of psyche and its telos leads me to suggest that his personal experience of individuation was also his personal version of the instinctual "song" that Ostriker's poem describes: his dreams served Jung as mysterious vehicles for that breath of life (spirit) that entered his chest, shaping itself for the remarkable "song" of all his work and writing, and those of us who follow in Jung's footsteps may hear "homing" reverberations of Jung's song as personal melodies of our own. Some call this reverberation Soul, others may call it the Holy Spirit (often imagined as feminine), and still others refer to feelings of Nostalgia, or call it Dreamtime. But all these designations try to describe archetypal experience that points two ways at once (as do all archetypal ideas), seemingly back toward an original taste of union and, simultaneously, forward toward an experience of feeling guided by some kind of "homing device" or inner compass toward an experience of feeling rightly "placed." Ostriker's complete poem articulates this whole idea beautifully:

Move

Whether it's a turtle who drags herself

Slowly to the sandlot, where she digs

The sandy nest she was born to dig

And lay leathery eggs in, or whether it's salmon

Rocketing upstream

Toward pools that call, Bring your eggs here

And nowhere else in the world, whether it is turtle-green

Ugliness and awkwardness, or the seething

Grace and gild of silky salmon, we

Are envious, our wishes speak out right here.

Thirsty for a destiny like theirs,

An absolute right choice

To end all choices. Is it memory,

We ask, is it a smell

They remember,

Or just what is it—some kind of blueprint

That makes them move, hot grain by grain,

Cold cascade above icy cascade,

Slipping through

Water's fingers

A hundred miles

Inland from the easy, shiny sea?

And we also—in the company

Of our tribe

Or perhaps alone, like the turtle

On her wrinkled feet with the tapping nails—

We also are going to travel, we say let's be

Oblivious to all, save

That we travel, and we say

When we reach the place we'll know

We are in the right spot, somehow, like a breath

Entering a singer's chest, that shapes itself

For the song that is to follow.

(Ostriker, 1989)

At a conference in Gersau, Switzerland, I referred to an early version of The Pillar of Isis by imagining the five levels of the model as keys, "sounding the chord of having a dream." If we read the model from the bottom up, like a hexagram from the I Ching, we can imagine that it sounds a psychoid chord of the experience of dreaming (Jung's term for the entangled inner and outer depths of psyche and matter.) Just like music moves, dreaming moves from the Deep unconscious up and out, spreading into unconscious body experience, into increasingly emergent connections with personal experience and memory, into connections with ego-agency and nascent consciousness, until—relatively embodied—the chord of dreaming reaches upper levels of the model where consciousness enters and dreams can be remembered, talked about, interpreted or not, and used creatively. I feel that The Pillar of Isis illustrates this progression upwards from being "placed in the world" (the Anima Mundi?) through unconscious, elemental, somatic experience into memory and imagination modulating into image, collective myth and narrative, unfolding into personal story and on up into higher levels of active imagination, individual consciousness, and presence. As I mentioned, The Pillar of Isis evolved through several versions, and Sounding the Chord of Having a Dream was one of them. Mark Richardson, an artist friend, illustrated the last two versions so I could use slides to make the complex nature of the conscious and unconscious mind comprehensible to myself as well as others. The name, Pillar of Isis, appeared in the same way Atmavictu's name appeared to Jung, perhaps because it out-pictures my own dawning recognition of what Jungians commonly refer to as mysteries of the "Feminine."

Myths from early Egypt tell us that Isis helped to raise the sun. Jung's interest in Isis (scattered throughout his alchemical studies) was in Isis as the Black One or the Old One, a personification of the embodied Feminine that was both murderous and healing, and known as a pupil of Hermes (Jung, 1959, 18-20). My interest was in Isis as a great teacher, as earth, vessel, and prima materia of transformative processes. I hear the common phrase, "mysteries of the Feminine," as referring to psyche's ability to create imagery capable of bridging dynamic, elemental factors we commonly experience as opposites—elements like mind and body, matter and spirit, or heaven and earth. Parallels to the figure of Isis and aspects of her myth include images of Gnostic Sophia, a feminine emanation of the Godhead, who falls into matter; Kabir, who sings from the heart of Islam to tell us of a "Secret One" inside us who runs the planets of the galaxies through her fingers as casually as if they were colored beads. A third example lives among indigenous peoples of New Mexico as First Woman of the Navaho Emergence Story, who—having fallen to the back of Turtle Earth—roams the galaxies as Turtle Spirit.

These generous myths contain both Life and Death. Aspects of the Pillar came together in my mind over time, and I felt as if Egypt's

Queen of Transformation herself waited upon me, in both senses of that word, mirroring Mind to mind, reflecting over and over again my growing awareness of how consciousness rises from darkest night and our earliest beginnings. In the midst of an evolutionary process we can't fully imagine, we still manage to trace our capacity to live meaningfully back far enough in time and down far enough through psyche's roots, that we've developed a burgeoning collective awareness of our planet as it is pictured in Isis' First Realm—a place where world and psyche merge in deep unconscious union with the earth. Jung placed the collective unconscious here, characterizing it as a place where we feel connected to everything and we experience unity—a "place" of archetypal affect, archetypal experience, and archetypal behavior—the seat of soul.

With only a vague idea that dreams of participants in small Jungian gatherings might reflect Jung's spirit of place, I offered my dream-tending gatherings over ten years, calling them "Dreaming in Place," and I coupled the name of the local venue with Jung's idea of a spirit of Place. The two or three morning dream-sharing meetings I scheduled before breakfast were enthusiastically attended, and I asked that there be no questions, cross talk, analysis of images, analysis of dreams or dreamers. I asked that people slowly speak their dreams aloud with whatever early-morning intimacy they could muster so I could write them down. We also met several afternoons to talk about dreams and dreaming, although in Ireland I spent that seminar time telling the story of Dream Angus, the Celtic God of Dreams.

When a gathering "feels right," dream sharing tends to evoke visceral, openhearted, and soul-enlivened images. I collected these images, hoping to track unconscious responses to places of meeting, presentations, and each other, and see what psyche had in mind. Dreams gathered from these sessions, and others written on paper scraps by sleepyheads who didn't rise early enough provided me with plenty of material. Did any dream reflect a literal Place of dreaming? Or might the gathering "place" be woven into weft and woof of tribal dream only? Tending and gathering are gentle activities that bespeak a gentle attitude capable of attending to images as well as dreamers without much meddling, so my project seemed worth a try.

I lightly pruned the dreams I gathered, weaving them into a recitation to read aloud to participants at the last morning's plenary discussion. To illustrate how we can engage all five levels of the Pillar of Isis through conscious ego participation in creative art forms like poetry or active imagination, I often read aloud Norah Pollard's "She Dreamed of Cows." Pollard's poem gives a beautiful example of how the "chord" of a dream, ostensibly fractured by trauma, returns psyche and dreams to creative harmonics, and this illustrates how levels of The Pillar of Isis re-establish themselves. Imagine Pollard's dreaming body as the inner landscape for Pollard's new beginning; her poem illustrates the "homing" instinct that took her out of mad mind into creative expression. Hearing Pollard's poem read aloud usually brought the group to silence and gratitude, as if we were experiencing her poem the way Pollard had experienced her dream: it licked us back to life.

She Dreamed of Cows

I knew a woman who washed her hair and bathed her body
and lay down with a .38 in her right hand.
Before she did the thing, she went over her life.
She started at the beginning and recalled everything—
all the shame, sorrow, regret and loss.
This took her a long time into the night
and a long time crying out in rage and grief and disbelief—
until sleep captured her and bore her down.

She dreamed of a green pasture and a green oak tree.
She dreamed of cows. She dreamed she stood
under the tree and the brown and white cows
came slowly up from the pond and stood near her.
Some butted her gently and they licked her bare arms

with their great coarse drooling tongues. Their eyes, wet as
shining water, regarded her.
They came closer and began to
press their warm flanks against her, and as they pressed
an almost unbearable joy came over her and
lifted her like a warm wind and she could fly.
She flew over the tree and she flew over the field and
she flew with the cows.

When the woman woke, she rose and went to the mirror.
She looked a long time at her living self.
Then she went down to the kitchen which the sun had
made all yellow, and she made tea.
She drank it at the table, slowly, all the while
touching her arms where the cows had licked
                                        (Pollard, 2009, 43.)

This poem is about being placed back into life when you have lost your way, and it moves me that dreams and poetry can do this. The root of her dream, her poem re-minds Pollard that she is a "who" among other "who's," a beast among other beasts, a body among other bodies. A dream remembered is remembered by a mind returning to itself, and a dream like the one that centered this poem lends the dreamer body, weight and gravity until she could reclaim these for herself. Despite all that grieved her and everything that pulled her toward despair, Pollard's dream carried her into what Ostriker describes as the "right spot," and hearing Pollard's poem read aloud "re-minded" us, her listeners, into our own animal sensibilities and out of daily mind.

Simple perceptions of psyche's images let us know we're hanging out in the Pillar's higher dimensions, perhaps Realms Three or Four, whereas the "feels right" feeling of helpful dream interpretation belongs in Realm Five, along with conscious feelings and values. Note that although the poet goes over the personal details of her despairing life while she is awake, dream and poem allow her to grieve as deeply as she can. Healing comes not from consciousness but from a bigger place that dreaming pulls us into. Healing came from Pollard's *larger sense of self* that is as deep and soulful as the sensate reality of how a cow's tongue feels and how the poet's skin felt beneath her own reflective hands in morning sunlight. Aristotle would have called the sensate, feeling reality that licked Pollard back into "true north" again, "thick time," as when a present moment (the "now" of sensation) is experienced with a paradoxical temporal extension and depth (Humphrey, 2011, 60, 90.)

> *"and is it the wind,"* asks poet John Burnside,
>   *or rainstorms,*
>   *or the sea*
>   *repairs a soul*
>   *or is it magnetic north*
>   *that brings us true*
>   *knitting the cut flesh*
>   *smoothing the creases*
>   *in dreams?"*

(Burnside, 2009, 70.)

Sometimes The Pillar of Isis reminded participants of Edinger's ego/Self axis (Edinger, 1972), helpful when thinking about traumatic interruptions to instinctual life. With a hurt ego/Self axis, for example, perhaps the "sounding chord of dreaming" loses harmonics and become dissonant, for evidence of trauma implies that unconscious self-interpretations are charged with emotions that are unable to proceed from deeply anchored feeling/thinking integration. Dissociative images lead us astray; we are like salmon, feeling blocked from returning to a birth stream. If we imagine trauma rupturing a "homing instinct" to the depth that dream imagery implies, we understand how dream work restores an instinctive capacity to "know the right spot." Life becomes meaningful again. We can almost feel our breath "shape itself" in our chests again, whatever the "song" may be that is to follow.

So the Pillar of Isis lends imaginative shadow imagery and important feminine components to clinical work. We may take it for granted that human loving requires *embodied* consciousness, but we are less aware of how traumatic defenses against loving have to be undone as we mature and learn from our mistakes. From time to time, Jung implies that real transformation occurs unconsciously, usually marked by the progression of a series of dreams, as if the kind of transformation Jung was after might have little to do with conscious experience. The presence of Isis and the feminine make for a bigger picture. As earth, vessel, and the *matter* of good and evil, Isis embraces all that is pictured here in Her Pillar. Old and Black, signifying the *prima materia* of transformation, Isis values nonlinear imagination, inclusivity, and a clear recognition of interdependence. Isis also embodies "feminine" attitudes of acceptance, endurance, devotion, and emotional engagement, involving us in an alchemical stage where the masculine spiritual principle of consciousness dies and the feminine principle of nature and the unconscious ascends to rule over spiritual transformation and resurrection (Jung, 1963, pp. 18-20). In psychotherapy, the presence of Isis initiates us into a healing, renewing, and nurturing experience of transformation that we undergo while we are *awake,* for "The Feminine" never defines problems or finds solutions, whether of technique, will power, knowledge, or medication. Dreams and unconscious bodies soak in the presence of Isis. Elements mix and match: masculine and feminine, collective and personal, psyche and soul, conscious and unconscious—all work together to call us back to foundations and toward a future at once. When Isis is present, we glimpse, sense, imagine, intuit, and feel, renewed capacity for life.

Most of us take it for granted that levels of moods, attention and perception occur at psychological depths that elude nets of image as well as language (Level 5 in the Pillar). Jung's creative mind proposed that the psyche is composed of these inarticulate dimensions and that our dreams originate in psychosomatic depths, as do poetic inspiration and song. Personal experience of somatically tuned "being" signals the presence of creativity to the inner world, as surely as do tracks in the outer world signal the passage of other species or our own. Jung named the deep, impersonal, psychosomatic layers of the psyche the collective unconscious or the objective psyche, insisting that a collective *somatic unconscious* lies cheek by jowl with the experience that we *do* remember, the images and memories that enter the storied-consciousness within which we craft personal life.

In conference settings The Pillar of Isis helped me think through different levels of mind/psyche through which dreaming and dreams, stories and personal life actually emerge. Much of the collective psyche of which we've become aware in past decades pertains to the multiple relational, historical memories of the passionate early attachments that undergird personal history. We know these early relationships matter, but they can only be imagined into personal history. Dreaming may bring wisdom and balance to our lives whether we attend to dreams or not, but more importantly, dreams help us imagine, and imagining happens only over time. While gathering conference dreams satisfied my personal urge to balance often-stimulating lecture material, by making a place for unconsciousness, I also claimed space for a slowly changing background of experience that included self-shifting across waking, dreaming, and even dreamless sleep. Honoring dream space makes Place for an entire way of Being, albeit in an older idiom—makes place for a slower, muted, pre-conscious process of psychic integration that is as mildly meditative as the slow moving jaws of a cud chewing cow.

The First Dimension of Isis' Pillar pictures this older way of Being as psyche's roots intertwined with elements of earth and animal soul, with the slow passage of seasons and aeons, and with personal and collective memories of long ago. When consciousness enters the picture as in Levels Two, Three and Four, dream associations become important, for in spite of knowing that we live on the passionate emotions we employ in our personal attachments, we can't begin to personally embody an "inner world" until we make use of dream associations to imagine a developmental history, as if we imagine psyche while psyche imagines us. *Only imagination places the unconscious in a past and in a body.* Maybe Jung's discovery of the complex through his Word Association Test first brought the extent of psyche's unconscious *embodiment* home to Jung and into collective consciousness. The fact remains that until we experience in an embodied fashion how psyche historicizes, we can't connect in mind (personal or collective) the invisibly-danced-over-time metaphor of how individual bodily being co-exists in the same world that is inhabited by Jung's archetypes—how these two worlds, separate worlds, also form a single world in which we live out psychological complexes.

I can imagine Jung's complexes like this: invisible psyche, etching living metaphor into lives that we perform as events in time, events that are as telling to the psyche as a waggle dance of bees. Other bees who "read" the waggle dance know that "sweetness is this way, not that;" "food (survival) is in this direction, not there . . . this way, not that, this tree here." Analogously, psyche, dancing in therapeutic relatedness, embodies the two-way, communicative "complex" of affect and image between two people that a complex *is*. Unless we maintain conscious, imaginative awareness of this dance, we "behave" our complexes into the world as unconsciously as bees dance. Dreams help us "see" how psychic contents from Level Five manifest in our personal histories.

What we call "enlargement of consciousness," William James called "expansion of the imagination." James, too, thought that imagination has to mature, just as a capacity for a rich and meaningful dream life has to mature. We may say that psyche in relationship "contains" complexes, but it is my experience that psyche also composes complexes on the spot, unconsciously instructing and *in-structuring itself,* as it were, fossilizing past experience of place and presence for presently-related review. Psyche provides in-sight and in-structuring as it historicizes, oozing personal histories out of collective memory, histories as translucent in time as honey is in sunlight, spun sustenance for awareness of self and soul.

Today we perceive our place in the world by imagining that we are evolving individual souls. Not like psyche, not like bees, we individuate. A dreaming psyche is an indigenous storyteller of personal life, the kind of life that individuates. Dreams, images, complexes, stories, myths—these ARE psyche. Grounded in this knowledge, we personally experience the psyche's impersonal capacity to link. Psyche's stories bridge past and present, link right and left-brain, history and imagination, body and mind, psyche and soul. Plumbing these depths, Jung wrote, "I must learn that the dregs of my thought, my dreams, are the speech of my soul" (IRSJA, 3). Embodied experience of paradoxically unknowable psychic reality transformed Jung and the nature of psyche, too.

In other venues I referred to The Pillar of Isis to help outline grammars of memory and sensation, perceptions, emotions, and feelings, as well as various ways of perceiving dream images, all familiar components of making sense of being human. Issues of place and world, psyche, soul and body reverberate in the deepest levels of this model, so The Pillar helped me articulate the "old" (collective) psyche as ground source of Creative Imagination. From this Place we draw our collective and personal stories, from within and without. By imagining ourselves in space-time, we imagine ourselves in Being. All the while, psyche tunes us in to soul and out again through individuating stories and dreams.

The Pillar of Isis also helped me differentiate collective clinical theory from personal experience so that I could match my personal experience with collective meaning. For an example of this, here is how Jung describes his own 1950s version of the presently haunting idea that we are nature's organs of nature's self-awareness. He writes: "'But why on earth,' you may ask, 'should it be necessary for man to achieve, by hook or crook, a higher level of consciousness?' This is truly the crucial question, and I do not find the answer easy. Instead of a real answer, I can make only a confession of faith. I believe that, after thousands of millions of years, someone had to realize that this wonderful world of mountains and oceans, suns and moons, galaxies and nebulae, plants and animals, exists" (Jung, 1959, p. 95).

Again I find the mythic image of Isis as earth and vessel generous. Adding to Jung's earlier perception, the psychological template of the Pillar explicitly calls on unconscious depths of feeling, masculine and feminine principles, psyche and soul. Feminine values of Isis expand Jung's confession of faith by asking, how do you *feel* about Jung's vast perception of consciousness? And what about the animals? Isis implies: how do you *feel* about extinctions happening all around us (Kolbert, 2014)? Can we, or do we, value Jung's perception of why consciousness comes about in the first place—that some mind has to register nature and nature's self-perception? Is our perception of earth's "is-ness," earth's existence as the beautiful blue planet that it is—and the "being-ness" of trees, plants and creatures that inhabit the earth—"message" enough, reason enough, that consciousness come about? Does the presence of instinct justify us in following instinct mindlessly, like salmon seeking home waters, even if movements and migrations, individuating or not, decimate our world? And if so, do we (and if so, HOW do we) shoulder responsibility for causing the planet's present plight?

If Jung's mature confession of faith in a vast sweep of human consciousness does not stand alone, Isis' transformative presence helps us ask: what do we *feel about* all that Jung's descriptive confession brings to our attention? Can we at least value a feeling awareness more deeply? Centering as it does on self-interest, of course, consciousness pertains to human maturation, but consciousness alone is limited, like spirit without matter, like disembodied psyche or un-embodied soul, like heaven without earth. Jung suggests that with consciousness comes choice. Are we making right choices? Not just for our well-being but the well-being of others? How well do we relate to "all our relations?" Where and how does love of Home enter? Do we still have the capacity to "re-cognize" a feeling of Original Unity?

Supposing that the numinosum makes itself known through the collective unconscious (Level One), and supposing that God speaks through dreams, Jung writes: "the whole world is God's suffering" (Jung, 2014, 5063). I seem to hear Isis murmuring alongside Jung's words: "Remember, you dreamed up the cultures that you live and suffer now. Remember, every grief that visits flesh and bone pains some one individual, some one person or animal who suffers that pain, willingly or not." The presence of Isis reminds me that we can't escape individual, personal responsibility to feel deeply—and have deep feelings about—all real outcomes that issue forth from how we live on earth and how we treat each other. Isis implies context, and context provides repercussions. We can't relegate archetypal feeling to a transpersonal realm or simply think about it in terms of statistics; each number indicates a person, a man, woman, or child. Nor can we rest upon the "collateral damage." The First Realm of The Pillar of Isis depicts personal and relational issues that are buried deep together in world and mind, as tightly interwoven as the roots of time.

Like spider's webs, our dreams are attached ever so slightly to personal life at all four corners. With something like magical thinking, I imagine that dreams begin as crucial hopes for survival in a world over which we have little control, for some dreams are not about individual identity as much as they are about the necessity to hide identity and protect one's true self. Psychotherapists spot psychological defenses in dreams like these, designed not to harm but to protect both body and mind. But in conference settings, dream tending seemed most important because as we gave dreams attention they reciprocated, and by exploring dreams together we intuited subjective mind-body connections that some of us called psyche and others called soul. Also, it was as if every time our interest in ideas and social preoccupations relegated psyche and soul to the background of attention, our dream work intervened, balancing our common fascination with ideas and prompting us to look both ways at cross walks of living that we usually navigate instinctively. Whether a dream was dramatic or insignificant, collective attention to psyche's offerings affected a kind of group homage to the collective and personal unconscious. In each fragment we glimpsed the individual attentions of the modern psyche. To include dreams generated beneath the flow of conference ideas began as my personal gesture toward living with psychosomatic integrity, but the dreams did the work. Like buoys marking deep water, every dream made place for psyche and opened a channel for soul.

And, on occasion, illuminated by personal associations, one or two dreams *did* reflect the "Place" of being dreamed. In Greece, for example, we had a dream of angry Poseidon rising from the waves, as if the black of Santorini's volcanic soil and the white of its gleaming villages conjured a tale of light and dark conjoined. Poseidon was brother to Zeus and god of the sea. He also raped Medusa, a human girl whose lovely visage warped to a snake-haired mask of rage. Carl Safina tells us that the human body is 70% fluid saline, the same percentage of liquid to mass as seas exhibit to land (Safina, 2012.) And oceans cover 70% of the earth. Imagine that each of us is a body wrapped around a sea: we can test this by tasting our tears. As an example of individual consciousness suffering nature as *numen,* this stormy dream felt sacred, spawned by the unconscious mystery of Place.[1]

Another time, traipsing over the dark green hills of Ireland, our hearts hammered at glimpses of Dana, Mother, distant as the silver sheen of river and sea—so beautiful we felt we were in a waking dream. Dana summoned us, unfurling like a dream, challenging each of us to find himself/herself in The Dream That is Her World (MacEowen, 2004, 97.) Encountering Dana opens the soul to sacred power and its own mystery. Like Isis, Dana inspires and does not explain. Such a dream-like experience affirmed my sense that we don't envision literal earthy places without simultaneously summoning an earth where human subjectivity takes hold, a

---

1 Remember the storm gods? Surely these ancient weather gods emerged out of ancestral encounters with the *numen* of Place: Thor hurling His Awful Lightning Bolts over the northern peoples, Yahweh sending Desert Plagues, early Zeus, harsh and inexorable, and Dagda, roaming the Celtic Isles, club in hand. Weather Gods punished with sudden raging storms, then send days so fair and mild that fear was forgotten. Perhaps long ago the human soul experienced weather as collective consciousness of Place. To describe them as being birthed by the collective psyche in no way makes light of the power of these Old Gods. Perhaps Poseidon's dream appearance accompanied the distress many of us felt about Santorini's empty seas: Homer's *wine-dark sea* has been over-fished and dynamited to a point of lifeless desolation, an appalling, heart-breaking reality. God of sea, storms and earthquakes, Poseidon lost out early to the ruling aspect of Greece's patriarchal culture, the part that worked at keeping everything rational and under control, and our culture represses him too. Storms of bottled up emotion expressed as psychological complexes that attack and rape the *feminine.* Poseidon began as a fertility god—who sent up springs of water to nourish life—but as he grew/ tempestuous and dominating, he becomes a fitting metaphor for our collective preoccupation with dominating the natural world today.

psychological earth. This sense of depth in time, or dual perception, correlates dream space with psychological space that deepens into Jung's idea of a "third" space, a paradoxical "in between" experience of outer place and inner space as both separate and One.

Perhaps the human psyche delights in geographical Place because in localizing a truth of experience, a locality helps us grasp the abstract and invisible by way of something concrete. Perhaps this is how (and why) many particular places became (and still are) powerful anchors of tradition in the ancient world. Perhaps that's why those of us familiar with Carl Jung's work can be so moved when we visit Bollingen, the place he lovingly built by hand. Perhaps a deep desire for proximity to Place expresses psyche's dreaming more than ours: remember the birth-loyalties of salmon, the long seasonal journeys of whales, the persistent high-flying patterns of migrating birds.

At times I have been asked, was anything *accomplished* by tending dreams? Aside from our usual ways of using dreams to find personal meaning, I suspect that many of us feel that we ought to be *doing something more* with dreams—like Freud, say, using his own dreams and those of others as a means to an end, a Royal Road to the unconscious mind. Tending encourages something earlier and deeper than doing, something simpler. Tending dreams involves turning the mythic level of the psyche on its head in order to prowl among its roots and read it from the bottom up. This upside-down attitude quickly became an imaginative *expectation of space* for psyche and soul—a place that is seldom held, found, contained or captured by other theories and models.

This is how the act of tending can become more important than dream content, even content that is useful, helpful, striking, alarming, or unforgettable. Tending reminds us that psyche's images do not derive from consciousness any more than a dream does, nourishing awareness of the inner life of body and mind. Tending sows within us implications of attentiveness to spirit within and beneath ordinary life. Because it represents soul tracking from the inside out, tending attunes us to the rhythms and tides of heart.

Nothing can align us more closely with the destiny of soul and the spirit of life around us than to become more supple in how we track individual perceptions and projections and how we refine what we find. Just as we discover genetic ancestors, we discover a mythic ancestry of elders *behind* our elders, uncovering archetypal mystery behind all form. We are nurtured by mythic images of reality night after night. By day, a willing attention to dreams can teach us that the deepest elements of our creation stories are the same elements that explore the making of our human minds, the makings of structure itself, and the makings of all our attempts to understand. Whatever we feel about our dream, they manifest mysterious processes that bridge dimensions of Being and restore biogenetic integrity, *and they do this for us by affecting us long before we do anything with them.*

I imagine tending as a feminine animating principle like Isis Herself—a kind of life focus that adds to our ability to dream, a gentle attentiveness that all of us do well to cultivate. Just as dreaming nourishes the psychosomatic integrity of body and soul, tending dreams may even help our world. For as important as finding meaning is, we know in our bones that dreams are really about something else. On the most basic level we can imagine, we need our dreams and we need our dreaming for physical wellbeing and psychological sanity. Keeping body and psyche, soul and world, ego and self together, dreaming is easily its own reward.

References

Burnside, J. (2009) *The Unprovable Fact: Part III The Mediciners.* In The asylum dance. Cape Town, S. A.: Jonathan Cape Random House. Quoted with permission.

Edinger, E. (1972) *Ego and archetype: individuation and the religious function of the psyche.* New York: Penguin Books.

Humphrey, N. (2011) *Soul dust: the magic of consciousness.* Princeton and Oxford: Princeton University Press. Quoted in *The IRSJA bulletin board,* Vol. 2 #9. September 2015, 3.

Jung, C. G. *The collected works.* CW I-XX. Edited by Sir Herbert Read. London: Routledge.

Jung, C. G. (1959) *The archetypes and the collective unconscious.* CW 9i. New York. Bollingen Foundation.

Jung, C. G. (1963) *Mysterium coniunctionis.* CW 14. New York: Bollingen Foundation.

Jung, C. G. (1989) *Memories, dreams, reflections.* Recorded and edited by Aniela Jaffe. translated by Richard and Clara Winston. New York: Vintage Books.

Kolbert, E. (2014) *The sixth extinction: an unnatural history.* New York: Henry Holt & Co.

MacEowen, F. (2004) *The spiral of memory and belonging: A Celtic path of soul and kinship.* Novato, California: New World Library.

Montgomery, S. (2015) *The soul of an octopus: A surprising exploration into the wonder of consciousness.* New York: Atria Books.

Ostriker, A. (1989) "Move," in *Green age.* Pittsburgh: University of Pittsburgh Press, 70-71. Quoted with permission.

Pollard, N. (2009) "She Dreamed of Cows," in *Death & rapture in the animal kingdom: New poems by Norah Pollard.* Simsbury, Conn: Antrim House. Quoted with permission from author.

Safina, C. (2015) *Beyond words: What animals think and feel.* New York: John Macrae Books/Henry Holt and Company.

Safina, C. (1999) *Song for the blue ocean: Encounters along the world's coasts and beneath the seas.* New York: John Macrae Books/Henry Holt and Company.

van Löben Sels, R. (2003) *A dream in the world: Poetics of soul in two women, modern and medieval.* New York & London: Brunner-Routledge.

van Löben Sels, R. (2011) "The story of Angus, the Celtic god of dreams. Part I: Story and storytelling," *Jungian odyssey 2010: Trust and betrayal: Dawnings of consciousness.* Jungian Odyssey Series, Vol. III. Edited by S. Worth, I. Meier & J. Hill. Spring Journal Books. New Orleans, Louisiana, 131-38.

van Löben Sels, R., "The story of Angus, the Celtic god of dreams. Part 2: Angus: Poet, lover, and bringer of dreams," *ibid,* 139-152.

van Löben Sels, R., "Dreaming in Gersau, Switzerland," *ibid,* 153-62.

van Löben Sels, R., (2015) "Dreaming in place: Santorini, Greece," in *Ancient Greece, modern psyche: Archetypes evolving.* Routledge Press, 155-181.

Chapter 8

Tracking the Wild Poem
Three Great Cats

by Naomi Ruth Lowinsky

> *In the very essence of poetry there is something indecent:*
> *a thing is brought forth which we didn't know we had in us,*
> *so we blink our eyes, as if a tiger had sprung out*
> *and stood in the light, lashing his tail.*
>
> (Milosz, 1988, "Ars Poetica?" p. 211)

Introduction: The Mouth of the Underworld

Poems are wild things. Milosz' tiger springs out of the unconscious, with all the vitality and fierceness of that realm. This wild beauty, this dread creature, personifies the "reality of the psyche." The mouth of the underworld has spoken. But messages from the depths must be translated into language accessible by day. The wild poem must be tracked through many visions and revisions, draft after draft. This requires much of the poet: patience, tenacity, frequent descents to the underworld. In revising the poem, the poet is revised; a relationship is formed with an aspect of Self hitherto unknown. The transcendent function—to use Jung's language—has been constellated, meaning that the unconscious and the conscious have joined to create a third thing—a poem. When a poem feels finished to me, my world feels larger, wilder, full of feeling, color, and spirit.

Working on a poem, then, is not so different from the Jungian practices of active imagination and analytic listening. One must make room in oneself for what Allen Ginsburg calls "The Lion for Real," though the lion is terrifying. One must be able to tolerate extreme states of discomfort, of not knowing—which Keats famously called Negative Capability— "capable of being in uncertainties, Mysteries, doubts, without any irritable reaching after fact & reason..." (1959, p. 261). One must allow oneself to be propelled from world to world—from the night world of shadow and dream, to the day world of love, work, and history, to the eternal world of the gods and myth, back down to the underworld roots of language—without getting the bends.

Part One: Tiger

...what creates an artist...is exposure to the tiger...
(Hirshfield, 1997, p.156)

Big cats have stalked me since I was a girl. I did not know what they would demand of me as I laid myself down to sleep under a large oil painting of a tiger every night. This was the mark of my grandmother, my Oma—the painter Emma Hoffman—who imprinted me with her hungry artist eyes. It was the mark of Erich, a dying tiger in the Berlin Zoo, painted by Oma as a young woman, before she married, had six children—lost three—before Hitler and her life as a refugee.

Oma told my brothers and me the story of Erich over and over in our childhood. We demanded it, wanting to hear Oma's guttural growl as she became the tiger, greeting the young woman she used to be, with her easel and brushes. She did not paint the bars of Erich's cage; she painted his glorious reclining body, his fine old head on the ground, his life ebbing. Was she painting her own wildness ebbing as she approached domestic life?

Oma knew her wild nature. Watching her paint, I saw her eyes go dark and inward—predator eyes, tiger eyes. In the act of creation, I saw her become a creature. The magic of word roots, which reach down into the collective unconscious, reveals this primal connection: the words "creation" and "creature" come from the same etymological root, meaning "to grow," to "bring forth." Tiger came forth when Oma was in the act of creation. She became tiger. I saw it. It scared me. But in the night of my girlhood sleep, tiger comforted me, held me in some mysterious way, associated in my young child reverie with Blake's "Tyger Tyger burning bright/ in the forests of the night." This "Poem of Experience" with its dread vision of the "menacing blaze of a tiger's eyes" (Frye, 1969, p. 237), did not frighten me. Rather, it visited me as a lullaby might, with its trance inducing rhythms and rhymes. As is so often true of the unconscious, I was being tracked by a dangerous inner creature who would eventually bring both wild energy and trouble to my creative life. But I was a child on my way to sleep, and the double natured tiger/Tyger was the guardian of my soul.

My Familiar

> *Poems do not make appointments with their subjects—they stalk them, keeping their distance, looking slightly off to one side. And when at last the leap comes, it is most often from the side, the rear, an overhead perch, from some word–blind woven of brush or shadow or fire.*

(Hirshfield, 1997, pp. 107-8)

Poems surprise their poets. They take us places we didn't know we were going. They track us, leaping out when they are least expected, for example in the form of a forgotten dream in a long ago journal. When I was a young mother, recently divorced, a starving tiger showed up in a dream, left the mark of its claws on my writing hand. Much of a lifetime later, going over notebooks from that time, the tiger leapt into my poem, insisting on a dialogue with the mother in me. The tiger, it turns out, has been a fierce advocate for my writing life.

Your Familiar

You were so full of your own
deep dance   so fascinated
by the revelations
of your hips

you never considered
the mess
you were making

His fury
His vendetta
His suit for custody
of the children   The truth was
you had no power

> *A starving tiger*
> *paces the kitchen*

Not to mention
the little matter
of money   how
to make it?

Was it all your fault?

What were you good for?
Mostly you followed words
tracking them deep in the woods

> *Should you feed it?*
> *Should you drive it away*
> *banging the lids of your pots?*
> *Will it attack the children?*

And what of the children?
Their severed days
every other weekend
on a little yellow plane
to visit Daddy

And when it leaps
leaving its mark
on your writing hand
is that a sign

of your guilt? Or
your promise?

(First published in
Cape Rock)

Tyger, Tyger

We stare into the fiery eyes of the Tyger and think ourselves
lost in the "forests of the night." But the Tyger is the face of
the creator, marvelous and ambiguous; he is not evil.

(Kazin, in Blake, 1946, p. 42)

Though an essay is not as wild a creature, for me, as is a poem—it is more rational, more domesticated—I experience some of the same creative dynamics in writing prose as I do with poetry. So, beginning this essay, following the track of my associations to the big cats of my inner life, I am surprised by that double natured Tiger/Tyger—the marks of Oma and Blake in my childhood reveries. They are so opposite, one caged and dying in an earthly zoo; the other, a mythical sky tiger, "burning bright"—one the creation of my personal grandmother; the other, the creation of "one of the most prophetic and gifted rebels in the history of western man" (Kazin, in Blake, 1946, p.6). Something shifts in me. I become aware of an unwelcome feeling, like Milosz' "tiger"—an indecent, embarrassing, intrusive thing I didn't know was in me. For heaven's sake, I was an English Major; I studied Blake. Yet I have no idea what that strange little poem of Blake's is all about. As a child I remember feeling held by Oma's tiger in concert with Blake's Tyger, as I wandered the "forests of the night." But rereading "The Tyger" I can't see how. It's scary. It's not the paean to the creator's artistic talents I thought it was. For the creator has made a dreadful creature, which, as Kazin points out, is a self-portrait:

> And what shoulder, & what art,
> Could twist the sinews of thy heart?
> And when thy heart began to beat,
> What dread hand? & what dread feet?
>
> (Blake, 1946, "The Tyger," p. 109)

My Jungian training has me ask, who is the tiger in me? That starving tiger who showed up when I was a single mother was my own famished, wild nature, shadowing my overly domesticated life, leaving its mark on my writing hand. The tiger is the creator in me, both terrible and enlivening. It is embattled with the nurturer I also am. I don't like to acknowledge my predatory nature. But over the years I've learned that when I'm not feeding my creative nature, not tracking the wild life of poems, tiger will show up and make trouble. I get short tempered with the people I love and with myself. This happened recently, when I was struggling with family and health issues. A dream gives me a different point of view. In the dream I live in a large house with many rooms full of people and activities. But I am locked in a small room with a tigress. She has expressive eyes and long hair, and leaps against the walls, trying to break us both out of there. She claws me—again, my writing hand—that mark that bridges over forty years of my life. As Kazin says of Blake:

> ...he will not let us off with anything
> less than...the fact that the Tyger
> exists—a fact that includes all its
> ambiguity and all our wonder and
> fear before it.
>
> (Kazin, in Blake, 1946, p. 46)

I stand in awe before this mystery, that I have been tracked by tiger all my life, tiger has been at once daemonic and devoted; she has shown me my path.

Mystery

I ask my dream to tell me a story, show
me an image, send me a message, anything to free
my trapped spirit—caught in some old woe
Dream gives me a tigress. I foresee she'll hurl me
to the ground. Am I her meat?
Is she the essence of that girl
who prowled the woods, talked to the trees
watched the river swirl?

O tiger it is spring! Wisteria
and mountain laurel bloom. I have this only
life but you appear in many forms—mystery,
familiar. Last night you lurked about the center
of the town. Am I supposed to wake from sleep
$\qquad$ and let you enter?

$\qquad$ (Lowinsky, 2013, p.64)

Letting the tiger enter one's life is dangerous. One has to be very careful with wild animals, be they inner or outer. If you scare them they'll disappear. If you let them get too close, they'll eat you or your children. I have learned to be watchful, receptive, alert—grounded in my own wild nature. For, as Jung writes:

> The unborn work in the psyche
> of the artist is a force of nature...It
> is a split off portion of the psyche
> which leads a life of its own.
> $\qquad$ (1978, para. 115)

This process requires an ongoing relationship—vision and revision—a hunt, or being hunted, a wrestling with the angel, usually requiring many versions, being in a state of semi-possession, letting fierce energies into consciousness, often in the middle of the night, awakened by some creature from the depths. Like a woman in labor I have learned not to resist the power of what wants to come through. Jung says it well:

> The artist is not a person endowed
> with free will who seeks his own
> ends, but one who allows art to
> realize its purposes through him.
>
> (1978, para. 157)

Creating a bridge between the mouth of the underworld and what can be recognized in the day world requires sacred time—in my case morning time. A candle is lit. I drop down into a short meditation to clear my psyche and invite the wild things in. Jung knew this process. For him it was not about art, but about the development of consciousness. He called it Active Imagination, and his inner figures were his guides and psycho–pomps. It was Jung's passionate belief that the "creative imagination is...the real ground of the psyche, the only immediate reality" (Jung, 1973, p. 60). Blake held a similar passionate belief: "This World is a World of Imagination and Vision" (Kazin, in Blake, 1946, p. 29). In his Introduction to *The Portable Blake* Kazin writes:

> [Blake] wrote and drew, as he lived,
> from a fathomless inner window, in
> an effort to make what was deepest
> and most invisible capturable.
>
> (1946, p.21)

I had not understood until I began working on this paper, that long before I had heard the name Jung, I was under the influence of Blake, who evoked my poetic nature—my tiger nature. Tiger can slip through the jungle, disguised by dark stripes and tawny hide which look like sun and shadow, at once powerful and hidden, light and dark, "here and not here, the tiger is like spirit or wind" (*The Book of Symbols*, p. 270) transporting us back into the realm of the Divinity, who, in Judaism, is associated with breath and wind (Schwartz, 2004 p. 20).

Both Kazin and Northrop Frye—who wrote the monumental work on Blake, *Fearful Symmetry,* borrowing his title from Blake's poem, "The Tyger"—make a distinction between mystic poets and visionaries. They see Blake as the latter.

> *Vision is [Blake's] master–word, not mysticism or soul. For*
> *vision represents the total imagination of man made tangible*
> *and direct in works of art.*
>
> (Kazin, in *The Portable Blake,* 1946, p. 16.)

Jung made a similar distinction, though in the other direction. What he was up to, he insisted, was not art, but psyche—soul. I have written elsewhere about my quarrel with Jung concerning that split (Lowinsky, 2012, pp. 151-164). It has been the fruit of my creative development to break through the cultural divisions between the visionary and the mystic, between imagination and psyche, between art and the spiritual. Big cats have been my familiars and my guides.

Part Two: Lion

> *Lion that eats my mind now for a decade knowing only your hunger...*
> *O roar of the Universe how am I chosen*
> *In this life I have heard your promise I am ready to die I have served*
> *Your starved and ancient Presence O Lord I wait in my room at your*
> *Mercy*
>
> (Ginsberg, 2007, "The Lion for Real," p.183)

Ginsberg is a poet in the prophetic tradition. He moves fluidly from the carnal to the sacred. His lion is a manifestation of the ancient Lord of the Hebrews—the "roar of the universe." He is a mystical poet praying to a "starved and ancient Presence." Jane Hirshfield, who writes eloquently about Ginsberg's poem in her book *Nine Gates,* puts it this way: "For giving oneself to the lion, or to poetry, is a vow, nothing more, nothing less than one's entire life will be asked"

(1997, p. 159). It is an act of surrender to something much larger than oneself, or in Jungian terms, to the Self.

Ginsberg's poem portrays how unbearable that wild blast of daemonic energy can be. The lion has invaded his living room, terrified him, sent him into a panic. Possessed by the god Pan, he calls up his old Reichian analyst, panting, "there's a Lion in my room." The Reichian is no help. He runs to his old boyfriend, gets drunk with him and his girlfriend, announces "I had a lion with a mad gleam in my eye," and ends up masturbating in a jeep moaning "Lion." He finds Joey, his novelist friend and roars at him "Lion!" Joey reads him his "spontaneous ignu high poetries." Ginsberg figures Joey understands him "when we made it in Ignaz Wisdom's bathroom" (2007, p. 182). Ignaz Wisdom's bathroom and many other astonishments in this poem illuminate Jung's comment:

> A great work of art is like a dream:
> for all its apparent obviousness
> it does not explain itself and is
> always ambiguous...To grasp its
> meaning, we must allow it to shape
> us as it shaped [the artist]. Then
> we also understand the nature
> of his primordial experience. He
> has plunged into the healing and
> redeeming depths of the collective
> psyche.
>   (1978, para. 162)

"The Lion for Real" is Ginsberg's version of being in the grip of the creative daemon—an ecstatic state that is at once awe–full and awesome, combining panic and passion, longings of the flesh and longings of the spirit—a very Jewish vision of the divine as both marvelous and terrible.

Doing the Wild Thing

...a poem is a living thing
made by living creatures

Alexander "Ars Poetica #1002:
Rally," 2010, p. 175

Though I had known and loved Ginsberg's *Howl* since I was teenager yearning to be a beat poet, I didn't know his "Lion for Real" until I read Hirshfield's discussion of it in *Nine Gates*. Years earlier, during my candidacy at the San Francisco Jung Institute, I dreamt of a lion who leapt through the window of the Institute library, told me he loved me, told me he'd eat me.

> you
my hottest familiar
true cat
of my sun
and my rising
flash of fierce father's tail
in the brew
of creation
no wonder
I feared...

> you'd leap
through the library
window
sever my head
from my body
crunch bone
feed on what's soft
maybe you'd burn me up
in your yellow corona
maybe you did...

(Lowinsky, 2000, "what the spirit requires" pp. 50-51)

Being eaten by a lion is not a pleasant experience. But looking back over the quarter century since that terrible visitation, I can see that the numinous shadow creature from the other side devoured my false self, crunched me down to my essence. Ginsberg and I had both been visited by the same archetype. In every archetypal image, Jung writes,

> there is a little piece of human psychology and human fate, a remnant of the joys and sorrows that have been repeated countless times in our ancestral history...It is like a deeply graven river–bed in the psyche, in which the waters of life, instead of flowing along as before in a broad but shallow stream, suddenly swell into a mighty river. This happens whenever...[a] mythological situation reappears [and] is...characterized by a peculiar emotional intensity.
>
> (1978, para. 127-8)

After that lion devoured me I became somebody I would not have recognized when I was younger. Fiercer, more focused, more "selfish," my younger self would have said. I set aside territory and time for my creative life because when I didn't my inner carnivore would roar. That great cat was my own essential Self, which had been severely muzzled in childhood and early adulthood. Astrologically Leo is my "sun and my rising"—my nature is mostly fire with a bit of earth and air—no water.

When the core Self emerges, libido runs wild. Working on a poem is erotic in the broadest sense—an arousal of the senses, a passionate exchange of energies and desire with a creature or creator on another plane of being. I often feel turned on, excited, when the work is going well, as though in the arms of a ghost lover. Jung understood libido as psychic energy—a much broader and many faceted libido than Freud's narrowly sexual one. Jung writes:

> Libido is creative and procreative..., possesses an intuitive faculty, a strange power to 'smell the right place,' almost as if it were a live creature with an independent life of its own...This libido is a force of nature, good and bad at once, or morally neutral...[It] is the dark creative power of the unconscious...

> Libido creates the God–image by making use of archetypal patterns... Man in consequence worships the psychic force within him as something divine. (1976, para. 182)

Thus Ginsberg, having been invaded and terrified by the lion, turns around to worship and pray to the Lion. The creative process becomes a way to flush out the image of the divine, which has been shaped by the unconscious forces within. I too pray to the Lion.

a leo prays

lion
be with me
your burning heart   your leap
                            of certainty
sun knows your body
ocean smells you coming
you are not divided against your fierceness
any more than is the turkey vulture
                    against his bone cleaning

the spider   against her web

so if I have teeth
if my heart is a big thing that beats
    if it burns for word of you
        let me not be divided against such passion

some say we are made of fragments
    we drift in and out
      without core
      no god the conductor
      no imprint   no plan
        nothing from forever visits the dream
        nothing from tomorrow remembers
          the dead stag
        that coven of black vultures we startled
            cleaning his bones

O my animal soul
    let them not sever me   from you
      who are green and glowing
      whose eyes are burning coals

      who danced in the planets at my birth

      my life is   your keep!

(2005, pp. 66-7)

For me, and I would imagine, for Ginsberg, the animal soul who demands a poem organizes experience, gives it shape and meaning. I did not know, when the sight of a coven of vultures cleaning the carcass of a stag, began this poem, that it would lead me into a theological consideration of my own Sun Sign, of my dislike for the atheist's "no imprint no plan" and my passionate need to know the nature of the god "who danced in the planets at my birth." To write such a poem renews the God within, signifying "a regenerated attitude, a renewed possibility of life...because, psychologically speaking, God always denotes...the maximum sum of libido" (Jung, 1977, para. 301).

Freaked in the Moon Brain

When I'm working on a writing project, be it a poem or an essay, it visits me at night. Sometimes it wakes me up and yells at me. As I was working on the Lion section of this paper, I awoke to Ginsberg's voice in my ear, yelling: "You're leaving out the nasty part. You want to avoid it. What really terrified you about being eaten by the Lion was being torn into fragments, 'without core,' without plan, you were afraid of going mad, just as I was afraid of going mad, because my mother, Naomi, had gone mad":

> ...to have been here, and changed, like a tree, broken, or flower—fed to the ground—but mad, with its petals, colored, thinking Great Universe, shaken, cut in the head, leaf stript, hid in an egg crate hospital, cloth wrapped, sore—freaked in the moon brain...
>
> (Ginsberg, 2007, "Kaddish," p. 219)

Often the day world requires a "tough love" intervention from the night world to knock down defenses and face a humiliating truth. Ginsberg named my truth: my fear of the terrible mouth of the underworld, my fear of the teeth of the lion, kept me from committing myself to my art for many years. It had spooked me, as a teenager with dreams of being a poet, to learn that my hero, Ginsberg, had a crazy mother with my name.

Many years ago I heard Ginsberg chant his poems. As an aside he remarked that he didn't do much revision: "First thought, best thought," he said. Not true for me. First thought is often constipated thought, shallow thought, fearful thought. It usually takes a long conversation between conscious and unconscious for a poem of mine to spring to life. Learning to revise, like the long conversation between analyst and patient, is for me, where the healing happens.

It also happens in the Jungian library. My lion did not show up unbidden in my living room as did Ginsberg's. My lion jumped through a window of the Jung Institute and landed on the library table. I was on fire with the Jungian Weltanschauung; it devoured me, gave me a way to name my experiences, often ones that others thought quite mad, such as conversations with inner figures or with the dead. Jung understood the profound problem of "divine madness—a higher form of the irrationality of the life stream through us...a madness that cannot be integrated into present–day society" (2009, p.295). The Jungian tradition held me, understood me, both in the library and in the consulting room. My calling as a poet would converge with my training as an analyst and each would amplify the other.

I began to trust that I could tolerate the intense onslaught of libidinal energy—that "roar of the universe"—that I could contain and channel it into my writing. The lion could indeed have made me crazy—"freaked in the moon brain"—but the wisdom of the ages I found in the Jungian library, two long Jungian analyses, and the practice of poetry, taught me how to work with the awesome presence of the lion.

Part Three: Leopard

Sometimes, Before First Light

I hear hobgoblin music—elf lyre, fairie fiddling, banshee harpist plucking every note of dread out of a slow dawn. My right breast could be harboring an enemy. The doctor points to a suspicious shadow on his imaging machine, amidst galaxies of magnified crushed flesh. This shadow, in the shape of a cigar, is just the size an elf might smoke, while dreaming up a trick to play upon a body trying to get back to sleep...

Lowinsky (first published in *Caveat Lector*)

That enemy took me unaware, attacking first my husband Dan, who was diagnosed with lymphoma, and then me, diagnosed with breast cancer. That was the bad news. The good news was that both our cancers were treatable and, for the moment, we are both cancer free. That phrase—"for the moment"—announces our initiation into a new phase of life, in which that trickster elf is always with us, and life cannot be taken for granted.

Big Cat Medicine

> Poems…transform fate. They make of intransigent outer circumstance something workable, softened.
>
> (Hirshfield, 2015, p. 245)

Leopard is my initiator, my psycho-pomp into this new realm. She did not come to me in dream, or vision. She came in the most ordinary day–world form—in clothing and accessories. On the day I was scheduled to go to the Breast Center for a biopsy, I reached for my leopard print bra. I wasn't remembering the Goddess dressed in leopard skins, found with her animal epiphany at Çatal Hüyük, dated between 7100–6300 BCE (Johnson, 1981 p. 102). I wasn't remembering the Mother Goddess sitting on the "lion throne of birth, her hands resting on the heads of two flanking leopards…," from the same Neolithic period and site (Johnson, 1981 p. 102), nor was I remembering the Goddess riding her leopard found at nearby Halicar, from 6000 BCE (Daniélou, 1982, p. 117). My choice of bra did not come from my Jungian library, but from the leopard in my soul.

At the reception desk of the Breast Center a woman with a kind face greeted me, saw the fear in my eyes, took my hand and said: "Honey, it's going to be alright." She was wearing a leopard print blouse. I said: "I love your blouse." Leaning in conspiratorially, I whispered, "I'm wearing my leopard bra, for courage." An intense charge of energy passed between us—two women wearing the ancient markings of the Goddess in her leopard epiphany. The Kabbalah says:

> An epiphany enables you to sense
> creation not as something com-
> pleted, but as constantly becoming,
> evolving, ascending. This trans-
> ports you from a place where there
> is nothing new to a place where
> there is nothing old, where every-
> thing renews itself, where heaven
> and earth rejoice as at the moment
> of creation.
>
> (Matt, 1996, p. 99)

I sat in the waiting room and marveled at the synchronicity of leopard prints on jackets, iPhone holders, purses; my creative process raised its great cat head, and the poem, which insisted on being a prose poem, began:

Wearing Leopard to the Breast Center

Big cats have always stalked your dreams. When did they spring into fashion, flinging their markings on cottons and silks, imbuing your legs and your breasts, with their jungle heat? They're every-where—wrapped around the receptionist's neck, flaunting their glamour on handbags and iPhone all over the waiting room. You've got your leopard bra on, for courage, before you hand your tender old girls to the technician—to be crushed.

This is no maidenform fantasy. This is the leap of a pred-ator—her grace, her glory, her claws that rip flesh. This is no ten-thousand-dollar fur, requiring a great cat to die for your glamour, as you stride down some Avenue in Vogue Magazine. This is you wrapped in wild evocation—animal prints on your bed sheets, your bathrobe, your faux leopard vest.

There's a reason those big cats stalk you—track you deep into dreaming. They smell your nature. Remember the starving tiger, clawed at your writing hand? The lion in the library, said he loved you, said he'd eat you? The sad–eyed tigress, flung herself against your four walls, frantic to break you out? Oh you've been broken and entered, opened and eaten, ripped and reborn. Big cat medicine—breathing the dark in some feline belly—waking to joy, bruised and weeping.

Grandmother Leopard come lie with me, lick me where everything aches, rough tongue me back to my rainforest senses. Remember me to the base of my spine, where tail begins its slow motion. Remember my nose—what it knows—of earth smells, fungi, green growth and scat. Remember the delicate hairs of my ears, the breeze as we leap through the trees. Track me through dances of shadow and light, from sunset to luminous bodies of night. Mark me as one of your own.

(First published in Diverse Voices Quarterly)

Why a prose poem? I had been reading Robert Bly's astounding prose poems, poems that seemed able to leap from world to world as fleetly as a leopard. Bly writes:

> ...the urgent, alert rhythm of the
> prose poem prepares us to journey,
> to cross the border, either to the
> other world, or to that place where
> the animal lives.

(Bly, 1986, p. 88)

The urgency of cancer, its bodily threat, called forth potent animal imagery in dreams and in waiting rooms. I understood that my husband and I were in serious need of animal medicine, an ancient shamanic system which holds that our "brothers and sisters of the animal kingdom" can reveal "our role in the Great Mystery" (Sams & Carson, 1999, p. 13). Poems are my medicine, and the animal images that possessed me wanted to be expressed in prose poems. This process culminated in a series of poems full of wild creatures; they emerged in response to my husband's illness as well as mine. The act of writing the poems shifted our relationship to the ordeal we were suffering. The act of reading the poem to my husband made him laugh or cry, and that opened up space for us to experience the

Great Mystery together. Jane Hirshfield writes eloquently about the transformative powers of poetry:

> In dark times...what restores the
> capacity for humanness is the re-
> alignment that comes from finding
> ourselves simply, decently, *moved*.
> For this, we need the connection
> forged by poetry's singing.
>
> (Hirshfield 2015, p. 254)

As I was working on this paper a dream showed me a sign reading: "Leopard wants to sing." *The Book of Symbols* tells us:

> The Leopard is shy and solitary,
> the most nocturnal of the big cats,
> and so elusive that the sighting of
> the beautiful snow leopard living at
> altitudes exceeding 10,000 feet and
> rarely glimpsed...represents the
> mystic goal of spiritual journeys...
> An arboreal hunter, the leopard
> is associated with the magic and
> shape–shifting of shamans for
> whom the treetops were initiatory,
> numinous openings to the land of
> the spirits.
>
> (*The Book of Symbols*, 2010, p. 270)

As with so many of my poems, leopard sang to me at night, insisting I go deeper into her jungle. She sang me a shape–shifting journey from the Breast Center's waiting room, where leopard's marks were flung round women's necks, breasts, handbags, iPhone holders, to the world of fashion and the boudoir. Leopard sang me my history of great cat encounters in dreams and in poems. Leopard is a close relative of Panther, whose medicine is: "Embracing the Unknown" (Sams & Carson, 1999, p. 245). Leopard sang me of Grandmother

Leopard, recasting a Hindu fable that had long ago leapt out of a book in my library and marked my psyche. It is a teaching story told by the nineteenth century Hindu saint Śrī Rāmakrishna and retold by Heinrich Zimmer (Zimmer, 1989, p. 6–7) about a baby tiger who, orphaned and adopted by goats, is convinced he is a goat. A fierce old tiger comes along one night, grabs the cub by the neck, carries him to a pond and insists he look "into the mirror surface, which was illuminated by the moon." The jungle tiger says:

> Now look at those two faces. Are
> they not alike?" You have the pot–
> face of a tiger; it is like mine. Why
> do you fancy yourself to be a goat?
> Why do you bleat? Why do you
> nibble grass?
>
> (Zimmer, 1989, p. 7)

The baby goat, like the ugly duckling of European fairy tale, is initiated into his true nature and his kin. This story expresses ancient Hindu ideas about the "rediscovery and assimilation of the Self" (Zimmer, 1989, p. 8). Jung, it must be remembered, borrowed heavily from the Vedas and the Upanishads in his early writings, as he was beginning to articulate his concept of the Self. Jung quotes a description of Brahman from the Katha Upanishad:

> That Self, smaller than small,
> greater than great, is hidden in the
> heart of this creature here. Man
> becomes free from desire and free
> from sorrow when by the grace of
> the Creator he beholds the glory of
> the Self. Sitting still he walks afar;
> lying down he goes everywhere.
>
> (Jung, 1977, para.329)

Jung writes that Brahman is "not only the producer but the produced, the ever–becoming..." (Jung, 1977, para. 330). Quoting from the Brihadaranyaka Upanishad, Jung continues, "Brahman is... 'the thread by which this world and the other world and all things are tied together, the Self, the inner controller, the immortal'" (Jung, 1977, para. 334). The Brahman concept, he continues is "a dynamic or creative principle which I have termed libido. The word Brahman means prayer, incantation, sacred speech, sacred knowledge..." (Jung, 1977, para. 336). This idea that Brahman is at once Self, libido and sacred speech, articulates my experience of coming through many drafts to the pleasure of a completed poem. Things have been tied together. Grandmother Leopard has had her say. A prayer has been answered.

Leopards in the Temple

> Leopards break into the temple and drink to the dregs what is in the sacrificial pitchers; this is repeated over and over again; finally it can be calculated in advance, and it becomes a part of the ceremony.
>
> (Kafka, 1971, p. 472)

In my library meanders I came across this parable by Franz Kafka in a favorite reference book of mine, *The Tree of Souls: The Mythology of Judaism,* by Howard Schwartz. He comments:

> Kafka wrote a number of parables that closely follow biblical and midrashic models...Here...Kafka transforms the myth into a universal one, where it is no longer certain that the temple in Kafka's parable is the Temple in Jerusalem.
>
> (Schwartz, 2004, p. 423)

I haven't read Kafka since I was a teenager, and his parables, which I've never read, are a revelation. In her Introduction to this collection Joyce Carol Oates helps me understand my intense response to

Kafka later in life:

> Perceptive teenagers love him not
> because he is "one of the great
> moderns" but because he speaks
> their private language by speaking
> so boldly in his own.
>
> (Kafka, 1971, p. ix)

The fierce energy and bold talk of adolescence—tempered by life experience—is enlivening as we pass out of the everyday cares of midlife into the realm of the mysteries. Kafka's modern myth moves me as a big dream does, or a good poem. It has what Jane Hirshfield calls the "poetic concentration [which] allows us to bring the dream mind's compression, displacement, wit, depth and surprise, into our waking minds" (Hirshfield, 1997, p. 18). And Kafka himself, writes:

> All these parables really set out to
> say merely that the incomprehen-
> sible is incomprehensible, and we
> know that already. But the cares
> we have to struggle with every day:
> that is a different matter.
>
> (1971, p. 459)

Poems strive to say the unsayable. They do this through image, rhythm, sound, song. Kafka's parable helps me grasp the ungrasp-able: the sacred nature of my Leopard experience. The leopards have broken into the temple of my body, the temple of my husband's body; they have broken into the holy of holies and they drink the sacrificial vessels dry. They are what Joseph Henderson calls:

> Mythological guardians of thresh-
> olds..., both friendly and fierce,
> showing that what is aroused from
> the unconscious by the approach of
> a new threshold of consciousness is

> a feeling of ambivalence, a mixture
> of attraction and repulsion.
>
> (Henderson, 1987, p. 43)

The leopards have broken into ordinary life, their markings are blooming all over the bodies and sanctuaries of women; they have broken into the temples of beauty, of culture, of medicine. They drink dry the vessels of sacrifice, as if to say one has to suffer the terrible thirst for the sacred; the ordeal must be embodied. Henderson writes:

> Sacrifice is an act of submission expe-
> rienced as a meaningful initiatory
> ordeal, to be distinguished from the
> trial of strength appropriate to the
> accomplishment of heroes.
>
> (1987 p. 71)

I am certainly far past the heroic initiations of young adulthood. Leopard's power—which shamans know to be associated with birth and with death—is what I must now submit to. In Kafka's parable the leopards become part of the ritual. Leopard initiation ushers me into a Temple which is not separate from the animal realm—the realm of body, instinct and earth—or from leopard's association with the night, the uncanny, the unknown. Jane Hirshfield comments that the arts partake "of something that lies at the core of ritual: the reenactment of and entrance into a mystery" (Hirshfield, 2015, p. 193). Writing the poem became a ritual of integrating Grandmother Leopard, though I had no idea she'd show up when the poem began in the waiting room of the Breast Center. As Hirshfield says, such "a ritual must be passed through with the whole body, not glimpsed through a door" (Hirshfield, 2015, p. 198). When the words of prayer to this great spirit animal come to me: "*lick me where everything aches, rough tongue me back to my rainforest senses. Remember me to the base of my spine, where tail begins its slow motion*" I can feel, in my body, that I have become Leopard, as my Oma, the painter, became Tiger.

In Conclusion

> And the beast which I saw was like
> unto a leopard...and his mouth as
> the mouth of a lion: and the dragon
> gave him his power, and his seat,
> and great authority.
>
> (Revelation 13:2)

What if the mark of the tiger's claw on my writing hand is not just about tiger's concern for my creative life, but concern for All Creation. What if tiger wants to waken me to the fate of the earth, the loss of species, especially of tiger? What if leopard's marks flung round women's necks, breasts, on handbags and iPhone holders, are signs of the swan song of leopard: "Remember me...?" What if the big cats were gone from the jungle, the desert, the forest; what if there were just a few left dying in zoos or in poems—Rilke's weary panther, pacing "in cramped circles," whose "mighty will stands paralyzed" (Rilke, 1982, p. 25)? Does our animal being stand paralyzed in the face of such unbearable loss? What becomes of Big Cat Medicine when all the big cats are gone? What is the role of the human creator, the poet, for example, as the great cats disappear from their habitats because the jungles and forests are being cut down, because the ancient wisdom of animal medicine that sees us as part of the Great Mystery has been hacked to shreds? Is our role to witness, to prophesy, to protest, to channel the great authority of the dragon—a mythical beast, a reminder of the extinct realm of the dinosaurs?

As I was working on the conclusion of this paper, asking these questions, I found myself at a conference on eco-psychology, giving a paper to a roomful of people at the Los Angeles Jung Institute. It was not lost on me that the conference brochure displayed a striking image by the artist James Griffith of a great cat descending a steep rocky mountain. The room became a sacred space in which we could descend into our grief and fear. I found myself in conversation with a woman who told me about a series of alchemical paintings she had made during a time of terrible crisis in her life, when her husband had surgery for brain cancer. She showed me her final image: a woman with the head of a cat. This cat was buff, raised her heavily muscled arms in a gesture of power and pride and declared: "Look, I am woman! Meaowhhh..." (Tauber, 2012, p. 65).

This alchemical painter/cat woman is Marianne Tauber. In a different medium, in a different life situation, her work demonstrates the power of the archetype. Lion–headed humans have been found in ancient sites, expressing "a dual nature..., harnessing...the lion's independence and fierceness to protect the...world." (Moon, 1991, p. 109). Tauber found her medicine in a painting practice that held her as she and her family descended into a dark time. Through her creative process Tauber claimed her animal nature, her instinctive female power and authority, her sense of self, and transformed what had been a patriarchal marriage. She lived out a version of what is the great drama of our times—the return of the goddess, with her animal epiphanies, her wild nature, her wisdom about earth and her creatures.

In her book she describes herself as a "servant of the invisible" (Tauber, 2012, p. 2) and describes her painting practice as at once "deadly serious prayer and a playful dance of soul" (Tauber, 2012, p. 22). It struck me that Tauber has named our role as Jungians and artists: to be servants of the invisible, to practice rituals which are "deadly serious prayers" as well as "playful dances of soul." The leopards have broken into the temple, and if we have the courage to let them, they will teach us their animal ways.

References

The Book of Symbols: Reflections on Archetypal Images (2010). Cologne, Germany: Taschen.

Alexander, E. (2010). Crave Radiance: New and Selected Poems 1990–2010. Graywolf Press.

Blake, W. (1946). Kazin, A. (Ed.). The Portable Blake. New York: Viking Press.

Bly, R. (1986). Selected Poems. New York: Harper & Row.

Daniélou, A. (1982). *Gods of Love and Ecstasy: The Traditions of Shiva and Dionysus.* Rochester, Vermont Inner Traditions.

Frye, N. (1969). *Fearful Symmetry: A Study of William Blake.* Princeton University Press.

Ginsberg, A. (2007). *Collected Poems: 1947-1997.* New York: HarperPerennial.

Henderson, J. (1987). *Thresholds of Initiation.* Middletown, CN. Wesleyan University Press.

Hirshfield, J. (1997). *Nine Gates: Entering the Mind of Poetry.* New York: HarperCollins.

Hirshfield, J. (2015). *Ten Windows: How Great Poems Transform the World.* New York: Alfred A. Knopf.

Johnson, B. (1981). *Lady of the Beasts: Ancient Images of the Goddess and Her Sacred Animals.* San Francisco: Harper & Row.

Jung, C.G. (1976). *Symbols of Transformation, Collected Works v. 5.* Princeton University Press.

Jung, C.G. (1977). *Psychological Types, Collected Works v. 6.* Princeton University Press.

Jung, C.G. (1978). *The Spirit in Man, Art and Literature, Collected Works v.15.* Princeton University Press.

Jung, C.G. (1973). *Letters*: v. I. Princeton University Press.

Jung, C. (2009). *The Red Book.* New York: W.W. Norton and Company.

Kafka, F. (1971). *The Complete Stories and Parables.* New York: Schocken Books Inc.

Keats, J. (1959). Bush, D. (Ed.) *Selected Poems and Letters.* Boston: Houghton Mifflin Co.

Lowinsky, N. (2005). *Crimes of the dreamer: poems.* Oakland CA: Scarlet Tanager Books.

Lowinsky, N. (2013). *The Faust Woman Poems.* Il Piccolo Editions, Fisher King.

Lowinsky, N. (2012). "Drunk with Fire: How the Red Book Transformed My Jung," in Damery, P. and Lowinsky, N. (Eds.). *Marked by Fire: Stories of the Jungian Way.* Fisher King.

Lowinsky, N. (2000) *red clay is talking*. Oakland, CA: Scarlet Tanager Books.

Matt, D. (1996). *The Essential Kabbalah: The Heart of Jewish Mysticism*. HarperSanFrancisco.

Milosz, C. (1988). *The Collected Poems: 1931-1987*. Hopewell, N J: The Ecco Press.

Moon, B. Ed. (1991) *An Encyclopedia of Archetypal Symbolism*. Boston: Shambhala.

Oliver, M. (2014). *Blue Horses: Poems*. New York: The Penguin Press.

Rilke, R. M. (1982), Mitchell, S. (Ed. and trans.) *Selected Poetry*. New York: Vintage International.

Sams, J. & Carson, D. (1999) *Medicine Cards*. New York: St. Martin's Press.

Schwartz, H. (2004). *Tree of Souls: The Mythology of Judaism*. Oxford University Press.

Tauber, M. (2012). *The Soul's Ministrations: An Imaginal Journey through Crisis*. Wilmette, Ill: Chiron.

Zimmer, H. (1989). *Philosophies of India*. Princeton University Press.

Chapter 9

Witnesses of the Other

by Ian Livingston

Introduction

This paper uses a synthesis of Jungian and Lacanian approaches to explore the relationship between the artist and her art as a profoundly devotional act of adoration for the Other. The actions of the artist emerge as responses to the ineluctability of the natural creative imperative inherent in being in existence. Jung's inquiries in alchemical literature figure as foundational to understanding art as the active pursuit of communication in the language the artist speaks most articulately, whether that language is musical, aesthetic in terms of color and form, kinesthetic, or scientific. The artist here is accepted as an individual possessed of some subjective insight that can only be expressed in the most metaphorical terms, while metaphor is understood as the nature of all apprehension and communication.

Roots

What do we know of beginnings, of the roots that spring from them, and the appalling immensity of the sources of human creative engagements? All we have learned, made, and acquired has taught us that we know precious little, indeed. The sciences know some things about how things change, about the generation of organisms from conjugation, like sentences growing from a vocabulary, but we know very little about sources, beginnings, the first roots, and observe only the surfaces of the growing thing, whether vegetable, or animal, and the roots of becoming, of being, and of making elude us. Still, we are not utterly clueless, even the preacher of Ecclesiastes (1:14) bemoans the ancient complaint that he is familiar with everything done under the sun, that everything returns eternally to the same point. Even so, it is clear that every instant is new, and holds the promise of potential for the novel instant to follow because nothing ever returns to the same point, only, perhaps, to the same axis, just as one does not derive from zero. We know these things when we take the time to think about them, but maybe we know them, too, even before we take the time to think, just as we know the source of those thoughts. Beneath every endeavor, says Freud (1920, 1961, pp. 45—46), an impulse to completion derives from a sensed expulsion out of some state of contentment. But, how can that be?

The source of our search, the quest that lures us always forward into every new day, the creative imperative, drives us in search of new knowledge, insight, discovery, even when the knowledge sought is as basic as knowledge of the wherewithal to continue the daily struggle for survival. If the pressure to return to a familiar state of being—or to an imagined state of grace—is compelling, so, too, the allure of the unknown is irresistible. It is not a drive to return, but a drive to novelty tethered, perhaps, to an imagined recollection of safety.

Given this premise, it seems necessary that the soul in search of the roots of creativity must certainly pass at some point through the gates of motivation, for the quest asks not only whence, but, especially, why humans create art and artifacts, and why they pursue learning. Is the creative act peculiar to the rational being, or is it more basic, more elemental to the nature of *being* than even to the edifice of rationality? Might creative impulse be the foundation of reason?

It is generally accepted now that the operational center of what we recognize as human identity is the human brain and that the human brain is a sense organ. Through the miracle of evolution, the brain has developed from a purely reactive instrument, responding simply to external stimuli, to the awesome power of the human being to creatively respond to not only external stimuli, but also to the subjective syntheses of projected possibilities. What we know as ideas are complex responses to stimuli which give shape and meaning to sensations, feelings that are born of emotional states in the brain (Damasio, 2003, p.70).

Possibly the rational itself is but a creative response to the overwhelming abundance of stimuli that confront the human being. Contemporary research suggests that all that arises in consciousness originates in perceptions, sophisticating through physical processes in the brain. Where, from that perspective, shall we mark the line between "conditioned response" and "creative act?" How a person goes about answering these questions may reveal somewhat of their position on the *ex nihilo / ex materia* dialectic, but still more is revealed about perspectives regarding resistance and flow than is intended, perhaps, in the substance of those arguments. To argue creation *ex nihilo* requires an element of magical thinking, an acceptance that what cannot be understood is without cause; whereas *ex materia* perspectives on human thought, for instance, incline to limit the range of possibilities for truly new ideas.

Resistance is clearly a natural response to change, all sentient beings startle defensively before they test something new in their environment, but the ease with which they assimilate the capacity to flow with novelty increases with experience. These aspects of development, resistance and flow, mark out the channels of human social and psychological enterprise. We create in order to resist impermanence and to affect the direction of the inevitable flow of continuance.

The record of human artifacts ranges from the variety of primitive tools and weapons early hominids made to the vast cities of aggregate, glass, and polymer towering over altered land as monuments honoring the physical sciences, and to the remarkable human understanding of molecules, electronics, gravity, particles, stars. Humans have always, we might adduce, struggled to create, to express some aspect of themselves in the world, even when that expression manifests destructively.

Maybe the struggle to create is more elemental even than that; maybe it is the nature of nature itself to create, and we, as children of that creative impetus, are powerless to successfully will resistance to the creative impulse endemic to being. If that is so, every person is a creative person, will ye, nill ye. It just is simply, irresistibly, so.

However, there is a zone of demarcation between the impulse to create and the will to create beautiful or expressive art. It is the products of conscious will that endure, for through the disciplined attention of the artist, the artisan, or the scientist whose skill, insight, and ability come at some cost, that these works accrue cultural value, and cultural value reflects the inherently social nature of creativity.

Nothing new arises in a vacuum; the artist or artisan always works in a social context, even when that context is ascetic in nature. Certainly, the attention required for the creation of an arrow from raw materials is much less than that required for creating a novel, a bronze figure, or a psychotherapeutic approach to treating an adaptive disorder, but all require disciplined and creative attention and resourceful interaction with others and the environment. These are complex activities engaged in over spans of time, often involving interrupted sequences over periods of separation from the project, therefore requiring the efforts of will, of memory, and of the ability to focus on ideas without immediate material tethers.

Why individuals tether their attention where they do, then, seems central to the question of the source of complex, intentional creativity. What is the source of that intention? What moves the soul to her work? There might be a broad array of responses to such questions, but the focus here is upon such creative acts as draw, and are intended to draw, the regard of others. In these cases, the creative response is clearly focused in the fields of communication, intrasubjective, intersubjective, and interobjective.

Necessity and Will

Jung, in *Psychological Types* (1921 / 1971, pp 242-253), draws upon Meister Eckhart's religious metaphors to equate the libido with the soul as the "organ of perception," thus as the intermediary between the conscious and the unconscious functions of the mind, and that in this role the libido speaks in symbols and images. "The organ of perception," he writes, "apprehends the contents of the unconscious, and, as the creative function, gives birth to its *dynamis* in the form of a symbol" (para.426).

Of the ways this *dynamis* manifests itself in intentional conscious activity the first is artistic, the second philosophical. It seems appropriate to include the scientific as a third affirmative function, born of the synthesis of the first two. After follow the fair and foul of religion, and the sacred and profane of pleasure. These emerge from the individual's interior conversations between the self, or ego, and the unconscious, through the translative participation of the libido / soul. It is necessary to note that Jung does not identify the libido with the negative connotations Freud does in his discussions of *ego* and *id* (1923 / 1960, pp. 44—5). For Jung (1921 /1971, para. 424), the libido (soul) is a relational function that derives its virtues and value from the dialog it facilitates between the ego (self) and the unconscious (God).

It seems well-advised, therefore, to take up the question of otherness in the Lacanian terms of Subject and Other in a discussion of the roots of creativity. Because nothing comes from nothing, and creative art is clearly something, it follows that when we talk about creativity we are in fact talking about creative synthesis, the creation of one thing from another, or a set of others in combination.

Humans begin, in Lacan's view (Fink, 1995; Lacan, 1966, 2005), acculturating to the processes of synthetic sophistication with the discovery of others, usually beginning with the caregiving parent, and the role others play in the aggregation of understanding and confusion over time can best be understood in dialogical terms, as a multivalent conversation the self carries on both internally and externally, with subjective and objective "others." Over the course of childhood development, these "others" soon enough present themselves through the flaws and syntheses of memory and sensation as an Other that includes and transcends all individual others in the child's experience.

The Lacanian Other is the force that informs the dialectical tensions that formulate the subjectivity of the self. Self and Other remain bound in lifelong dialectical dialog, a set of conversations occurring along the interface of consciousness and unconsciousness (Fink, 1995; Lacan, 1966, 2005; Smythe, 2013). In the practice of daily life, the otherness of the Other is a function of the subject. How we regard events, their scenes, and their agencies and agents in our experience depends upon the degree to which we integrate experience through language. Fink (1995) specifically refers to that language as the "m(O)ther tongue;" Lacan (1966, 2005) settles for "native."

But, what language might that be? Does it not likely vary as much between individuals as it does between cultures? Antonin Artaud (1938, 1958, p. 107) famously questioned whether the language of words is the best of languages, and many artists have echoed that sentiment. Indeed, the languages of form, color, rhythm, notation, and movement convey much that seems incommunicable through words. Certainly, metaphor operates far beyond the range of words.

The Big Bang is a metaphor. However mathematically and scientifically likely or unlikely it may seem, it stands untestable, immeasurable, speculative. It is not a bad metaphor, though, given the workings of the human mind. A primal instant of unsurpassable destructive force gave rise to the synthesizing power of stars and all else we regard as materially "real." Destruction and creativity are mystically and mathematically bound in this single instant of cosmic thrust. The mysterious force of gravity gives birth to the stars, their nuclear syntheses produce all the matter which composes our world and our bodies, and by that same mystery, galaxies form and are consumed. From this instant emerges all form and all that derives from form, including human perspective, perception, thought, synthesis, and creativity. We are thus creatures inhabiting a brief ground of violent tensions between creation and destruction, an image Jung (1944 / 1953, para. 436) discusses in relation to the alchemical imagery of the father as body devouring the son as spirit and thereby uniting the body and spirit, being and prehension, newly created as one entity in a violently destructive act.

The question arises here of where to draw the line between the conscious and the unconscious states of the mind. Borrowing a phrase from Robbins' title (2012. p. 225), we might call the interface a "porous boundary," as neuroscience and phenomenology alike often remain uncertain as to what functions belong to which state. Even in the deepest of sleep stages the brain is busy attending to autonomic functions and to the business of clearing away cellular and chemical detritus from the neural pathways. These functions merge seamlessly with dream states, and with semi-conscious dream states such as lucid dreaming and the foggy state experienced in waking from dreams, where coherent cognitive functioning blends with the dream state. These states correspond to positions in an ongoing symposium the topic of which is defining what is real and what is important at the intrapersonal level.

It may be that some obstacle, or set of obstacles, prevents an individual from fully engaging in this dialog, and that it thus becomes imperative for that person to engage in symbolic dialog with an other of another sort. We here move from talking about the subjective agent to the purposive creative act, for it is incumbent upon the individual to discover how best to uncover and integrate the material that motivates them. This is clearly a creative endeavor. No set of instructions is generally available to which people may refer regarding how to manage and perform the activities involved in intrapersonal inquiry. So it is that people use projection, which is generally more unconscious than conscious, in order to give form to what they otherwise experience as randomly or spontaneously arising obstructions to their intentions.

Jung (1960 / 1971, para. 417) refers to this failure of libido's translative function as projecting the religious (godly) function of the libido on external objects, thus impairing the dialog of the subject (ego) and the Other (unconscious). Of the ways in which people deal with these failed conversations, the creative arts offer a plethora of valuable insights. It seems convenient in this case to follow Eliade (1957 / 1987, p. 15) and divide these into "the sacred and the profane" arts as the prevailing ways in which people regard the Other as divided. We reach out to or against the numinous, or we reach out to or against our fellow beings, and the audience thus frames at some level an informing reference for the work. Thus the seed sends its root into the unconscious, and the plant begins its growth toward its ultimate flowering in the world of shared otherness. A well-tethered inquiry will follow a course that affords some harmony to its parts, whereas random projection of misapprehended discontentment produces dysfunctional fits of disordered activity. Humans seem to negotiate a range within that dialectic.

FIGURE 1. *TRAVELLING HERMIT* BY COLETTE CALASCIONE.

Opening the door to speak with the stranger

If the arts represent any sort of transmutation of unconscious material into corporeal knowledge, then the artist is the agent who opens the door to allow the incursion of what was enshrouded in darkness thus into the light of conscious regard. Each participant in creative activity finds some means of opening that door. Even the theorist in the sciences must gape into the darkness beyond that doorway, where are hinted mysteries of origin, of causes for the effects she witnesses in the laboratory. These require stories no less than does religion, because the human mind seeks order in the incomprehensibly vast field of stimuli presented its limited means of interpretation. That which cannot be compassed seems chaos, and that infinite field of the unknown presents itself as darkness before a process of creative endeavor redefines that darkness as the realm of possibility.

St. John of the Cross called this process of discovery the "Dark Night of the Soul," in his profound poem by that name (1979) or, we might infer by way of Jung as per the discussion above, the dark night of the libido. Here on the cross of motivation, between the unconscious (God) and conscious awareness of solution (Earth) hangs pinned the libido (soul) of the inquirer, whose method will determine the form of her product (progeny). A Lacanian way of stating this puzzle might argue that the subject regards the Other in reference to the other, wherein the subject stands as the libidinous self (soul), the other as the objective goal (temporal form), and the Other as the realm of possibility (God). Manifold methods, sometimes messy, sometimes precise, from the arcane to the scientific, present themselves as available to the inquirer in search of creative response to any situation, but these all meet certain formulae. First must come some sort of recognition that some sort of demand for action exists. A synthesis is then required of tethered discipline, of courageous inquiry that moves in spite of the fear of inadequacy toward the problem, and of patience for the frequent failures and repeated attempts to discover the means to bridge the distance between the perceived need and its fulfillment in order to produce novel functions, art, and artifacts in the shared world.

A method is the tool whereby the inquirer works to redefine the unknown as that which is potentially to be known. It is the language both of the inquiry and of the product of the inquiry. That language might be words, form, color, sound (music), numbers, and so on. The purpose of expressing discovery in transmittable form is that a subject (self) may communicate a felt state or condition to another self or group of selves. It may be argued that the purpose of every act is to achieve intersubjectivity such that between I and Thou something common is recognized, whether fleetingly or in some enduring understanding.

FIGURE 2. *INTERNAL LANDSCAPE* BY COLETTE CALASCIONE.

At the root of our stories, our homages, our temples, we find the myths and religions, and at the root of myth and of religion, we come upon the door where the unconscious knocked to enter. Each transition is more difficult to discover as the soul pries open the doorway onto the shadowed regions before which our hearts flutter as we venture from the safety of the accepted into the emptiness implicit in the presence of the creative instinct. Awe cows and inspires the soul. It is fruitless to hate what we fear, but where fear and desire conjugate the realm of possibility opens. This is the vestibule where the artist, the mystic, and the scientist mingle with the depths outside the known; it is the studio, the desk, the hermitage, or the laboratory where the creative midwife gives form to what was previously only felt. Where the subject and the Other conjugate is where creatives deliver God into the world in the most primal of all dynamics.

References

Artaud, A. (1958). *The theater and its double.* (M. C. Richards, trans.) New York, NY: Grove. (Original work published 1938).

Cassirer, E. (1955). *The philosophy of symbolic forms.* (R. Manheim, trans.) New Haven, CT: Yale University Press.

Damasio, A. (2003). *Looking for Spinoza: Joy, sorrow, and the feeling brain.* Orlando, FL: Harcourt.

De Sousa, A. (2011). Freudian Theory and Consciousness: A Conceptual Analysis. *Mens Sana Monographs,* 9(1), 210-217. doi:10.4103/0973-1229.77437

De Yepes y Alavarez, J. (1979). *The collected works of St. John of the Cross.* (K. Kavanaugh and O. Rodriguez, trans.) Washington, DC: Institute of Carmelite Studies. (Original work published c. 1579 – 1591).

Dougherty, M. (2008). Subjective education in analytic training: drawing on values from the art academy. *Journal of Analytical Psychology,* 53(5), 607-614. doi:10.1111/j.1468-5922.2008.00753.x

Ecclesiastes. (1952). In *The holy bible: Revised standard edition.* New York, NY: Thomas Nelson & Sons.

Eliade, M. (1959). *The sacred and the profane: The nature of religion.* (W. R. Trask, trans.) Orlando, FL: Harcourt. (Original work published 1957).

Fink, B. (1995). *The Lacanian subject: Between language and jouissance.* Princeton, NJ: Princeton University Press.

Freud, S. (1960). *The ego and the id.* (J. Strachey, trans.) New York, NY: Norton.(Original work published 1923).

Freud, S. (1961). *Beyond the pleasure principle.* (J. Strachey, trans.) New York, NY: Norton. (Original work published 1920.)

Freud, S. (1961). *Civilization and its discontents.* (J. Strachey, trans.) New York, NY: Norton. (Original work published 1929).

Gullatz, S. (2010). Constructing the collective unconscious. *Journal of Analytical Psychology, 55*(5), 691-714. doi:10.1111/j.1468-5922.2010.01878.x

Jameson, F. (1991). *Postmodernism: Or the cultural logic of late capitalism.* Durham, NC: Duke University Press.

Jung, C. G. (1953). *Psychology and alchemy.* (R. F. C. Hull, trans.) Princeton, NJ: Princeton University Press. (Original work published 1944).

Jung, C. G. (1959). *The archetypes and the collective unconscious.* (R. F. C. Hull, trans.) Princeton, NJ: Princeton University Press.

Jung, C. G. (1971). *Psychological types.* (H. G. Baynes and R. F. C. Hull, trans.) Princeton, NJ: Princeton University Press. (Original work published 1960).

Jung, C. G. (1983). *The essential Jung.* A. Storr (Ed). Princeton, NJ: Princeton University Press.

Koskinen, C. A., & Lindström, U. Å. (2013). Listening to the otherness of the Other: Envisioning listening based on a hermeneutical reading of Lévinas. *International Journal of Listening, 27*(3), 146-156. doi:10.1080/10904018.2013.813259

Lacan, J. (2006). Écrits. (B. Fink, Trans.) New York, NY: Norton. (Original work published 1966).

McGrath, S. J. (2010). Schelling on the Unconscious. *Research in Phenomenology, 40*(1), 72. doi:10.1163/008555510X12626616014664

Meredith-Owen, W. (2011). Winnicott on Jung: destruction, creativity and the unrepressed unconscious. *The Journal of Analytical Psychology, 56*(1), 56-75. doi:10.1111/j.1468-5922.2010.01890.x

Mrnarević, P. (2011). Creativity—Vice or virtue?: A study of different visions of creativity. *Politicka Misao: Croatian Political Science Review, 48*(4), 7-25.

Robbins, A. (2012). Playing along the porous edge of chaos and discipline: Pathways to the creative analytic process. 07351690.2011.609049

Smythe, W. E. (2013). The Dialogical Jung: Otherness within the Self. *Behavioral Sciences (2076-328X)*, *3*(4), 636-646. doi:10.3390/bs3040634

Spinoza, B. (1994). *Ethics*. (E. Curley, Ed. and Trans.) New York, NY: Penguin.

Stebbins, M. (2010). Lacan for Jungians: a response to S. Gullatz. *Journal of Analytical Psychology*, *55*(5), 715-721. doi:10.1111/j.1468-5922.2010.01879.x

Wayne, J. (2012). A Lacanian suggestion to contemporary psychoanalysis regarding the talking cure. *International Journal of Psychoanalytic Self Psychology*, *7*(3), 458-461. doi:10.1080/15551024.2012.686161

Chapter 10

Unconscious Compensation and Integration: Art Making for Wholeness and Balance

by Jordan S. Potash, PhD, &
Lisa Raye Garlock, MS

> *"Below the threshold of consciousness everything was seething with life."*
>
> (Jung, 1965, p. 178)

In this chapter, we investigate the unconscious roots of creativity as they relate to the psychic processes of compensation and integration. The heart of our investigation entailed a heuristic arts-based inquiry in which we deliberately attempt to illuminate the psyche's propensity for creative activity. In so doing, we hoped to complement Jung's (1965) account of his creative process as detailed in "Confrontation with the Unconscious" in *Memories, Dreams, Reflections.*

Psychic Processes of Creativity

In "Conscious, Unconscious, and Individuation" Jung (1939) wrote, "The collaboration of the unconscious is intelligent and purposive, and even when it acts in opposition to consciousness its expression is still compensatory in an intelligent way, as if it were trying to restore the lost balance" (para. 492). The unconscious creatively produces images, re-organizes disparate parts, and translates impulses into symbols that can be understood. Evidence of these actions are seen in dreams, but also mirrored in art making when mysterious aspects of the self come into awareness. These processes are evident when we view images as both compensatory for what is lacking and integrative for what is unknown.

Wholeness, Balance and Creativity

The content of the unconscious represents a myriad of experiences including repressed memories, personal wishes, unformulated ideas, and archetypes. Given this variety, Jung (1971) hypothe-sized, "that at its deeper levels, the unconscious possesses collective contents in a relatively active state" (p. 83). Such perpetual activity allows contradictory experiences to interact, combine, and sepa-rate until they emerge in consciousness as seemingly spontaneous insights. Such inspirations are useful for solving problems, but constant unconscious reorganization reflects a central tenet of Jungian thought. The psyche achieves wholeness through the union of opposites and maintains balance through the self-regu-lating function. Instead of attempting to deactivate incongruous components, Jung (1943) explained, "There is no balance, no system of self-regulation, without opposition. The psyche is just such a self-regulating system" (para. 92). This notion suggests that juxta-positions in the unconscious are not nuisances to nullify, but are necessary as corresponding elements that fuel the psyche's devel-opment and regeneration in its quest for individuation (Jung, 1939).

Such activity is directly related to creativity. Through inter-views with highly creative people, Andreasen (2005) identified four elements of the unconscious creative process: entering a state that is apart from reality, working as if someone or something else is directing the work, having a wandering mind, and feeling invisible. Likewise, Jung (1933) stated, "Whenever the creative force predomi-nates, human life is ruled and molded by the unconscious as against the active will, and the conscious ego is swept along on a subterranean current, being nothing more than a helpless observer of events" (p. 170). Creativity is rooted in the unconscious, but requires consciousness as a translator.

Relation of Art to the Unconscious

One of the ways in which individuals can understand the creative process of the unconscious is through art making. In Jungian practice, active imagination engages creative pursuits to give form to and make sense of unconscious images brought to consciousness (Chodorow, 1997). Jung (1933) described the relationship between art making and the unconscious as:

> The secret of artistic creation and of the effectiveness of art is to be found in a return to the state of participation mystique—to that level of experience at which it is man who lives, and not the individual, and at which the weal or woe of the single human being does not count, but only human existence. (p. 172)

Essentially, the personal life of the artist does not matter. Art, like the unconscious, takes on a life of its own, needing to be in the world and using the artist for that purpose.

Fully appreciating the relation between art making and the unconscious requires attention to the distinction Jung (1933) made between two types of artists, the visionary and psychological. The visionary draws from archetypal experiences, whereas the psychological draws from individual consciousness. Visionary artists serve as conduits for society by channeling the collective into symbolic form in order to express and point to new directions. The visionary artist concept is also useful for understanding how individuals draw from the unconscious to further individuation (Matthews, 2015). What we find is a connection between individual self-understanding and how the individual connects to others through archetypal experiences. To fully appreciate how the unconscious directs artistic activity, we can turn our attention to the psychic processes of compensation and integration.

Compensation

Jung (1933) investigated the compensatory function as it related to spontaneous internal images such as those found in dreams:

> The psyche is a self-regulating system that maintains itself in equilibrium as the body does. Every process that goes too far immediately and inevitably calls forth a compensatory activity... We can take the idea of compensation, so understood, as a law of psychic happening. Too little on one side results in too much on the other. The relation between conscious and unconscious is compensatory...and a means of self-regulation. (pp. 17-18)

The act of compensation explains that the psyche generates opposites in order to ensure wholeness by creating that which is missing. Neumann (1959) saw this tendency as a "natural curative power of the unconscious" (p. 156). Such a theory of the unconscious has parallels to Csikszentmihalyi's (1996) research on creativity in which he discovered Ten Dimensions of Complexity defined as "pairs of apparently antithetical traits that are... integrated with each other in a dialectical tension" (p. 57-8). These dimensions include: 1) physical energy and rest, 2) smart and naïve, 3) playfulness/irresponsibility and discipline/responsibility, 4) imagination/fantasy and reality, 5) extroversion and introversion, 6) humble and proud, 7) masculine and feminine, 8) traditional/conservative and rebellious/iconoclastic, 9) passionate and objective, 10) suffering/pain and enjoyment. By drawing on the various trait pairs, individuals can sustain an overall balance and discover innovative ideas.

Taking the opportunity to understand the specific symbols that result from compensation promotes broader understanding of one's self and situation. Neumann (1959) continued:

> the law of psychic compensation leads to an
> unremitting dialectical exchange between the
> assimilating consciousness and the contents that
> are continuously being newly constellated. Then
> begins the continuous process characteristic of
> creative transformation—new constellations of the
> unconscious and of consciousness interact with
> new productions and new transformative phases of
> the personality. The creative principle thus seizes
> upon and transforms consciousness as well as the
> unconscious, the ego-self relation as well as the
> ego-*thou* relation. (p. 165-166)

As further explanation as to how compensation arises from an
unconscious process, but requires conscious involvement, Stein
(1998) described, "The individuation process is driven by the self
and carried out through the mechanism of compensation. While
the ego does not generate it or control it, it may participate in this
process by becoming aware of it" (p. 194).

Integration

For compensatory images to become actualized, they need to be
incorporated into the psyche. Unconscious elements can invoke
anxiety, but it is important to follow Jung's (1933) advice:

> The unconscious is not a demoniacal monster, but a
> natural entity...the anxious division of the day-time
> and the night-time sides of the psyche, cease with
> progressive assimilation. What my critics feared—
> the overwhelming of the conscious mind by the
> unconscious—is far more likely to ensue when the
> unconscious is excluded from life by being repressed,
> falsely interpreted, and depreciated. (p. 17)

Assimilating unconsciousness into consciousness completes the
creative process by identifying embedded archetypes. Rowland

(2015) cited Jung's conception of the symbol as, "dynamic instances of the ensouled world invoking in us reciprocal healing and transformation" (p. 92). Art that is allowed to manifest spontaneously and intuitively has the potential to act as a gateway to both the personal and collective unconscious, which when brought to consciousness promotes well-being. Similarly, Neumann (1959) compelled us to discover the eternal qualities within art. We are instructed to reconnect with the archetypes that give the art its timeless character. When these are discovered, we have the potential to become inwardly integrated, while also moving "toward a universal humanism" (p. 130) in relation to others. Perhaps that is why Neumann wrote art "is a great fulfillment and still greater hope" (p. 134).

By following the creative impulse, we move closer to individuation and a greater awareness of our connection to others, even if this process cannot be fully articulated:

> What happens within oneself when one integrates previously unconscious contents with the consciousness is something which can scarcely be described in words. It can only be experienced... Whether a change has taken place as the result of integration, and what the nature of that change is, remains a matter of subjective conviction. (Jung, 1965, p. 287)

Both compensation and integration represent unconscious creative acts that promote awareness and innovation. Since they are unconscious processes, they are elusive and only seen in retrospect or through parallel activities. As the processes are creative, creative activity can serve to demonstrate them.

Heuristic Arts-based Inquiry

As both artists and art therapists, we investigated the unconscious roots of creativity through our own art practices. Heuristic research (Moustakas, 1990) invites researchers to immerse themselves in personally meaningful questions that have archetypal significance, whereas arts-based research (McNiff, 2011) grounds inquiry in researcher generated art making. Both processes require researchers to vacillate between periods of absorption, generativity, and reflection. This sequence mirrors Jung's process of active imagination, which according to Chodorow (1997) entails beginning with an emotion, impulse, or internal image; observing how it naturally transforms itself; giving the image form through the creative arts; and reflecting on the resulting image. We chose this method of inquiry in order to mirror Jung's artistic investigations that led to the creation of *The Red Book* and subsequently to many of his seminal theories.

We each created and described our own art, in order to reflect on the question, "How do compensation and integration manifest themselves in creative activity?" We wanted to understand how the transcendent energy of creativity nurtures wholeness and balance. We each independently engaged in our own art making by working on visual art for a minimum of 30 minutes daily for 14 days. After completing the daily activity, we documented our creative process, associations, and reflections in writing. We did not share our art with each other until we both finished. The images and the writings became data for further analysis.

Lisa's Art Making

In order to explore my creative process, I at first started to do what was familiar—painting on paper—and found that I could not do it. Though I'd used this media for years for meditative art-making it felt contrived and unnatural, awkward and I could not stop my conscious mind from editorializing, questioning and censoring. Rather than work through those feelings, I chose different media— textiles, my current medium of preference—and primarily embroidery. Normally, my process of working with textiles requires coming up with an idea or image—a story I want to tell using this media. When I have that, I usually draw it out on paper, choose the fabrics, other materials, and colors, and begin a systematic process of creating. After I start, then I can let the piece take over and develop itself. However, for this project, I chose to have no plan. I would approach the blank, white canvas, and let the needle and thread move itself; I would add to the canvas each day, rather than create a new piece each time.

Without a plan, or story to tell, I did, however, start most embroidery sessions with a structured process of "imaginative layering" (Ayres, 2014, p. 710). This exercise is designed to create the seeds of inspiration with which to write. Writing is an art form, and one that does not come as easily to me as does visual art, so I felt this would help that process by clearing my mind of current distractions. In this exercise, categories are chosen, such as sounds, people, colors, places—things from which to create stories and engage the creative imagination. I chose arbitrary topics–colors, animals, *New York Times* (*NYT*) headlines and song titles–and set them into a four-square layout (Fig. 1).

Red	Yellow
Crow	Fox
Firebomb Kills Palestinian Toddler in West Bank	Perdue Sharply Cuts Antibiotic Use
I Never Promised You a Rose Garden	Born in the USA
Blue	Black
Cat	Hedgehog
Suspect in Charleston Shooting Rampage Indicates Desire to Plead Guilty	Tiny Texas Songbird at Center of Fight Over Listing as Endangered
We Are the Champions	Imagine

FIGURE 1. SAMPLE FOUR-SQUARE EXERCISE.

The four-square was appealing to me because of the symbolic number four. Jung (1964) saw four as a recurring number, starting early in human history: there are four directions, four discreet cycles of the hero's myth, four seasons. He (1974) felt that "there is some psychic element present which expresses itself through the quaternity" (p. 294). While I prefer asymmetrical or odd numbers, there is something very solid and grounded about the number four. The idea of combining random words and phrases intrigued me and I felt that since I was flying without a plan in my embroidery, starting with something that felt fairly concrete would add structure to my process. I was also curious to see if that exercise would relate overall to, or perhaps help illuminate, aspects of the unconscious creative process.

After my daily four-square was completed, I started working on the fabric. Instead of setting a time limit, I decided that I had to use four colors. In that way, four new colors were added daily, and the amount of time varied. Even though I can work fairly quickly, working with textiles slows down the making process, providing time and space for fantasizing and active imagination.

My materials included many colors of embroidery thread, organized along the color wheel, in a way that could travel easily; other materials included fabric, fabric paint, wool roving for needle felting, beads and buttons. I worked within 12-inch embroidery hoops, creating a circle or mandala. The locations where I worked were my studio, at my office and outside on a patio. I used the computer to outline my four-square and write my process notes afterwards, however on three days, due to time and space constraints, I only worked on the piece and did not do the four-square or process notes afterwards. During two of those days, I was with family members, so was focused on the exterior conversations, rather than the ones in my head when I worked alone.

When finished with the 14 days, I reviewed my embroidery (Fig. 2), four-squares and process observations. I went through the observations and circled words that stood out for me. Because the textile piece was unfinished artistically, I completed it (Fig. 3), and added my observations of the whole. Using the words from the process observations, I found I had two main categories: descriptive words and symbolic objects.

FIGURE 2. EMBROIDERY PROCESS.

FIGURE 3. *FINISHED PIECE / MANDALA.*

Some of the descriptive words were flow, connections, wanting to make substantial, filling, developing, expansion, separation, grounded and flowing upward. I was also struck by the opposite words: beneath, above; bisecting, whole, divided; calming, disturbing; uncomfortable, soothing. The symbolic object words included sun, moon, ocean, face-like, water, ebb/flow, stars, alive and earth. Using these words, I distilled my observations into two different poems, and then combined the two into one. The final poem is my art process describing itself in words:

Dancing thread makes tiny stitches flow
Hands overlapping
as they create expansion, asymmetry, separation, connections
Flowing/floating upward,
seedlings and stars balance and divide themselves

Strange, creature-like shapes and face-like images mirror the moon,
filling in, compensating in the circle and leaving the sun to ebb and flow
Above and below: disturbing, calm, odd, whole, unrecognizable yet
familiar shapes, balance
While earth anchors the cactus,
linear dots and the yellow line submerge,
alive and floating into vivid colors,
conscious and unconscious striving
for substantial and solid ground

"If you do this, then you must do that…"

Compensating within the medium of embroidery can be seen very concretely. To begin with, a blank canvas feels like the impetus for compensation—"I must fill or cover the emptiness!" Throughout the process, I was consciously and unconsciously striving for visual balance within the 12-inch circle. My embroidery process started with grounding the circle, setting a foundation from which I felt the need to start from or add to each day. When looking back at photos of each stage, I see efforts to fill in, expand, solidify and balance. This is seen from day to day, as lines, shapes and colors are added in such a way as to not feel awkward, ugly, or strange. Even so, there were days where part of the image felt odd, unfinished or bizarre, and I was left with the feelings of confusion or mild anxiety. An example of this is the image that looks like a brain stem and amygdala, in the upper right-hand corner. In an effort to make sense of this image, I went back to the four-square and my process notes for that day. All of the *NYT* headlines I used were disturbing, evoking images of incarceration, a state of emergency and death. My process notes reflected thoughts unrelated to any of the four-square topics, however, the four-square practice may have set the stage for some of the variation in unconscious imagery, even though I was not thinking of the topics while working.

If I were to compare this concrete and abstract imagery to what was happening in my life, I can see parallels in the constant efforts to make meaning of puzzling situations (particularly current events), continuing the process of balancing work life/personal life, leisure time/busy time, and aging parents/relationships. As my piece took form, I seemed to feel a need to work on the whole circle, yet I also felt a need to connect the lines and forms. There was a subconscious voice constantly saying, "If you do this, then you must do that..." If I made a line on the left, then I had to match it with something on the right, in a quest for balance.

In my final poem, certain lines distinctly illustrate the unconscious compensatory urge:

> "seedlings and stars balance and divide themselves,"
> "filling in, compensating in the circle and leaving the
> sun to ebb and flow," and "While earth anchors the
> cactus, linear dots and the yellow line submerge..."

Balance of the Elements

As my mandala developed, I was not conscious of trying to integrate the lines, patterns and shapes, but it was happening constantly. One of my strongest urges was to fill the white background with color. When I reached the final day of our project, I was quite disappointed that I was not finished. However, the imagery in the mandala was balanced as much as possible at that time. Again, I am being concrete in seeing Jung's concepts of compensation and integration take form in my art process. I was not thinking about Jung's ideas while working, but rather allowed my mind to flow freely. All the things that came to mind, such as family relationships, death and dying, news events, dark imaginings, normal issues of life, become integrated into the developing imagery in my mandala. The spiral, or curling line, or solid dots became imbued with conscious and unconscious thoughts and feelings. When looking at the completed piece, part of me was alarmed as I wondered if it had become an illustration of my unconscious. On the other hand, I was curious at the way the canvas was divided: the circle is loosely squared, with an obvious bisection, and less obvious quadrants.

The overall imagery is organized and calls to mind accretions of corals; above are expansions of what is below, spreading out and growing through water and air.

How might this relate to my unconscious? Pert (1997) suggests that "the body is the unconscious mind" (p. 141). If this is the case, what might this somewhat disturbing imagery be saying? There are at least four shapes within my mandala that are disturbing to me. The green, organic shape in the right-hand lower quadrant was discomfiting to me because I had a thought to make a standing stone; it was clearly not what I had in mind, and presented itself as something else entirely. The sharp, dotted shapes sticking out from the right-hand side in my mind evoked prickly growths, giving me a physical sensation of aversion. The amygdala/spinal cord shape in the top right-hand quadrant was a mystery, and somewhat amusing while also being alien-like. The split intestine-like shape in the left-hand top side felt awkward, lacking flow or elegance. The odd shapes are integrated with circles, symbols of wholeness, and flowing lines that are pleasing to the eyes. Perhaps this is an attempt to hide their awkwardness, helping them fit into the whole.

Within the poem, integration is seen by these lines: "Dancing thread makes tiny stitches flow," "as they create expansion, asymmetry, separation, connections," "Above and below: disturbing, calm, odd, whole, unrecognizable yet familiar shapes, balance." Each line contains conscious and unconscious material, open to interpretation by both the viewer and the creator. Balancing between compensation and integration was happening constantly during my process, both on the canvas and in my conscious and unconscious. The "proof" of the presence of the unconscious may be in the images, while the conscious can be seen in the balance of the elements making up the imagery.

Jordan's Art Making

I worked on my art each evening as the last activity of my day during the two-week period. I decided to use a new sketchbook that was relatively small in size (6" x 8.75") with durable paper that could accommodate a range of materials. For my first piece, I used masking tape to create a 5" x 5" square in which to work. I had not planned on doing so, but it was the first spontaneous action. After completing the first piece, I decided to start each piece the same way. Even though I intended to use a range of art materials, I used oil pastels (Holbein, 48 count) for the entire series. Despite the wide choices I had intended to give myself, early in to the process, I limited my way of working in both size and art materials.

I began each piece by taking a breath and looking at the fresh white square of paper within the frame. After several meditative breaths, I turned to the open box of pastels and scanned the range of colors. When a color called my attention, I took another breath to see if indeed the color felt right for that moment. When I had the right one, I began to make spontaneous lines, shapes, or scribbles. Sometimes, I worked quickly and other times slowly, but the goal was to allow images to form without intellectual direction or planning. These initial moments of the image were intuitive. Although I tried to clear my mind, occasionally thoughts would enter. "What's happening here?" "How could this become anything?" "What does this have to do with me?" Each time they did, I acknowledged the questions, let them drift and returned to the movements. When it made intuitive sense, I switched colors, changed direction, or created patterns. Ultimately, the seed of an image would be planted and I would develop it more fully from there. I tried to maintain focus on just the image and creative moment and indeed there were several sessions in which I did not remember having a single thought at all.

When the image felt complete, I stood back, took a few more breaths and made sure that it felt finished for the moment. After art making, I began a phenomenological description of what I literally saw that ultimately led to a more metaphoric one. I decided to link these poetic writings with the images by writing them in the remaining space on the page. This immediate creative writing helped me to make sense of the image. After both the visual and written aspects were complete, I sat down to write reflective notes. At the end of each session, I put the oil paste back in the box in color order for the next use.

Even though none of the pieces were planned, some led to surprise or discovery more than others. This feeling came about during the creative process, but often later upon reflection. Rather than describe all 14 pieces chronologically, I will now describe the three themes I noticed either in the images themselves or in my creative process. The direct quotations in the remainder of this section are from either my post-art poems or reflective writing.

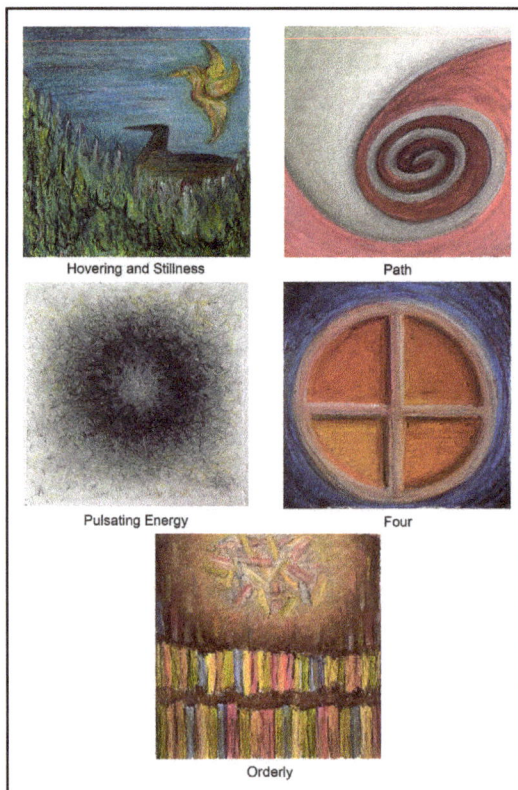

Hovering and Stillness

Path

Pulsating Energy

Four

Orderly

FIGURE 4. *DYNAMIC BALANCE.*

Dynamic Balance

Several of the artworks described a dynamic balance, which I noticed as the image and poem containing opposite tendencies or complementary aspects (Fig. 4). The first artwork, *Hovering and Stillness* depicts two birds. One is hovering in flight, the other sits in a shadow, but "Both are motionless. Both are ready." Part of the tension of this piece was captured in the sentiment, "The idea of hovering and stillness captivated me. I generally think of myself as having direction." The image, *Path* shows a grey spiral against a background that is pink-red at the outer, but becomes progressively darker towards the center. I described it as, "Traveling into the dark, the path is smooth leading me deeper. I trust that it will also guide me back out." Upon further reflection, I noted "alternate moments of clarity and obscurity." *Pulsating Energy* depicts small energetic scribbles that take a circular form. The piece changes in gradations of color from white in the center to rings of black, grey, and back to white with specks of green of all shades. The writing for this piece reads, "Being pulled into the dark and back into the light supported by green embers. A lot is happening, but it feels comfortable." The image *Four* depicts the balanced image of the quadrisected circle. In my reflection, I noted my frustration with the stereotypic image, but my comfort with it seeming to be the right image for the moment. *Orderly* contains the question, "Are they falling in line or are the rows coming apart? I can see a constant ordering and re-ordering."

Each of these images contains two extremes. I am struck that the images themselves do not necessarily appear balanced, but that the feeling they promote was one of homeostasis. These images alerted me to the fact that there were extremes at play, but they countered one another. The idea of countering one another is different from canceling each other out. I did not have the sense that the opposing elements initiated a sense of neutrality, but rather an energetic movement between the states that allowed me to learn from each. Even the most static of the pieces, *Four*, has a slightly off-centered cross with variations of color in each of the quadrants, which lends it subtle energy. Looking at all of these pieces together, I am struck that they do not seem like an obvious grouping.

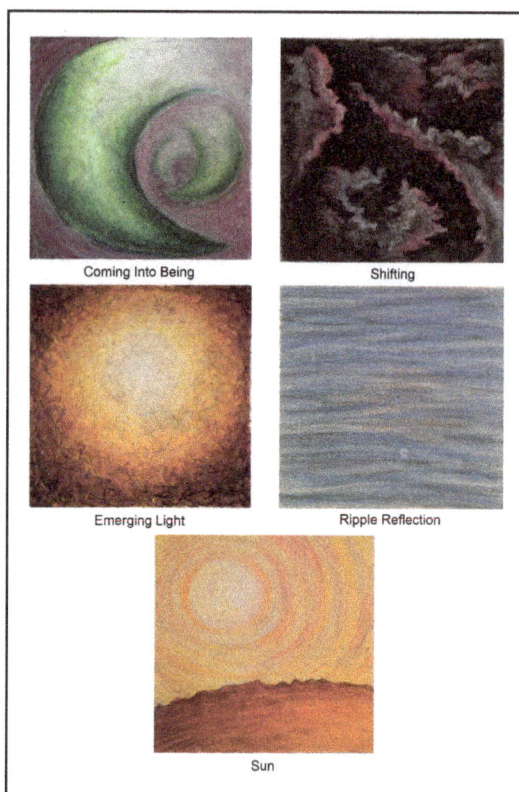

FIGURE 5. *COMING INTO BEING.*

Coming into Being

Another theme pertained to the sense of formation (Fig. 5). The image *Coming into Being* summarizes this theme with the reflection, "I have no sense as to where it's all going. I know it will be good, but where it actually ends up, I can't see yet." Similarly, *Shifting* depicted amorphous and gaseous shapes that seemed to appear and recede more than take specific shape. The uncertainty of the image was captured in the poem, "Who sees moments of light as they come to be, disappear and reform, morph, twist and fade?" The artwork

Sun shows a bright yellow sky, but the appearance of a shadow from the bottom left caught my attention and made me wonder what was casting it. The wonderment evoked by these pieces was captured in the description of *Emerging Light*, "I look forward to see what it becomes and what it reveals." In contrast, *Ripple Reflection* depicts mostly smooth water with the hints of orange in the wave crests towards the center of the image. I imagined the orange as the sun, but I wrote, "The ripples disrupt the full reflection of the sun, but my focus is on the pattern of the water more so than the sun." From this line of the poem, I noticed that I was less interested in the emerging image and more so on the current state.

Each of these pieces left an impression of an unfinished moment. That is not to say that the art was unfinished or that I was left with a state of incompleteness. Instead, the image seemed to be pointing to something that is emerging, but that I could not yet name. Even though I did not know what was coming to fruition, creating these images helped me to see that something was fluctuating. What was notable to me as that on the surface I would not have imagined anything changing.

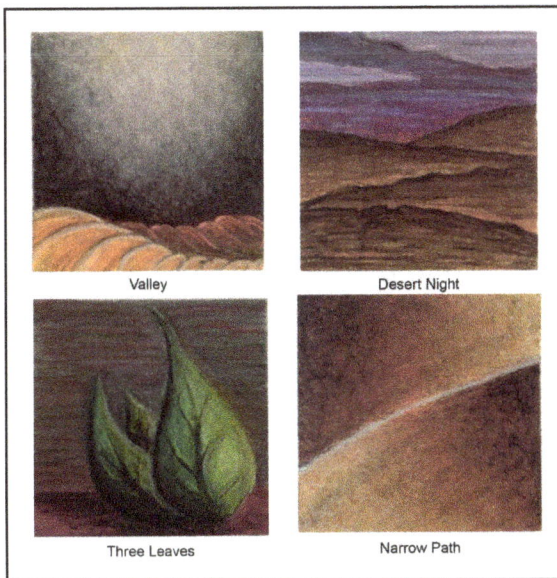

FIGURE 6. *What I Need.*

What I Need

Several images contained ideas of what seemed to be missing from my life at that moment (Fig. 6). The night sky with a glowing light titled *Valley* is a landscape of two red-orange rolling hills. What I focused on in my writing was the narrow valley dotted with green. In my reflective writing, I noted that I had not remembered creating it, but realized, "The idea of the valley is comforting to me. It may not be easy to reach or easy to leave, but comforting. I wonder why I might need this in my life at this moment. I feel like I'm being called to a place of rest and reflection." The image *Desert Night* had a similar reflection as the description stated, "Needed quiet and solitude, but not to think—just to sit and be." In contrast to these needs, *Three Leaves* was described as, "Three leaves bunched together. They are cut off from their source. Still, they are fresh and carry the possibility of the full tree within. They are cut off, but they thrive." In my reflective writing, I noted ways in which I feel separated and a desire to seek community. Lastly, in *Narrow Path*, I wrote, "Continuing on the path brings darkness and light. I still have to go." Although this image also has an element of balance (dark and light), the lasting impression of this piece was the urge to keep going despite potential difficulties ahead.

Before creating each of these images, I had not set out to create that which was missing or to even try to resolve a concern. It was the process that brought them to mind. My reflection notes from *Narrow Path* highlighted this sentiment, "Seeing this image makes me realize how much this weighs on me. I guess I know that's often under the surface, despite how good other things seem to be." Some of these images indicated needed states of being, while others pointed to directions to remedy a situation.

Discussion

After our respective forays into the world of colors, textures, and the unconscious, we returned to our question: "How do compensation and integration manifest themselves in creative activity?" It is striking to us how using art materials seems to embody many of Jung's concepts. This should not be surprising when we look at Jung's (1965) description of his artistic explorations, which informed the *Red Book* and subsequently many of his later ideas. As our art series demonstrated, within the unconscious there is much activity, but generally, "We allow the images to rise up, and maybe wonder about them, but that is all. We do not take the trouble to understand them, let alone draw ethical conclusions from them" (p. 192). Following Jung's lead, we took "the trouble" to analyze our creative processes and identify themes that parallel and complement Jung's ideas on creativity.

Structure: Promoting Compensation and Integration

We both felt compelled to set up a structure, perhaps because our plan to immerse ourselves in the unconscious creative process provoked some anxiety. Within our established meta structure, we both chose to set up micro-structures. Jordan taped off boundaries and used the same materials when initially he had left it open for multiple mediums. Lisa started with the four-square of random words and phrases within set categories and required the use of four colors each day. This was setting up a structure that seemed arbitrary, but was comforting. Within our respective boundaries, we both chose to follow our imagery with words as part of the creative process, which added to a sense of comprehension and order. Given the psyche's need for compensation, imposing such structure may have been a necessary act to ensure expression.

As the unconscious is active, it will seek opportunities to come to the surface. When not given proper outlet, energy may erupt, as in what happens in psychosis. Too much structure can result in constriction. Either way some people struggle with how to set a flexible enough structure within themselves. Jung (1965) noticed this possibility when he encountered:

> the same psychic material which is the stuff of psychosis and is found in the insane. This is the fund of unconscious images which fatally confuse the mental patient. But it is also the matrix of a mythopoeic imagination which has vanished from our rational age. (p. 188)

Often compensation makes itself known in dreams when the conscious mind is asleep. These artistic processes demonstrate, as in active imagination, that it is possible to create a waking environment in which the ego is in the position of observer. Doing so requires a safe, structured space in which the unconscious is encouraged to present itself.

Aesthetics: Blending Compensation and Integration

Not only did Jung (1961) note the difference between visionary and psychological artists, he also distinguished between "aesthetic creations" and art. In discussing his practice of making daily mandalas, he denied that they were art, but rather they "were cryptograms concerning the state of the self" (p. 196). In another example, Jung (1929 as cited in van den Berk, 2012) said, "Although my patients occasionally produce artistically beautiful things that might very well be shown in modern 'art' exhibitions, I nevertheless treat them as completely worthless when judged by the canons of real art" (p. 77).

As artists and art therapists, we can draw a distinction between these two roles, but we can also choose to integrate them. We created our artworks using an intuitive, unplanned, emergent process. At the same time, it was impossible to ignore the aesthetic qualities as we worked. We were both unhappy with some of the images, feeling they were ill composed (Jordan's *Coming into Being*) or inelegant (Lisa's strange green, organic shape). Jung (1965) might have argued that what we did was not art, as evidenced by his statement:

> fantasies of the unconscious as art, they would have carried no more conviction than visual perceptions,

as if I were watching a movie. I would have felt no moral obligation toward them. The anima might then have easily seduced me into believing that I was a misunderstood artist, and that my so-called artistic nature gave me the right to neglect reality. (p. 187)

We, however, did not share this sentiment. We live in a different social-cultural context than Jung, which includes a wider definition of art, but our experiences demonstrate that the question of "what is art?" is clearly very complicated.

The tension between spontaneous creation and practiced artistic skills highlights the interaction between the conscious and the unconscious. Perhaps this was an indication of the interplay between the unconscious well that led to compensatory images and integrative strivings related to aesthetics. We both noticed how our initial impulses and early fragments of imagery were unplanned. These represent the spontaneous expressions of the unconscious. As they developed, our conscious understanding of arrangement, color, and composition entered into the creative process. Rather than see this as ego-driven, it seemed to be ego-supported. That is, our artistic knowledge and sensibilities allowed us to bring the image into form and awareness.

Uncertainty: Doubting Compensation and Integration

When images arise, it is obvious to ask what they mean and to what are they related. We both empathized with Jung (1965) when he said, "I was writing down fantasies which often struck me as nonsense, and toward which I had strong resistances. For as long as we do not understand their meaning, such fantasies are a diabolical mixture of the sublime and the ridiculous" (p. 178). There were several points in our art making where we each wanted to exclude or erase an image. These images sparked annoyance, discomfort, frustration, or simply a dislike of the aesthetic qualities. It seemed impossible to discern their meanings, at least in the short-term.

There were and continue to be images that are unknowable. For Lisa this occurred throughout the process, as odd forms presented themselves. It appeared that on the days the strangest forms arose, her thoughts while working were darker than on other days. She is still in the process of trying to understand them as they do not seem to be anything that she would consciously choose to make. Jordan worked on the piece *Shifting* before ultimately turning it upside down and rotated *Valley* 90 degrees before seeing them as completed images. All of the images within his Coming into Being theme demonstrated a lack of concrete ideas that did not reveal their meanings in the same way as those images grouped as What I Need. At these moments, we both noticed a hesitation or uncertainty with the progression of our images. It would be fair to say that we forgot Jung's (1965) advice:

> when I was working on the fantasies, I needed a point of support in 'this world,'...No matter how deeply absorbed or how blown about I was, I always knew that everything I was experiencing was ultimately directed at this real life of mine. I meant to meet its obligations and fulfill its meanings. (p. 189)

Our resistance to certain images or doubting that they would lead to messages revealed an inability to appreciate the role of compensation in balancing the unacceptable with what our ego selves deemed as acceptable. This tension is necessary for the creative process, though impedes integration. We also came to accept the possibility of living with not knowing the meaning, not liking the image, and not being able to change it in a satisfactory way. The images will continue to inform, assuming we are willing to hear them, and their meanings may deepen over time.

Commonalities: Appreciating Compensation and Integration

While we, as individuals, have a lot in common, there is much about us that is different from each other including our genders, ages, life experiences, and chosen art materials. There seemed to be elements that appeared in both of our work. Overall, the color palettes of both are similar. The circle is the most obvious symbol that appears, and is repeated within our individual pieces. The spiral and quaternary structures showed up in both, as well. The symbols identified in both included: celestial objects (sun, stars), water, light/dark, plants, paths, four, and seeds. Linear qualities are also similar where there are flowing, jagged, stepped and diffused lines. Whereas Jordan's individual pieces are infused visually with emotion, it is harder to see in Lisa's. This could be related to the media—oil pastels are immediate, and can be layered, blended and mixed to create a mood. Using thread is more controlled and takes longer. Emotional content is embedded in the stitches, but identifying the moods or emotions is more elusive.

We suspect that the collective unconscious is at work here. Our artwork speaks to the archetypal language of common images. Jung (1965) addressed this phenomenon when he wrote, "the contents of psychic experience are real, and real not only as my own personal experiences, but as collective experiences which others also have" (p. 194). The images are common, but they arise when individually needed, reflecting the process of compensation. Their integration in the psyche indicates their acceptance in awareness. This point was particularly relevant as even though we had similar images, they had different meanings and purposes. The psyche may have an infinite vocabulary of images, but they consolidate around recognizable forms. Jordan noticed this in the creation of the quaternary mandala, which caused him to struggle with the appearance of such a stereotypic image. Lisa also discovered the appearance of the quaternary form in the squaring of her overall circular piece. Seeing these similarities in each other's art making recalled the importance

Neumann (1959) put on identifying the essence of art that allows images to connect to each other and to collective ideals.

Conclusion

Our goal was to explore the unconscious roots of creativity through compensation and integration in order to understand how they work to promote wholeness. Through both of our art making processes, we were able to feel, see and think about the unconscious through conscious aspects of creating visual art. Materials played a confounding role for Lisa, as it felt like a deeper and more unfathomable process than using a more traditional art medium. Her apparent need to preface her art making with the four-square exercise may have added complexity, as writing down random topics could have activated the unconscious in unexpected and unknown ways. Her process illustrated almost constant compensation in various forms. Embroidery also affected the imagery in that what arose from this process was surrealistic, and far from her usual style. Her attempts to integrate the imagery was on-going, but only felt complete for her after the 14 days were over and she was able to finish it. However, the actual making was absorbing, relaxing and stimulating, and meditative, all leading to a sense of wellness.

Despite Jordan's familiarity with his materials, there were still revelations. Perhaps what was more surprising was that the range of images or types of reflections surprised him. Having created artwork for many years and facilitating art making with clients in the service of healing, spontaneous images for discovery frequently occur. Of course, so do creative lulls. Regaining appreciation for these times as indications of impending change offered an important lesson. The study re-awakened the core idea that images that are unclear should be met with wonder and curiosity as they represent compensation and impending integration. We can allow ourselves moments to welcome these unconscious processes to the surface, but ultimately they will make themselves known when needed.

In some ways, more questions were raised than were answered. We discovered some ways that compensation and integration promote, combine, and appear even when their power is obscured. Undertaking a heuristic process provided us both with first-hand accounts of two of Jung's important concepts related to creativity. Experiencing them brought us to a new level of awareness, however, these unconscious processes are still mysterious. We have more of an appreciation for them and how to encourage their active manifestation for well-being. As Jung's theories and our art-making series demonstrated, part of understanding creativity is to understand that it is in some ways incomprehensible. We were informed by our own irritations and discoveries while creating even though we can look back at the process and see all of it as just part of the natural ebb and flow of the exaltation and frustration of creativity.

References

Andreasen, N. (2005). *The creative brain: The science of genius.* New York, NY: Penguin.

Ayres, E. (2014). *Writing the wave: Inspired rides for aspiring writers* [Kindle version]. California, MD: Veriditas Books.

Chodorow, J. (Ed.). (1997). *Jung on active imagination.* Princeton, NJ: Princeton University Press.

Csikszentmihalyi, M. (1996). *Creativity: flow and the psychology of discovery and invention.* New York: Harper Collins.

Jung, C. G. (1933). *Modern man in search of a soul* (W. S. Dell & C. F. Baynes, Trans.). London, UK: Lund Humphries.

Jung, C. G. (1939). Conscious, Unconscious, and Individuation. *The archetypes and the collective unconscious, Part I, Collected Works Vol. 9.* London: Routledge.

Jung, C. G. (1943). On the psychology of the unconscious. *Two Essays on Analytical Psychology, Collected Works Vol. 7.* London: Routledge.

Jung, C. G. (1965). *Memories, dreams, reflections.* London: Fontana.

Jung, C.G. (1971). *The portable Jung. The relations between the ego and the unconscious.* (Hull, R.F.C., Translator). New York, NY: The Viking Press.

Matthews, R. (2015). An analytical psychology view of wholeness in art. *International Journal of Jungian Studies, 7* (2), 124-138. doi: 10.1080/19409052.2104.954753

McNiff, S. (2011). Artistic expressions as primary modes of inquiry. *British Journal of Guidance & Counselling, 39* (5), 385-396. doi:10.1080/0306 9885.2011.621526

Moustakas, C. E. (1990). *Heuristic Research: Design, Methodology, and Applications.* Newbury Park, CA: Sage.

Neumann, E. (1959). *Art and the creative unconscious: Four essays* (R. Manheim Trans.). New York, NY: Harper Torchbooks.

Pert, C. (1997). *Molecules of emotion: The science behind mind-body medicine.* New York, NY: Scribner.

Rowland, S. (2015). Jung, art and psychotherapy re-conceptualized by the symbol that joins us to the wildness of the universe. *International Journal of Jungian Studies, 7* (2), 81-93. doi: 10.1080/19409052.2104.905487

Stein, M. (1998) *Jung's map of the soul: An introduction.* Chicago and La Salle, IL: Open Court.

Van den Berk, T. (2012). *Jung on art: The autonomy of the creative drive* [Kindle version]. New York, NY: Routledge.

Chapter 11

Art, Aesthetics and Ethics:
An impossible troika according to Jung

by Tjeu van den Berk

Translation by Dr. Petra Galama

> *"This re-immersion in the state of participation mystique is the secret of artistic creation and of the effect which great art has upon us.... That is why every great work of art is objective and impersonal, and yet profoundly moving."*
>
> (Jung 1978a, p.105)

George Steiner's nagging question

Literary scientist and philosopher of culture, George Steiner, raises a pressing issue in an interview: "So often I have asked myself the question, and it is entirely related to beauty and consolation: How can people who in the evening read Rilke or play Beethoven, slaughter other people in the morning as if stamping forms?"

This question has dominated my work. Nearer the end of my life, I find no theory acceptable: not the idea of a collective schizophrenia, not the idea which Koestler in this very room always said to me:

> But I have the answer, part of our brain is prehistoric, sadistic, animal. It is a lovely story, but there is not a shred of evidence for it. I have been even more

> pessimistic... I have no answer. I know that for me,
> without the Allegretto of the Schubert posthumous
> quintet (opus 163) much in life would not be worth
> living...The presence of such a work defines for me
> the inexhaustible magic and terror of Europe; the
> coexistence of the highest that man has achieved
> and of the lowest, of the most inhumane and
> sadistic. If we knew that music like that made you
> incapable of doing certain things, we would be safe.
> But perhaps man is not meant to feel safe. (Kayzer,
> 2000, pp. 60-61)

Steiner's haunting question, let us not forget that he comes from an Austrian Jewish family, which fled from France in 1940, includes several sub-questions. I will mention two.

A first is: does a bad inclination hinder a person's enjoyment of art? Obviously not. The second is: if, however, Schubert's music really deeply affects the camp commander, should that not restrain him from continuing on his sadistic path? That apparently is also not the case. There are people who react radically different to both questions based on the conviction that someone with a bad conscience is simply not capable of truly appreciating Beethoven. Steiner assumes that the camp commander does, but exactly this is incomprehensible to him.

In this contribution Jung's answer is fundamental. It is rather categorical. He thinks that art is not intended to protect us from evil nor to incite us to do good, he thinks that art can affect both good and evil people in an authentic way. According to him there is no intrinsic relationship between art and ethics. He always emphasised this perspective.

For example, it is well-known that Jung went through a spiritual crisis in 1913. At a certain moment, he became aware that it was healing to give the images and voices in his mind a chance to get on stage and have a conversation with them in some way. He wrote down whatever appeared in his imagination as stories or drew them as images. In *Memories, Dreams, Reflections* he describes how an inner female voice tried to seduce him to see this work as a form of art; he absolutely refused this. He gives several reasons to explicate his viewpoint. At a certain moment he says: "If I had taken these fantasies of the unconscious as art... *I would have felt no ethical obligation toward them*" (Jung, 1989, p. 187 italics mine). In other words, if I had been at work as an artist, I would have been working amorally. I do, however, feel deeply morally engaged with what I am doing here and therefore my mandalas are not art.

Jung formulates very accurately what he does or does not mean, since we can construe from the context that if his anima had whispered to him: "You have created a beautiful *aesthetic* product," therefore not an artistic product, he would have fully consented. Why this sharp distinction between art and aesthetics and why, apparently, can ethics be combined with aesthetics but not with art? To this point, I want to find answers in this contribution.

Of course this theme--art and aesthetics in relation to ethics-- treats only one aspect of Jung's entire vision on art. The latter will not be discussed here. The reader, being interested in Jung's entire theory of art, is referred to existing literature (*cf.* Vivas, 1974; Mayo, 1995; Gaillard, 2008; Van den Berk, 2012). One will notice that this theme forms a coherent part of these works.

Jung's vision has strong classic papers to draw from, although rather recent. His view is accurately formulated by philosophers like David Hume and Immanuel Kant and by several others during the two following centuries. However, during the last decennia, one can hear several counter-sounds not so much literally directed against Jung (he is unfortunately as good as absent in the circuit of art-critics), but against the opinion that art and ethics do not have an intrinsic relationship. Often, this criticism leads to the conviction that authors like Jung hold an art for art's sake perspective (*cf.* Levinson, 1998; Devereaux, 2003; Gaut, 2007). I hope it will become clear that Jung's view is definitely not an art for art's sake perspective. I am even convinced that Jung's nuanced, albeit complicated vision, can clarify the existing discussion on several points.

Before I explicate Jung's vision, it will be good to tackle two misunderstandings. The first is that an amoral work of art couldn't correspond with the fact that the artist indeed always has ethical aspirations. We know from experience that an artist's personal ethics does not influence his art. These artists, are they not of such different kinds of moral plumage! But whether they are virtuous or not, whether a murderer, a paedophiliac, a whoremonger or an obedient citizen, a rich capitalist or a poor loser, an anti-Semitic like Wagner, a follower of Mussolini like Pirandello or a brave catholic like Messiaen, the moment a work of art sprouts from their pen, chisel or brush, its beauty stands, ethically integral on its own two legs.

A second possible misunderstanding, that might be overlooked here, is that the content of artworks, for example literature or film, can discuss ethical themes, like the weal and woe of adultery in *Anna Karenina* by Tolstoy. However, it is not the ethical theme itself which shapes this novel into a work of art. Picasso's *Guernica* is not exhibited in a museum because of Picasso's personal indictment against the war. This work is exhibited as an artistic product not as an ethical product. For, is it possible that a painter who portrays war as something admirable will no longer be exhibited? And if ethics and art would have an intrinsic bond, what should we do with a piano sonata by Mozart?

This contribution is about all forms of art, about what shapes all these arts into art. The fact that in certain forms of art (for example music and abstract art), simply nothing can be distinguished as explicitly ethical. Although there is something identifiable as art, the implication is that ethics is not inherent to art, nor to a certain form of art, as for example literary art. Oscar Wilde writes in the introduction to *The Picture of Dorian Gray*:

> There is no such thing as a moral or immoral book. Books are well written or badly written. That's all...No artist has ethical sympathies. An ethical sympathy in an artist is an unpardonable mannerism of style. (Wilde, 2001, p. 273)

Great art is essentially numinous in nature

The German theologian Paul Tillich mentions several times in his writings that as a privileged and carefree young man art had never interested him, despite the educational efforts of his parents and teachers. When World War I started, he was mobilised. While being in Berlin on a temporary leave from his battalion (of which three quarters died), he went into the Kaiser Friedrich Museum to avoid a gust of rain. There, in a small upstairs room, he came upon *Madonna with child and singing angels* by Sandro Botticelli and to his surprise he burst out in tears. He experienced a moment of "approaching ecstasy," as he called it (*cf.* De Botton, 2007, pp. 22-25).

Tillich assures us repeatedly that it was not the subject (the angels, Maria with her child) that affected him but the painting itself, not the nature of the object but the nature of the painting. He experienced something that filled him with awe, something completely different than what he had encountered in his theology books. "There was Beauty itself. It shone through the colors of the paint... Something of the divine source of all things came through to me. I turned away shaken" (Tillich, 1987, p. 235).

In my view, he describes here the quintessence of experiencing art. Whatever an artwork may express, one experiences in essence something like delight and emotion. And whatever forms of delight and emotion there might be (from the most silent to the most expressive), in that instant one feels oneself to be placed outside oneself. One is in a sort of *ec-stasy*. Being delighted evokes something of a seizure. We all have our own personal examples in that we experience the sublime and are perplexed.

This is an experience called "numinous" by the religious phenomenologist Rudolf Otto, an experience of a *mysterium fascinosum et tremendum*, a secret that is fascinating and awe-inspiring at the same time. At times the one or the other feeling can be more present, but there always is this contrasting experience. Rilke mainly had the terrifying aspect in mind when in his first *Duino Elegy* he wrote: "For beauty is nothing but the beginning of terror, that we are still able to bear" (Rilke, 2009).

Such an experience is not predictable let alone controllable, as it is full of gratuity. It is possibly only after years that a certain artwork incites us with delight or that after years it no longer incites us with delight. This is of course related to our own situation in life, to our individuation process, but also to the phase wherein our culture finds itself.

Where was Tillich affected? At the unconscious irrational level of his soul. Where originated Botticelli's' work of art? Also precisely there. The conscious worlds of the Italian Catholic and the German Protestant, with almost five centuries in between, are incomparable. But at an unconscious level, in the collective unconscious of both, they are impelled by identic, millions of years old archetypes. Out of that depth Botticelli created and in that depth Tillich experienced his creation. A deep yearning and motivation captured him at that level. Jung writes: "That is the secret of great art, and of its effects upon us. The creative process, so far as we are able to follow it at all, consists in the unconscious activation of an archetypal image, and in elaborating and shaping this image into the finished work" (Jung, 1978b, para. 130).

Let me give another example of an authentic art-experience. The professor of practical theology at the Free University of Amsterdam, Marcel Barnard, received such experience in his childhood:

> I must have been seven years old and it was evening. I was allowed to join my father who was going to Rotterdam, to the Museum Boymans van Beuningen. He went there because of his work, which brought him into contact with artists and museums. My mother stayed at home. That evening was the opening of an exhibition, as I recollect, of the work by [the Dutch painter] Peter Struyken. However I do not have that aspect clearly in my mind. It is

obviously not important. We stayed in a huge room on the first floor of the museum. Abstract works of art were displayed on the walls and on temporary freestanding walls. It was full of people, but not too crowded. There was enough space to move freely. I strolled there between the people whilst my father kept busy in a conversation. No one paid any attention to me, I stood there alone. Something happened that is hard to describe.

The somewhat desolate boy I was, became completely absorbed by the large museum room with the abstract artworks whilst standing between people who paid no attention to me. A presence which cannot be named, let alone explained, came towards me and it was larger than the people strolling there and than the room where we were. In that busy room, where I was left to myself, I was at the same moment included in a larger reality which fully understood and knew me. I never forgot that evening. Since that evening I know what I have to do. In that moment and place I have learned what I should do with my life, even though at the time I was not able to give words to that vocation. And I still cannot. It is a vocation without targets. A gratuitous mission. And if I have to say anything, it will be this: I encountered a presence and a trust that give direction to my life. (Barnard, 2005, p. 17)

We can recognise a similar experience in Tillich's story. The child experienced a mission within a grander encompassing reality even though he evidently could not observe an explicit message in these abstract paintings. Tillich likewise says that Botticelli's Madonna brought him "the keys for the interpretation of human existence, brought vital joy and spiritual truth" (Tillich 1987, p. 235).

He saw one of the highpoints of *figurative* painting. Barnard saw *non-figurative* masterpieces, but that made no difference. As works of art, neither is giving any explicit message. They have no logos, certainly no ethos, but they do have mythos, a symbolic meaning.

In Jung's view, this mythos rises up from a state of *participation mystique* (he derives the term from the anthropologist Lévy-Bruhl), "an a priori oneness of subject and object," wherein the human being is born, in which all individuals are without boundaries as well as identical (*cf.* Jung, 1990. para. 781). During their later life many adults, rushed as they are by their self-consciousness, have great difficulty staying in touch with this matrix of creativity. The artists knows how to descend into it.

Jung says,

> This re-immersion in the state of *participation mystique* is the secret of artistic creation and of the effect which great art has upon us, for at that level of experience it is no longer the weal or woe of the individual that counts, but the life of the collective. That is why every great work of art is objective and impersonal, and yet profoundly moving. And that is also why the personal life of the artist is at most a help or a hindrance, but is never essential to his creative task. He may go the way of the Philistine, a good citizen, a fool, or a criminal. His personal career may be interesting and inevitable, but it does not explain his art. (Jung, 1978a, para. 162)

The same is true for the beholder of his work, he may go the way of a Nazi camp-executioner!

Ceci n'est pas une pipe

In 1928, the Belgian painter René Magritte painted the painting which later became world-famous: *Ceci n'est pas une pipe*; This is not a pipe. The Dutch theologian and expert in gnosis, Gilles Quispel, once confided to me that Jung was deeply moved by this painting. What caused a landslide in Jung was the insight which hit him like a flash of lightning, that you can never say of any artwork: *Ceci est...*"Abraham" in a painting by Rembrandt is not Abraham, "Jesus on the Cross" is not that by Grünewald or Bach. Van Gogh knew like no other that his "cypresses" are not cypresses, but stirrings of his soul. Modern art is characterised by a deep resistance against this traditional, yet improper appreciation of art. If we do not know how to appreciate abstract art as we do figurative art, it could be that we like figurative art for the wrong reasons. Of course, a work of art is not a work of art *because* it is abstract, but Magritte taught us an important lesson, especially regarding our moral aspirations: a rape on a painting is not a rape, an act of war on a painting is not war, an immoral act by De Sade is not an immoral act, and when we watch Shakespeare's *Julius Caesar* in the theatre, we do not walk up to the stage to prevent his murder by Brutus. *Ceci n'est pas un meurtre.* The waterfall in a film can fall down heavily, but it is not a waterfall. That water will not make us wet.

Of course, the question that should be asked here is: if *ceci* is not a pipe, what is *ceci* then? According to Jung the answer is that *ceci* is a symbol, seen objective-empirically: an illusion. Art does not depict anything. Artwork can therefore be seen as a dream, which despite all openness never interprets itself. No dream says: "You should," or "that is the truth." Art offers a representation, like nature grows a plant. Art and nature show themselves to us with disinterest; they have no message. "Perhaps it [art] is like nature, which simply *is* and 'means' nothing beyond that...It needs no meaning, for meaning has nothing to do with art" (Jung, 1978b, para. 121).

If artworks are dreams, then the artist is a dreamer. In dreams it is not that "I" dream, but that "I" am being dreamt. My unconscious dreams. The Dutch painter Karel Appel tells us that he almost literally dreams during painting:

> So I enter my studio and look at my paintings and then
> work some more on them or I don't. Then suddenly
> I start on a blank canvas. And the inspiration flows

whilst I am working and I dissolve into nothing. The solitude, that emptiness is what I want; they create the best moments to work. When unexpectedly somebody enters, I am so to say taken out of my sleep. Suddenly somebody wakes me up and I have difficulty to fall asleep again when I want to sleep some more. In a painter's life it is annoying when you are disturbed, because you want to stay in it... you do not want to be awake. (Kayzer, 2000, pp. 160-161)

A Portrait of the Artist

The artist does not only feel any ethical obligation, he/she also does not feel religious nor political obligations, he/she is, sometimes against his/her will, pushed by a creative drive, a complex in the Jungian sense of the word. At this point, Jung cites a great inspiration, the German physiologist and painter Carl Gustav Carus:

> [The genius] is everywhere hemmed round and prevailed upon by the Unconscious, the mysterious god within him; so that ideas flow to him – he knows not whence; he is driven to work and to create – he knows not to what end; and is mastered by an impulse for constant growth and development – he knows not whither. (Jung, 1978a, para. 157)

Jung continually refers to this thought:

> Art is a kind of innate drive that seizes a human being and makes him its instrument. The artist is not a person endowed with free will who seeks his own ends, but one who allows art to realise its purposes through him. As a human being he may have moods and a will and personal aims, but as an artist he is 'man' in a higher sense – he is 'collective man,' a vehicle and moulder of the unconscious psychic life of mankind. That is his office, and it

is sometimes so heavy a burden that he is faced to sacrifice happiness and everything that makes life worth living for ordinary human being. (Jung, 1978a, para. 157)

Jung emphasised that extroversion and introversion are superficial appearances through which works of art become visible to us. They really are illusionary appearances! Extroversion and introversion are conscious attitudes; the work of art is of unknown origin. He expressed this in 1930:

It makes no difference whether the artist knows that his work is generated, grows and matures within him, or whether he imagines that it is his own invention. In reality it grows out of him as a child from its mother. The creative process has a feminine quality, and the creative work arises from unconscious depths – we might truly say from the realm of the Mothers. (Jung, 1978a. para. 159)

In the same year he wrote:

It is not Goethe that creates *Faust*, but *Faust* that creates Goethe. And what is *Faust*? *Faust* is essentially a symbol. By this I do not mean that it is an allegory pointing to something all too familiar, but the expression of something profoundly alive in the soul of every German, which Goethe helped to bring to birth. (Jung, 1978a, para. 159)

This is the core of Jung's theory of art: a creative process works autonomous, and the artist is standing under an unconscious, sacred obligation:

The unborn work in the psyche of the artist is a force of nature that achieves its end either with tyrannical might or with the subtle cunning of nature herself, quite regardless of the personal fate of the man who is his vehicle. (Jung, 1978b, para. 115)

In *A Portrait of the Artist as a Young Man*, James Joyce described an elaborate philosophy of art. Even though Jung had difficulty with Joyce's *Ulysses* (*cf.* Jung, 1978c), he completely agreed with his ideas about art. What is deeply distinctive of "true art," Joyce states, is a disinterested perception, while "improper art" always serves ethical, economic, sociological, political or religious interests. He discerns two kinds of improper art: art that elicits desire for the depicted object. He calls this pornographical art. All advertising art is in that sense pornographic, because its purpose is to excite desire in the beholder to possess the depicted object.

The second kind of improper art is that which elicits loathing or fear. He calls this didactic art. Critical satire, caricature portrayals and socially critical art are didactic and therefore, in Joyce's view, also improper. Fascist and Marxist art were and are of course consciously didactic, whereas, in some circles in Western-Europe and America since the last century, socio-political teachings are even regarded as the only *raison d'être* of art, otherwise labelled as "escapist," "ivory-tower art," or "l'art pour l'art."

In summary, Joyce writes:

> The feelings excited by improper art are kinetic, desire or loathing. Desire urges us to possess, to go to something, loathing urges us to abandon, to go from something. The arts which excite them, pornographical or didactic are therefore improper arts. The esthetic emotion (I use the general term) is therefore static. *The mind is arrested and raised above desire and loathing.* (Joyce, 1992, p. 158 italics mine)

Art experience and aesthetic experience

We will now look at the important difference which, according to Jung, exists between aesthetics and art. We already mentioned it briefly. To Jung, there is a vast difference between the aesthetic and the numinous character of art. A work of art is always aesthetic in nature, "a thing of beauty," but "above" in that it is essentially numinous in nature. Many art critics do not make this distinction, and if an individual does mention the numinous character, it usually remains an aesthetic aspect. To Jung this is an improper jumbling-up of concepts.

To begin with, aesthetics is not an exclusive aspect of art. There are many areas in life which potentially have an aesthetic nature: a landscape, for example, which is obviously not an artwork but an experience. Yet, one can also have an aesthetic view on life. According to Jung, the reason that art is constantly shaped as an aesthetic form is, astonishingly, strongly related with the amoral character of art. To see that clearly, we first have to understand what he meant by aesthetic. When does someone experience something as beautiful?

Aesthetics is a quality of sensory experience, not one of knowing or feeling. That is indeed the original meaning of the word *aisthèsis*. The an-esthetist is somebody who deprives us of all sensory experience during surgery. Tasting something really differs from understanding something. When we savour something as beautiful, says Kant, there is a disinterested delight irrespective of the fact that we do or do not possess that thing. We always keep an appropriate distance when we regard something as beautiful. To think that a peach is beautiful and subsequently eating it, testifies to another kind of taste than the aesthetic. "The mind is arrested and raised above desire and loathing," we read in Joyce.

Kant formulates stern and dry in 1790:

> In order to decide whether or not something is beautiful, we do not relate the representation by means of understanding to the object for cognition, but rather relate it by means of the imagination (perhaps combined with the understanding) to the subject and its feeling of pleasure or displeasure. The judgement of taste is therefore not a cognitive judgement, hence not a logical one, but is rather aesthetic, by

> which is understood one whose determining ground *cannot* be *other than subjective*. (Kant, 2000, p. 89)

Hume wrote in 1757:

> Beauty is no quality in things themselves. It exists merely in the mind which contemplates; and each perceives a different beauty. One person may perceive deformity, where another is sensible of beauty (Hume, 1886, p. 268).

Jung was entirely dedicated to this subjective viewpoint. Already in 1912 he plainly wrote: "Beauty does not indeed lie in things, but in the feeling that we give to them" (Jung, 1944, p. 107).

An experience of beauty is thus always subjective. It remains a mystery why we favor something as beautiful, and similarly why people like or dislike the same thing, and this ratio does not speak to how this sensory experience penetrates the unconscious.

Exactly this disinterested perception is, according to Jung, of eminent importance to the artist! If the artist does not have a distant sensory perception as a part of reality but is caught up by it, if he was morally involved for example, it would hinder him in bringing the work of art to birth. An artist has to leave his personal soul at home if he wants to create something at all. At first, this might sound strange and yet this is the inexorable conclusion of the previously stated. The artist has to leave all ethics aside. Jung tried to clarify this with an ordinary example. During a seminar held in 1933, he said he would illustrate the "aesthetic attitude:"

> I will give you an example of an extreme aesthetic attitude...On a snowy street an automobile skids, hits a child, and crushes its skull against the curbstone; you come along and see people standing about, and the blood on the snow, and you hear: "Awful accident! Child has been killed!" Naturally, you would be impressed. But if you have the gift of the aesthetic

attitude, you say: "What an interesting picture, how beautiful!" You see the beauty of the horror, which means you are shielded from the whole thing, you have experienced only the surface. The characteristic group of people around the place of disaster is very dramatic, and you can make a drawing of it which will be most artistic, most suggestive; and the contrast between the cold snow and the warm blood, the dead white and the bright red colour, is most remarkable, most suggestive and you can paint it. (Jung, 1997a, p. 919)

In this example, Jung emphasised that an aesthetic attitude gives an incomplete experience of reality. Such an attitude protects against an abundance of other sensations and is therefore per definition one-sided and superficial. Of course, he said, one can look aesthetically at everything, but no one would claim that the essence of something is known if one only approaches it aesthetically. To approach something in a purely aesthetic manner means: approaching it only in as far as one perceives it. Jung continually repeated that for the individuation process more is needed than an aesthetic attitude. *Above all it needs the question whether we regard something as good or true.* He described this succinctly in *Psychological Types.*

Just as the world of appearances can never become a moral problem for the man who merely senses it, the world of inner images is never a moral problem for the intuitive. For both of them it is an aesthetic problem, a matter of perception, a 'sensation.' (Jung, 1990, para. 658)

However, to the artist it is essential to have this (one-sided) aesthetic attitude. If he did not possess an aesthetic distance, he would simply not be capable to create art. In the example of the child's accident, it would have been impossible to portray this scene if the person who adopts an aesthetic attitude could not have estranged himself from the tragedy.

> The aesthetic attitude is a necessity for the artist, for he *must* shield himself against the object or the vision or the experience–whatever it is–in order to be able to reproduce it; if you are absolutely in it you are caught, destroyed, you are not an artist. (Jung, 1997a, p. 920)

The previous explorations let us understand that Jung took an ambiguous attitude to aesthetics. Is it a necessity for the artist, or for the individual person when it stands in the way of the individuation process. Jung distinguished two aspects of aesthetic taste: finding-pleasure-in and keeping-distance-from. It is possible to reduce one's whole attitude to life in this double disposition: finding pleasure in something while keeping a distance, *only* being able to find pleasure in something when keeping it at a distance. According to Jung, such a hedonistic view of life is by definition "superficial."

> Aestheticism is not fitted to solve the exceedingly serious and difficult task of educating man...It actually hinders a deeper investigation of the problem, because it always averts its face from anything evil, ugly, and difficult, and aims at pleasure, even though it [may] be of an edifying kind. Aestheticism therefore lacks all moral force, because *au fond* it is still only a refined hedonism. (Jung, 1990, para. 194)

For Jung, the aesthetic view of life is insufficient because it forgets, denies or represses ethics. This is inherent to aesthetic reduction.

And yet...it might surprise us that Jung persistently emphasised that aesthetics is important for the (mentally) sick person. This seems a paradox (becoming healthy demands a transcendence of aesthetics, being ill demands its integration), but it flows utterly from his vision on art and aesthetics. He spoke from his own experience. He encouraged his patients to use all kinds of crafts which an artist also uses: drawing, sculpting and making music. When people give shape to their nightly dream in a drawing or express their mental condition in a mandala, it has little to do with art, but it has with their therapy. The aesthetic craft enables them to be released from themselves for a while and look from a distance at what occupies them.

> The aesthetic approach immediately converts the problem into a picture which the spectator can contemplate at his ease, admiring both its beauty and its ugliness, merely re-experiencing its passions at a safe distance, with no danger of becoming involved in them. (Jung, 1990, para. 232)

Jung was always watchful that his patients did not consider their work "art." In 1929 he wrote:

> Although my patients occasionally produce artistically beautiful things that might very well be shown in modern "art" exhibitions, I nevertheless treat them as completely worthless when judged by the canons of real art. As a matter of fact, it is essential that they should be considered worthless, otherwise my patients might imagine themselves to be artists, and the whole point of the exercise would be missed. It is not a question of art at all – or, rather, it should not be a question of art – but of something more and other than mere art, namely the living effect upon the patient himself. The meaning of individual life, whose importance from the social standpoint is negligible, stands here at his highest, and for its sake the patient struggles to give form, however crude and childish, to the inexpressible...A patient needs only to have seen once or twice how much he is freed from a wretched state of mind by working at a symbolical picture, and he will always turn to this means of release whenever things go badly with him. (Jung, 1966, para. 106)

Jung wrote this from his own experience, while working on *The Red Book*. "As a result of my experiment I learned how helpful it can be, from the therapeutic point of view, to find the particular images which lie behind emotions" (Jung, 1989, p. 177). Jung was ill, he was trying to control the *symptoms*, he was rebalancing his (instinctual) nature. He was therapeutically engaged, not artistically. Jung was afraid that, if the artistic spirit would possess him, he would become a puppet of the unconscious. He did not want to lose the grip of his conscious I.

> In *The Red Book* I tried an esthetic elaboration of my fantasies, but never finished it. I became aware that I had not yet found the right language, that I still had to translate it into something else. Therefore, I gave up this estheticizing tendency in good time, in favour of a rigorous process of *understanding*. (Jung, 1989, p. 188)

Further (only in the German edition of *MDR*),

> *The aesthetic editing in* The Red Book *was necessary*—even though I was irritated and annoyed about it—because through this I received insight into the ethical obligation in the face of the images of the unconscious. This had a decisive influence on my way of life. (Jung, 1997b, p. 192 italics mine)

Here we read once more what we already saw at the beginning, that insight into the ethical obligation proved to Jung that this was not art. Very different laws were involved in the creation of aesthetic products of the active imagination which Jung and his patients practised during their crises. In those situations, an aesthetic attitude can be *a phase* in a curative process.

The mythological creative fantasy is a necessary matrix for the insane, and the ill, the religious, the artist, and the scientist. But how different this matrix works for each of them! An aesthetic view can help a relaxed person to uphold his conscious I, whereas for the artist, it is a means to bypass his ego via a numinous, autonomous complex.

Jung did not want to run away from his unconscious, animal nature. He would not allow himself to get lost in the "lovely appearance" of an aesthetic perspective. He did not want to "shed a deceptive aesthetic veil over the problem [of his life]" (Jung, 1990, para. 227).

It was, however, worthwhile to look from a distance to the objects which his insane mind produced. Depicting them in a lovely way enabled him to do this, for it brought into the spotlight what he needed to confront.

An attempt to formulate an answer to Steiner

In this contribution, I have not poured over the complex reality of good and evil, especially as it is focused on the concrete individual. Jung developed some thoughts on this subject which are worthy of consideration and heavily critiqued by both modern enlightened culture as well as the traditional culture of the church.

Of course it is possible that the individual camp commander did evil while thinking he was doing good. Of course principles which transcend our everyday moral codes are of influence in the formation of our conscience, and of course cultural educational ideals can conflict so strongly with other cultures that both think they have God on their side. But for our theme, these differentiations are not of much importance. The central question for us is whether there is an intrinsic relation between ethics and art, irrespective of the complexity of both realities.

Therefore, it is not appropriate to say to Steiner that perhaps the camp commander did not see himself as a sadist. If we did, there would no longer be a pressing question whereas there certainly is one! I accept the fact that the camp commander did evil, realised this, and still enjoyed Schubert, and yes, at that moment could have had a numinous experience. I agree that Steiner is convinced that he, in comparison with the other, feels himself to be a good person and similarly enjoys Schubert. That same taste for beauty together with this difference in humanity evokes the question in

Steiner and, to that question, I have tried to formulate an answer in the spirit of Jung.

Partially, that answer has to do with the wholly autonomous, numinous character of art. "When an archetypal situation occurs [Jung here discusses the experience of art] we suddenly feel an extraordinary sense of release, as though transported, or caught up by an overwhelming power" (Jung, 1978b, para. 128).

Suddenly there is an illumination!

To apply a comparison: the artist creates a work of art like God causes the sun to rise on good and evil people without distinction. Let it be a comfort to Steiner that the camp commander can never lower art to his existence as plebeian, but let it also be a warning to Steiner that art cannot be appropriated by the ones among human beings who are of noble mind. A work of art manifests itself like the *Tao* above all yin and yang.

That transcendental moment of illumination always comes to the fore when we experience the numinous beauty of a work of art. Joyce did not know otherwise than to consult Thomas of Aquino when he specifies the most typical characteristic of a work of art: *claritas*, radiance. For Aquinas, a work of art always "radiates" something of "divine splendour." The infidel Joyce cannot otherwise describe this *claritas* other than in spiritual terms.

> That supreme quality of beauty, the dear radiance
> of the esthetic image, is apprehended luminously
> by the mind which has been arrested by the whole-
> ness and fascinated by its harmony in the luminous
> silent stasis of esthetic pleasure, *a spiritual state.*
> (Joyce, 1992, p. 164 italics mine)

Tillich likewise mentions a similar light. It shines on saints and sinners, and it keeps shining in the darkest period of our culture. It keeps shining beyond good and evil even where jihadists destroy works of art.

In another respect, the answer is related to the aesthetic aspect of art. Steiner was not the first to be aware of the nagging theme he raises. It is a recurring story, how, amid the violence of war and at the most horrible places, all kinds of art were practised and enjoyed by the German *Wehrmacht*. This fact has almost become cliché. However, to me, this does not seem coincidental. Precisely, as discussed, it is characteristic of an aesthetic perspective to be able to distance oneself from the harsh, malevolent reality. Aesthetics empowered Jung to deal with his sometimes suicidal stirrings of the soul. Could it have been possible that precisely these aesthetic-artistic meetings in the families of camp commanders kept them going amid the hideous reality surrounding them? Someone like Nietzsche thought that one could only escape the harshness of reality through aesthetics and art. "The truth is ugly. We have art so we are not destroyed by the truth" (Nietzsche, 1997, p. 346). Further, he says, "As an aesthetic phenomenon existence is still *bearable* to us, and art furnishes us with the eye and the hand and above all the good conscience to be *able* to make such a phenomenon of ourselves" (Nietzsche, 2001, p. 104). Although Jung did not agree with Nietzsche's view on aesthetics, he understood this perspective well. He knew from experience that aesthetics could bracket good and evil for a short while.

When Steiner wonders why the camp commander could experience beauty even being such an evil person, then the answer is that exactly this aesthetic experience permitted him to transcend his evilness for the duration of Schubert's *Allegretto*. And maybe the same is true for Steiner, troubled as he was in his life by awful memories. These memories also disappeared during the *Allegretto*. Art and aesthetics made life more bearable for him. Perhaps, it is appropriate to stay silent, since we might already have come too close to Steiner's soul.

References

Barnard, M. (2005). Het Numineuze. *Interpretatie,* July (pp.17-19).

Berk, T. van den (2012). *Jung on art: The autonomy of the creative drive.* Psychology Press, Taylor and Francis Group, Hove and New York.

Botton, A. de (2007). *The architecture of happiness.* Penguin Books, London.

Devereaux, M. (2003). Where ethics and aesthetics meet: Titian's rape of Europa. *Hypathia*, Volume 18, no. 14 (Autumn-Winter).

Gaillard, C. (2008). The arts. In: R.K. Papadopoulos (ed.), *The handbook of Jungian psychology: theory, practice and applications.* Routledge, London/New York (pp. 324-376).

Gaut, B. (2007). *Art, emotion and ethics.* Oxford University Press, Oxford.

Hume, D. (1886). On the standard of taste. D. Hume, *The Philosophical Works*, Volume 3. Little, Brown, London (pp. 266-284).

Joyce, J. (1992). *A portrait of the artist as a young man.* Wordsworth Editions, Ware, Hertfordshire.

Jung, C. G. (1944). *Psychology of the unconscious: A study of the transformations and symbolisms of the libido. A contribution to the history of the evolution of thought.* Kegan Paul, Trench, Trubner and Co.

Jung, C. G. (1966). The aims of psychotherapy. *The practice of psychotherapy: Essays on the psychology of the transference and other subjects.* Princeton University Press, Princeton, NJ. Collected Works, Volume 16, 36-52.

Jung, C. G. (1978a). Psychology and literature. *The practice of psychotherapy. Essays on the psychology of the transference and other subjects.* Pantheon, New York. Collected Works, Volume 15, pp. 84-105.

Jung, C. G. (1978b). On the relation of analytical psychology to poetry. *The spirit in man, art and literature.* Princeton University Press, Princeton, NJ. Collected Works, Volume 15, pp. 65-83.

Jung, C. G. (1978c). "Ulysses": A monologue. *The spirit in man, art and literature.* Princeton University Press, Princeton, NJ. Collected Works. Volume 15, pp.109-134.

Jung C. G. (1989). *Memories, dreams, reflections.* Recorded and edited by Aniela Jaffé. Vintage Books, New York.

Jung, C. G. (1990). *Psychological types.* Collected Works, Volume 6. Princeton University Press, Princeton, NJ.

Jung, C. G. (1997a). *Visions: Notes of the seminar given in 1930-1934 by Carl Gustav Jung*. Edited by Claire Douglas. Two volumes. Bollingen Series XCIX. Princeton University Press, Princeton, NJ.

Jung, C. G. (1997b). *Erinnerungen, Träume, Gedanken von C. G. Jung* Aufgezeichnet und herausgeben von Aniela Jaffé. Walter-Verlag, Freiburg im Breisgau.

Kant, I. (2000). *Critique of the Power of Judgement*. Cambridge University Press, Cambridge.

Kayzer, W. (2000). *Het boek van de schoonheid en de troost*. Contact, Amsterdam/Antwerpen.

Levenson, J. (ed.). (1998). *Aesthetics and ethics: Essays at the intersection*. Cambridge University Press, Cambridge.

Mayo, D. H. (1995). *Jung and aesthetic experience: The unconscious as source of artistic inspiration*. Peter Lang, New York.

Nietzsche, F. (1997). *Herwaardering van Alle Waarden*. De Bezige Bij, Amsterdam.

Nietzsche, F. (2001). *The gay science*. Cambridge University Press, Cambridge.

Rilke, R. M. (2009). *Duino Elegies*: The first elegy. Translated by A. S. Kline. (http:///www.poetryintranslation.com/PITBR/German/The Fountain of Joy)

Tillich, P. (1987). *On art and architecture*. Edited and with an Introduction by John Dillenberger, in collaboration with Jane Dillenberger. Crossroad, New York.

Vivas, E. (1974). On aesthetics and Jung. In: *Modern Age*, Volume 18, number 3, pp. 246-256.

Wilde, O. (2011). *The picture of Dorian Gray* Edited by Nicholas Frankel. The Belknap Press of Harvard University Press, Cambridge Massachusetts; London, England (The 1891 Preface, p. 273).

Chapter 12

Art Subjects:
An Exploration of Imaginal Expression as Means of Individuation and Healing

by Heidi Sylvia Volf

Part I: Art as Intersection of the Transcendent and Immanent

> *An archetypal image has nothing but its naked fullness, which seems inapprehensible by the intellect. Concepts are coined and negotiable values; images are life.*
>
> Carl Jung, *The Collected Works:*
> Volume 14, 1963, para. 226

Art is truth manifest. Whether created or experienced, art acts as an initiator to individuation. Any kind of imaginal expression of archetypal motifs is interpretive and expressive of the highest reality. It is capable of conveying the experience of both the transcendent and immanent dimensions of mortal human existence by serving as a sort of mirror that pulls us out of our ego-based selves. Art serves to illustrate the tension between existence and beyond, the tension of the polarities of Logos and Eros, and the means of transcending them. It offers a means of glimpsing and exploring a kind of redemption in itself.

Described as poetry, fairy tale, dance, painting, and sculpture, even myth itself, artistic expressions of archetypal patterns carry metaphors that illuminate grand truths, dwarfing and even dismantling the ego. Jung understood this as essential to the therapeutic process. Not only did he insist a patient's individual story was necessary for analysis and healing, but he took it even further with his experiments in active imagination and drawing in *The Red Book* (2009).

Art is a means of accessing the oblivion of Other so as to embrace Self, it demands mutual experience of observer and observed. It depends on the notion of projection, drawing from the observer the experience needed and sought. As Joseph Campbell put it, "the symbol which you are ready for evokes a response in you" (2004, p. 93). The transcendent image echoes the immanent one. "Art, Jung suggests, is a material moment in which conscious and unconscious are in mutual embrace" (Rowland, 2010, p. 58).

Through the experience of Leo Frobenius' *Ergriffenheit* or James Joyce's "aesthetic arrest," we are drawn out by echoes and predictions of our potentialities, which serve to begin the catalyzation necessary to the discovery of the Self. The templates of our beliefs shift, our Gestalt is rearranged, our tiny solar systems collapse and nothing is ever the same as it was, it has evolved. Art allows entrance into the abyss, providing a moment to seize the opportunity to confront the Other and allow it to transform us, thus creating a new potentiality, a revelation.

Several verses of Robert Duncan's *Poetry, a Natural Thing*, aptly illustrate the journey of individuation, particularly the movement towards and through the abyss of Other.

> This beauty is an inner persistence
> toward the source
> striving against (within) down-rushet of the river,
> a call we heard and answer
> in the lateness of the world
> primordial bellowings
> from which the youngest world might spring,

> salmon not in the well where the
> hazelnut falls
> but at the falls battling, inarticulate,
> blindly making it. (1960/1993, p. 635)

Artists are visionary; they are heretics plowing through the hard earth of tradition, sewing it with seeds of revelation and revolution. Jung certainly fits into this category. He had the soul of a Romantic poet, reactionary in regards to the Reformation and Enlightenment. His theories were attempts to break away from ego-based individualism. He echoed the thoughts of Friedrich Nietzsche who declared, "there always emerges and has always emerged in the long run something for the sake of which it is worthwhile to live on Earth, for example virtue, art, music, dance, reason, spirituality—something transfiguring, refined, mad and divine" (1886/2006, p. 46).

Jung's relationship with artistic endeavors was ambiguous. This in itself illustrates his point. He could not define art, or rather state a definite opinion on it, as this would have relegated an experience to categorization and nullified the mystery of Other. In remaining vague, Jung acknowledged how art insinuates itself into the psyche, working from within. Jung

> points to psychology's use of the language of concepts
> and rational argument as offering an abstract cate-
> gorization of experience. Such language, he tells us
> in the poetry essay, is necessary for intelligibility,
> yet is also profoundly inauthentic in representing
> psychic experience. Abstract concepts move away
> from the feel of the living mystery of the psyche.
> (Rowland, 2010, p. 53)

With his writing, Jung demonstrated that it is simply not possible "to communicate, in sensible words, the fluidity, texture, and fantasy-fueled nature of the mind" (Rowland, 2010, p. 27). It is as if he wished to evoke the experience of the irrational unconscious, not merely explain it. Robert Romanyshyn's notion of "spiral reading" (2007) suits Jung's writing, giving the reader a "process captured in ideas and images, more than a definitive statement or conceptual argument" (Rowland, 2010, p. 32). This kind of writing (Jung's) and reading (Romanyshyn's) catalyzes individuation by provoking an encounter with the unconscious.

The spiral dismantling and resulting integration of the psyche is perfectly illustrated with Jung's experience reading James Joyce's *Ulysses*. Art induces an illness, starting a process that leads to self-discovery. Jung declared Joyce and Pablo Picasso to be "two great initiators ... masters of the fragmentation of aesthetical contents and accumulations of ingenious shards" (Bair, 2003, p. 407). Regarding *Ulysses*, an exhausted Jung stated:

> A world comes down in an almost endless, breathless stream of debris, a "catholic" world, i.e., a universe with moanings and outcries unheard and tears unshed because suffering had extinguished itself and an immense field of shards began to reveal its aesthetic "values." (Bair, 2003, p. 408)

These shards are what pierce the individual psyche, forcing an initiatory process, individuation and potential healing. Jung considered art, particularly in the form of narrative, as essential to the therapeutic process.

> In many cases in psychiatry, the patient who comes to us has a story that is not told, and which as a rule no one knows of. To my mind, therapy only really begins after the investigation of that wholly personal story. It is the patient's secret, the rock against which he is shattered. If I know his secret story, I have a key to the treatment. (Jung, 1963/1989, p. 117)

Artistic expression is a means of manifesting the unconscious. Creating or simply witnessing the varied signs and symbols allows for the harmonization of the outer world with the inner. According to Jung, "man's unconscious psyche has an irresistible urge to assimilate all outer experiences to inner psychic events" (Jung & Segal,

1998, p. 77). The outer experiences that resonate particularly, most beautifully, are the expressions of archetypal motifs.

Art is the greatest of initiators. The ritual of creation or observation and absorption of art reveals the ineffable. The shards of this beauty, this truth, prompt the sacrifice of the individual ego to a kind of collective, inner Self. In the trickster realm between Eros and Logos, lies the ineffable Other. Through this "hole" between the opposites, one can experience the whole. "Jungian art theory is an approach that recognizes art's potential for providing psychological wholeness through the serious business of facing and working with the Other" (Rowland, 2010, p. 64). Jung himself stated,

> As opposites never unite at their own level ... a supraordinate "third" is always required, in which the two parts can come together. And since the symbol derives as much from the conscious as from the unconscious, it is able to unite them both, reconciling their conceptual polarity though its form and their emotional polarity thorough its numinosity. (Jung & Segal, 1998, p. 89)

Imaginal expressions of archetypal patterns illustrate the essence of existence through a symbolic language and point through the spaces between two thoughts to the Other. This encounter, in turn, forms a direct route to the psyche. Symbolic expression and metaphor affect the psyche in a way that science and logic cannot. This sentiment is echoed by Thomas Schiller, who declared, "deeper meaning lies in the fairy tale of my childhood than in the truth that is taught by life," (cited in Campbell, 2002, p. 2). The symbols displayed in imaginal expression are concentrated pellets of meaning, starker, more vivid, and in higher relief than the events of day-to-day prose.

The kind of truth contained in artistic expressions needs no historicity. A massive stumbling block for Western civilization has been the concretization of these archetypal patterns. The motifs of Mother Earth have been appropriated by a patriarchal society.

There is no monotheism at all, dualism has become the religious norm, and anything that attempts to transcend this duality is seen as threatening. According to mythologist, Joseph Campbell, "one of the great calamities of contemporary life, is that the religions that we have inherited have insisted on the concrete historicity of their symbols" (2004, p. 88).

Through art, ancient beliefs have been and are preserved. Artistic expressions of the imaginal realm resurrect forgotten gods and demons, the "pregnant motifs" of myth that "are the purveyors of wisdom" (Campbell, 2002, p. 23). These "inherited iconographies" (Campbell, 2002, p. 22) illustrate existence, offering us the means of instruction in social adaptation and providing the requisite armor to survive and persevere. They are "phrases from an image-language, expressive of metaphysical, psychological and sociological truth" (Campbell, 2002, p. 23). According to Edmund Cusick,

> Since the age of narrative poetry has passed, we have learned to value verse precisely for its capacity not to drive us forward, but to abandon outward progress—to stand still and explore for us, the readers, the depth of meaning in a single scene, a single image. For this we borrow a word from religious experience: *epiphany*. (2008, p. 13)

God, Self, truth, beauty, is in each one of us, internal. However, it can often only be catalyzed by external imaginal expression. Salvation, redemption, and rebirth come with embracing the unknown, with the "mystic union of finite with its infinite ambient" (Campbell, 2002, p. 176). Art offers a threshold where one can glimpse redemption itself. According to Joyce, "any object intensely regarded may be a gate of access to the incorruptible eon of the gods" (cited in Campbell, 2004, p. 160).

The contact of the unconscious with the conscious through imaginal expression of archetypal motifs creates the possibility of joining together the ends of the continuum, of transcending polarities, and embodying the missing third. Artistic expression prompts "aesthetic arrest" and *Ergriffenheit*, which guide us towards sacrifice, figurative dismemberment and individuation. "Art heals consciousness by re-aligning the two creation myths [those of Earth Mother and Sky Father] and reconnecting them to our collective reality, understood as present time psychically imbued with the past" (Rowland, 2010, p. 61). We endure the experience in order to be reborn, reassembled, and reintegrated, ready to assume our *vita nuova*, following our own paths from the darkest points of the forest.

We are subject to and must subjugate ourselves to art, its creation and expression, as it can dictate our individuation. Jung knew that through the imaginal expressions of archetypal motifs, through "dialogical relation of transcendent and immanent qualities in differing amounts," (Rowland, 2008, p. 3) we could see beyond ego, to Self.

Familiar signs and mysterious symbols catalyze, shards pierce our ego, and the sacrifice of individuation begins. We shed prescribed beliefs and can begin to negotiate our own paths. Art initiates individuation, prompts dismemberment, and then motivates reintegration by providing examples, explanation, and a hint at the essence of salvation.

Part II: The Image

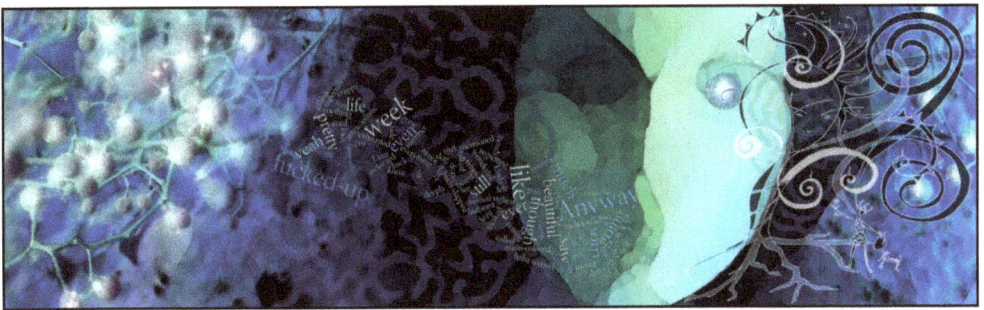

FIGURE 1. *CULTIVATING THE MOON.* SOURCE: AUTHOR.

Part III: An Irrational Exploration of the Image

There is both rhyme and reason in what I say, I have
made a dream poem of humanity. I will cling to it.

Thomas Mann, *The Magic Mountain*, 1961, p. 496

According to Edmund Cusick, "for the artist, contact with the
archetypes may be held—expressed or embodied—through the
emergence of the work of art, but cannot by definition be brought
under rational control" (2008, p. 13). I agree, and as such found it
difficult to "interpret" my imagining, preferring to explore it further
with a poem. Much as Jung felt ill as he read *Ulysses*, I experienced
a great deal of anxiety in "analyzing" the image I created and felt
as though I was ingesting a monster. Whereas the creation of the
image was cathartic and healing, I found attempted analysis of it to
have a much more painful effect.

I cannot view the image objectively as I am subject to it in more
ways than one. This is a case of necessary "immanent criticism" that
must take place *inside* the experience of the art, or in the interior of
the art itself. It needs to be partly ritual, an invocation to the power
of the work, the effect of meeting that ever-changing union of natural
and supernatural. (Rowland, 2008, p. 4)

The main image illustrates contact with the moon. The girl
is undergoing a kind of radical epiphany. It is painful and irrational. On the left are moonberries, growing and sparkling. They
are overlaid by a collage of tissue-paper snowflakes. On top of this
image is a collection of words; those of my last e-mail to someone
who had just broken my heart. The signs in the image, the girl, the
berries, the snowflakes, are knowable. However, for me, they evoke
mystery, something not entirely knowable. They become symbols
implying far more.

I am the girl in the image. It is based on a still from a film I did
a couple years ago, in which I portrayed a religious zealot postu-
lating on the horrors of "emo" and Goth culture. There is a horrified

expression on my face and something about it reminded me of Cassandra in Euripides's *Trojan Women* (415 B.C.E./1915).

> Where lies the galley? Whither shall I tread?
> See that your watch be set, your sail be spread.
> The wind comes quick! ... Three Powers—marks me thou!—
> There be in Hell, and one walks with thee now!
>
> (lines 456-460)

I began to play with the image in Photoshop, changing the colors, adding effects. The figure became more and more twisted, a greater embodiment of shock and horror, a highly-stylized enactment of nightmare. "She" began to remind me of the figure of Madeline I portrayed in Stephen Berkoff's adaptation of Edgar Allen Poe's *The Fall of the House of Usher* (1990), an epileptic, cataleptic shadow, a sickened anima figure to her twin Roderick.

Incorporated into this image is a photo I took of some tree branches with strange elderberry-like fruit, which I transformed into what appeared most meaningful, most reflective of my psychic state. In inverting the colors of the original image, the berries became white. They struck me as tiny moons being gently cultivated in a secret garden somewhere. The thought evoked John Keats' *Ode to a Nightingale* (1884). I was also reminded of Oscar Wilde's *Nightingale and the Rose* (1888), in which the nightingale pierces its heart on a rose thorn so as to turn a snow white rose red as a gesture of love for a forlorn young man. Like the nightingale, I felt my heart pierced by thorns, stabbed by the shards of epiphany.

I cut out a snowflake from tissue paper and scanned it so as to incorporate it into the image. The sign that is "snowflake" evokes the symbol of the Labyrinth. In fact, snowflakes remind me of a kind of fractalesque Labyrinth with the fierce Minotaur waiting inside any number of centers. They are also like so many cathedral rose windows, which are themselves indicative of the Labyrinths found inside. The Labyrinth is the classic psychoanalytical symbol of the journey to Self. We initially emerge from this Labyrinth, coming forth from a womb. A differentiation then occurs, a kind of transcendence, an initiation, a slaying, a sacrifice, and then a return to this womb where we integrate the wisdom of the Moon and the intellect of the Sun.

The image I initially intended to create consists of the marriage of Sky Father and Earth Mother as symbolized by the Sun and Moon in a tree. The scene is presided over by "the Fool," who represents what the human initiate must undergo in order to grasp the notion of cyclical birth, death, and rebirth. I included this preliminary sketch in the final image, on the right.

The girl in the image is a Cassandra, but also an Ariadne, both wronged by Logos-based gods or heroes. Cassandra is cursed and abandoned by Apollo, while Ariadne is abandoned by Theseus even though it is because of her that he is able to slay the Minotaur and find his way out of the Labyrinth. It is important to note that Ariadne is later rescued by Dionysus, an Eros figure. The girl in the image *is* "the Fool." This image is about embracing the irrational, even cultivating it. Reason rarely prevails; it is through emotional experience that salvation can be experienced.

My "critique" of this image, like Susan Rowland's definition of Jungian arts criticism, is "tentative about its own claims for understanding ... a practice against interpretation, and for imagination" (2010, p. 53). The irrational cannot be "interpreted," it must be further imagined so as to be ingested and digested. Below is not only an exploration of the image but of the circumstances that led me to create it, a "dream poem" of personal experience.

> Just once!
> I had begged.
> And
> Finally.
> Love knocked.
> (Heaven and Earth brought together by the Wise Fool!)
> The three witches were all swollen with promise.
> And I, a Hecate maybe?

Miniature moons everywhere,
Tangled in brambles, and I
Not knowing in which direction to turn...
But here I'd found another *puer*.
Another Little Prince who could manage only charm.
Mesmerized by the reflection of
Himself in my pupils.
Or had it been more?
Had he tried to love me?
Had I forced him to fail?
I take no prisoners.

What was I supposed to do when he said
He didn't love me
And then began to laugh,
Pointing out the writhing sardine
That had just been flung from the surf
Struggling to breathe on the sand?
The sand of the beach where I'd spent so many
Afternoons as a child.
I'd asked him to bring me here.
I was going to draw an
Octopus over the scar at the base of his spine.

But he had other plans.

I got up, ran to the sardine
And scooped it up so as to
Throw it back into the sea.
But it slipped from my hands
And skidded across the sand.

He continued to laugh.
I picked it up again.

Shining, writhing, my soul out of breath,
Out of its depths
Choking.

This time,
I managed to throw it back into the water.

Then I turned,
Ran towards him,
And pushed him hard to the ground.
I wanted to knock the wind out of him.
Just once!
But, he merely continued to laugh.

Jung created a theory that considers and envelopes objective and subjective experience. It dismantles logic with the irrational, and structures the irrational with logic. Anima and animus combat and complement each other in a dance of enantiodromia, bringing to light the wholeness of Other and Self. It is "dialogical between conceptual thinking transcendent of local conditions and an immediate embodied psychic experience" resulting in "a theory that is more properly a *form of storytelling* that weaves the contingent into meaning by reference to a scheme of ideas" (Rowland, 2008, p. 4).

In my image, my story, I imagine multiple moons, a string of pearls turned "heap of jewels unstrung" (Tate, 1680), terror and cyclical rebirth, as well as harvest. This harvest consists of irrational treasures, moonberries "gathered while ye may!" (to paraphrase Herrick, 1648), with which an elixir can be made; moonshine to soothe the reason-riddled soul. The story expresses terrifying and yet electrifying irrationality. The immediate categorization of the visual image is tempered by choosing to further explore the image through the verbal exercise of creating a poem, further "imagining" the creation rather than dryly "interpreting" it.

"For Jung, art materializes the past into imagination, which is to say, provides an embodiment of past consciousness that spiritualizes matter" (Rowland, 2010, p. 61). This artistic exercise was an attempt to spiritualize matter, to illustrate the healing intersection of Logos and Eros and the transcendent and immanent. At the heart of it all still lurks "the Fool," longing not just to understand, but *embody* the transformative journey all must take as they embrace Other. The "art" and "imagining" that has resulted stands as a record of my time spent in liminal space, striving for psychic rebirth.

References

Bair, D. (2003). *Jung: A biography*. Boston: Little, Brown and Co.

Berkoff, S. & Poe, E. A. (1990). *The fall of the House of Usher*. Oxford: Amber Lane Press.

Campbell, J. (2002). *The flight of the wild gander: Explorations in the mythological dimension*. Novato, CA: New World Library.

Campbell, J. (2004). *Pathways to bliss*. Novato, CA: New World Library.

Cusick, E. (2008). Psyche and the artist: Jung and the poet. In Susan Rowland (Ed.), *Psyche and the arts: Jungian approaches to music, architecture, literature, film and painting.* (pp. 12-21). London: Routledge.

Duncan, R. E. (1993). Poetry, a natural thing. In D. McQuade (Ed.), *The Harper American literature: Volume 2*. New York: HarperCollins. (Reprinted from *The Opening of the field*, 1960, New York: Grove Press).

Euripides. (1915). *The Trojan women*. G. Murray (Trans.). Oxford: Oxford University Press. (Original work performed 415, B.C.E.) Retrieved December 6, 2010, from http://www.sacred-texts.com/cla/eurip/trojan.htm.

Herrick, R. (1919) To the Virgins, to Make Much of Time. In A. Quiller-Couch (Ed.) *The Oxford Book of English Verse: 1250–1900*. (Original work published 1648) Retrieved December 6, 2010, from http://www.bartleby.com/101/248.html.

Jung, C. G. (1989). *Memories, Dreams, Reflections* (R. Winston & C. Winston, Trans.) (A. Jaffe, Ed.). New York: Vintage Books. (Original work published 1963)

Jung, C. G. (2009). *The red book: Liber novus*. (M. Kyburz & J. Peck, Trans.) (S. Shamdasani, Ed.). New York: W. W. Norton.

Jung, C. G., & Hull, R. F. C. (1963). *The collected works: Volume 14*. London: Routledge and Kegan Paul.

Jung, C. G., & Segal, R. A. (1998). *Jung on mythology: Selected and introduced by Robert A. Segal*. Princeton paperbacks. Princeton, NJ: Princeton University Press.

Keats, J. (1884). Ode to a nightingale. In *The poetical works of John Keats*. Retrieved December 6, 2010, from http://www.bartleby.com/126/40.html.

Mann, T. (1961). Snow. In *The magic mountain* (pp. 469-498). New York: Alfred A. Knopf. Retrieved October 22, 2010, from https://elearning.my.pacifica.edu/d2l/lms/content/viewer/main_frame.d2l?ou=12154&tId=127729.

Nietzsche, F. (2006). *Beyond good and evil*. (H. Zimmern, Trans.). Teddington, UK: Echo Library. (Original work published 1886)

Romanyshyn, R. D. (2007). *The wounded researcher: Research with soul in mind*. New Orleans, LA: Spring Journal Books.

Rowland, S. (2008). Introduction. In Susan Rowland (Ed.), *Psyche and the arts: Jungian approaches to music, architecture, literature, film and painting*. (pp. 2-11). London: Routledge.

Rowland, S. (2010). *C.G. Jung in the humanities: Taking the soul's path*. New Orleans, LA: Spring Journal Books.

Tate, N. (n.d.). (Original quote published 1680) Retrieved December 5, 2010, from http://www.enotes.com/literary-criticism/tate-nahum.

Wilde, O. (n.d.). *The Nightingale and the Rose*. (Original work published 1888) Retrieved December 5, 2010, from http://classiclit.about.com/library/bl-etexts/owilde/bl-owilde-nigh.htm.

Chapter 13

Art and Intersubjectivity

by Linda Carter

Introduction

The interaction of multiple complex systems is the source of the creative soul. The dynamism of mutual influence gives rise to emergent possibilities in the co-created third. In the context of the analytic dyad, psyche finds multiple modes of expression through word and image, dream and cognition. Relationship is co-constructed over time and new patterns of being and experiencing oneself as a member of the natural world emerges.

Here, I seek to bring together the art of psychotherapy with contemporary attachment science and the use of a painting by Leonardo da Vinci as an amplification of the therapeutic process. The clinical approach interweaves Jungian theories of image and archetype with intersubjective psychoanalysis with its focus on relational interaction in the analytic dyad. These different points of view are held together by Complex Adaptive Systems theory which focuses on the emergence of change in scale free networks; these are bottom up embedded systems such as the mind emerging from the brain which is embedded in multiple relational networks from the beginning of life. The baby/patient is influenced by the mother/analyst and the mother/analyst is influenced by the baby/patient in an embedded bidirectional system of mutual influence.

Case Study

The phone rang on a hot summer day. On the other end of the line was Helena who was calling while walking her 5-week-old baby on the boulevard, a local greenway in our small city. I could picture where she was. With the baby screaming in the background, she managed to tell me that she was struggling and wanted to be in therapy. Helena had heard about me 10 years ago from a former patient of mine who she had met when they both were hospitalized for depression. She wanted something different. For seven years Helena had been engaged in Cognitive Behavioral Therapy that was very helpful but recently her much-loved therapist had moved to the West Coast.

The transference and countertransference between Helena and I began before we met in the consulting room. She must have had imaginings of me from what she had heard, and I was positively disposed given my attachment to the patient who referred her.

From the first session, it was clear that Helena was overwhelmed. Her baby, Tanya, never stopped crying and didn't sleep; Helena was exhausted, depleted and run down. Her husband James was loving and supportive but only *she* could nurse the baby. The system was in crisis and in a constant state of dysregulation. At every level, resources were limited. It seemed that interventions were needed at multiple levels to steady the ship.

Helena readily agreed to come in 3-4 times a week, not for analysis, per se, but for help and support with regulation. She and James came in about 5 times not for couple's therapy but to try to strategize how to manage and support each other through this period of crisis. Eventually, I referred them to a couple's therapist for treatment. Further, I suggested that they participate in the local "crying clinic" whose goal is to help families with just a situation like theirs. With encouragement she joined a mothers' group and she, herself, initiated contact with a lactation consultant.

I was in action mode trying to assist her in finding resources to help with this overwhelming situation. At another level, I heard a voice from long ago saying: "Mother the mother." This was something I had learned working in a therapeutic nursery 30 years before. I deeply believed that this was a fundamental truth. I could offer a mothering presence to Helena.

From very early on, in my mind, I saw images of the Leonardo *Virgin and Child with St. Anne* (1498/1503) which you see below. This image was a powerful presence that accompanied each hour. I held back on talking about it or showing the picture to Helena. I needed time to metabolize and understand its significance for me and for the therapy. The image wafted through my mind like a thread of music; it was visceral, palpable, real and alive.

FIGURE 1. *Virgin and Child with St. Anne by Leonardo da Vinci, 1503.*
Leonardo da Vinci [Public domain], via Wikimedia Commons. Image obtained on 8/8/16.
https://en.wikipedia.org/wiki/The _ Virgin _ and _ Child _ with _ St. _ Anne _ (Leonardo)

In the meantime, Helena's moods were labile, shifting from one day to the next. She would feel fine and then abruptly shift into irritability, anger, depression and anxiety. However, even from the early days of treatment, Helena was able to settle into the therapy hour. She could use the relationship to calm down and feel comforted. Beebe's and Lachmann's (2002 p. 26) concept of mutual regulation was present and evident in noticeable decreases in anxiety, rate of speech and general distress. She was able to come closer to my more regulated state of being.

It unfolded that Helena has a significant history of depression, including psychiatric hospitalizations, and that she had tried a myriad of medications that she felt didn't work. Besides, she was breast feeding and didn't want to take any medicine. However, over time, I could see her depression deepening, and I was concerned that she had bipolar disorder and was being profoundly affected by hormones. I talked with her about this possibility. Eventually, she agreed to consultation with a very sensitive and thoughtful psychiatrist whom she has come to trust and value. Together, they settled on a combination of Zoloft and Lamictal which seem to work well for her.

As you can see, I was attempting to weave a network that would hold Helena and her baby. She was my patient but I was constantly aware of Tanya and her well-being. Helping them develop a secure attachment was what I was hoping for and it seemed that the best way to forge this connection was for Helena and me to develop our own significant attachment. Thoughts of earned secure attachment were in my mind. Given her history of trauma, I wondered if she had experienced an insecure attachment that could be moved toward earned security.

Earned security is a research term that has evolved through the administration of the Adult Attachment Interview (AAI). The AAI was developed by George, Kaplan and Main in 1984 and is made up of 20 questions; it takes an hour to administer and responses are recorded verbatim. Both coherence and content are evaluated by trained coders of this standardized test. It is used to describe a group of subjects who can speak coherently and collaboratively but who describe their parents as unloving (Hesse, 2008, p. 586). Their level of narrative coherence puts them in the secure-autonomous group but they differ in terms of deficits in the parental loving aspects of the AAI (ibid.).

Helena related well to me and could tell her stories of a traumatic early life with coherence and a sense of connectedness. Nevertheless, she tended to compartmentalize painful memories and limit time spent in discussing them. There was a natural affinity between us with an easy pattern of conversation. I found her bright, intelligent, motivated, curious, beautiful and thoughtful. She had good capacity for thinking psychologically, although reflecting through a depth perspective that was new to her. She had lots of questions about what I think, how I work, what methods I use, etc. Although I ask why she questions me at a given moment, I answer her. I feel that she needs grounding and a way to understand what is happening. Role models for how to be in a securely attached relationship with give and take seem to be quite limited. She needs to know how I think and how my mind works. I don't share personal history with her but I do tell her about how I understand what is happening between us. It has been clear that she is working on developing what Fonagy calls theory of mind and mentalization (2005). By exploring my mind, she is struggling to understand her own and to further develop reflective function.

As I have come to know her family history and relationships with parents, it's clear that Helena suffered significant trauma throughout her childhood. For the first six years of her life, Helena and her parents lived in a Communist controlled Eastern European country where she lived in close proximity to her paternal grandparents and extended family. Resources were sparse but she was part of a community where neighbors were friends and knew each other well. When the family moved to New England, her mother's birthplace, she lost the close connection with her grandmother and she lost the sense of belonging that comes with community.

They moved to an isolated area in Northern New England where they had no social contacts or sense of belonging. Both parents worked and her father's rages began. To this day, there are holes in the walls where he had thrown things. Helena was terrified of this behavior and frustrated that mother did nothing to protect them. Her mother began to drink and was affectively unavailable.

Helena's mother herself had a significant history of traumatic loss. At 17, she watched her brother drown, and within a week, Helena's grandmother suffered a fatal heart attack. In addition, Helena's mother had a first child born retarded who was placed in an institution and died at age ten. Helena was born somewhere between one and two years following the birth of this impaired older brother. One wonders if Helena experienced her mother as a "dead mother," to use Andre Green's terminology (Kohon 1999). One is also reminded of the replacement child concept first articulated by Cain and Cain (1964) relating to parents' failure to mourn the death of one child before having another.

Helena survived this difficult background through intelligence and capacity to do well in school. Teachers liked her and appreciated her significant talents and capabilities. Further, she was athletically inclined and showed an aptitude for acting. She got into an Ivy League school and left home.

College was difficult for Helena. She suffered crippling depression and was hospitalized on several occasions. Eventually, she withdrew from school as going forward was not possible. Meeting James seems to have been a turning point. Ten years older, he was mature, established and he thought she was wonderful. They forged a substantial and loving relationship. Helena finished school, worked successfully for several years in sociology research and then was accepted to graduate school. It seems that the relationship with James offered a platform from which she could launch into new aspects of her life.

It was through the relationship with James that a door opened for a new kind of attachment. He was steady, faithful and available—all welcome and new to Helena. They began to develop a secure base, a home and a way of living.

The history was reported in the midst of daily crises with sleeplessness, crying, and disruptions in the marriage. She was physically uncomfortable, her body hurt, and she related stories of the traumatic birth and caesarian section, a procedure that she did not expect. How could anyone understand what she had been through? And now, she had a screaming and demanding baby to care for who was five weeks when therapy began.

Leonardo's image of mother and child persisted in my mind along with the hope for a movement from insecure to an earned secure attachment capacity. Theory and image emerged through interaction with Helena. As we found a rhythm and way of being together in the implicit domain, I had a sense that we were contained within a co-created archetypal atmosphere symbolized by the image of *The Virgin and Child with St. Anne* (1503). There was something primal happening between us that was at the same time particular and unique to this new, emerging relationship. I would come to realize that the St. Anne stimulated a hope for coherence that was much needed by Helena and by the two of us in the analytic dyad. [I will henceforth refer to the images of *The Virgin and Child with St. Anne* in short hand as "the St. Anne."]

St. Anne, the Virgin and Child by Leonardo

Through my early experiences with Helena, I didn't realize that Leonardo had done both a sketch called a cartoon, known as the "Burlington House Cartoon," (1498) located at the National Gallery in London and separately a painting located at the Louvre which is similar in content but differs in detail. Before learning these facts, I saw in my mind Mary seated on the lap of St. Anne caring for the baby Jesus. The image had a sense of substantiality, support, presence. Perhaps, *I* needed this image in the background in order to support Helena who was on the front line with an upset baby.

FIGURE 2. *BURLINGTON HOUSE CARTOON BY LEONARDO DA VINCI, 1498.*
LEONARDO DA VINCI [PUBLIC DOMAIN], VIA WIKIMEDIA COMMONS. IMAGE OBTAINED ON
8/8/16. HTTPS://EN.WIKIPEDIA.ORG/WIKI/THE _ VIRGIN _ AND _ CHILD _ WITH _ ST _
ANNE _ AND _ ST _ JOHN _ THE _ BAPTIST

When I researched these pictures I felt captivated by their profundity. They are primal, gripping as they capture both the intensity of attachment and the struggle with separation.

The archetype of attachment and separation is fundamental for all; it is inescapable as a pivotal axis for life and relationship. This core dynamic configuration can be characterized through process and structure both of which profoundly influence intra-psychic development and coherence *and* interpersonal relationship systems throughout the lifespan. Research regarding security of attachment has helped us to appreciate the quality of interaction in adult psychotherapy.

We know from research by Beebe and Lachmann (2002), Tronick (2007) and others that security of attachment at four months predicts security of attachment at a year. Attachment at a year predicts young adult attachment. Internal working models are laid down early and affect the contours and quality of relationships going forward. Many of our patients have not had the substantial secure base that Leonardo so well conveys.

Attachment is not a diagnosis but a research description. We can imagine what a patient *may* have experienced and we can reflect on the quality of the current attachment capacity. Understanding that there is a human inclination to repeat interactional patterns allows us to infer what may have happened historically. We can use attachment designations phenomenologically as a way to appreciate a patient's way of being with themselves and another in current circumstances.

Amplification

As a way to think about this case and as a way to think about attachment in general, I suggest that we consider the St. Anne painting and cartoon as visual amplifications. These fundamental images resonate at the personal, cultural and collective levels of the psyche and remind us of the creative roots of human experience through artwork, clinical practice and science.

The sculptural, pyramidal shape of the figures conveys solidity and substantiality. Together the figures form a triangular mountain mimicked by the mountains in the background of the painted version. A structure is created through the interweaving of bodies; and simultaneously we can observe dynamic process and movement.

Touch and physical contact weave the figures together into a whole. Complex emotions are evoked as we watch St. Anne look on as her daughter attends to Jesus who moves out from his mother's grasp; he is held by her but is moving toward John the Baptist in the Cartoon and the lamb in the painting. Both imply the future destiny of his passion, death and resurrection where he joins his father in heaven. Mary is left to mourn the death of her beloved son. (One thinks here of the *Pieta*.) In the Cartoon St. Ann points to heaven with her left hand reminding us that the father may not be visible but is eternally present. We are reminded, here, of the archetypal role of father who often leads the way to separation between mother and child. These symbols together convey the complexity of mutually influencing nested systems where separation and attachment play out side-by-side through body, affect, interaction, presence and absence.

From his prolific writing we learn that Leonardo had an approach to sketches and drawings that we would today think of as working with the implicit domain, that which is known, felt and experienced usually outside conscious, verbal interaction. Leonardo sketched in order to capture the psychological state and feeling tone of his work and carefully followed up later with technical aspects of the construction. This approach to the sketch is evident in his own words as follows:

> Now have you never thought about how poets compose their verse? They do not trouble to trace beautiful letters nor do they mind crossing out several lines so as to make them better. So, painter, rough out the arrangement of the limbs of your figures and first attend to the movements appropriate to the mental state of the creatures that make up your picture rather than the beauty and perfection of their parts.

Leonardo in Gombrich 1966, p.59

Further he says: "Sketch subject pictures quickly and do not give the limbs too much finish: indicate their position, which you can then work out at your leisure" (ibid., p. 60). (See sketch for the Cartoon below)

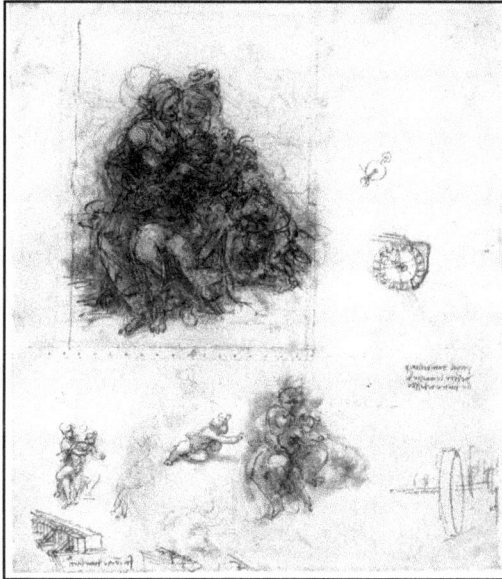

FIGURE 3. *SKETCH OF THE BURLINGTON.*
HOUSE CARTOON BY LEONARDO DA VINCI, 1498.
WIKIART IMAGE OBTAINED ON 8/8/16. HTTP://WWW.WIKIART.ORG/EN/
LEONARDO-DA-VINCI/STUDY-FOR-THE-BURLINGTON-HOUSE-CARTOON-
THE-VIRGIN-AND-CHILD-WITH-ST-ANNE-AND-ST-JOHN-THE-
I?UTM _ SOURCE=RETURNED&UTM _ MEDIUM=REFERRAL&UTM _
CAMPAIGN=REFERRAL

Study for Burlington House Cartoon

Notice in the Cartoon that the hands and the feet of the Virgin and St. Anne are not well articulated or specific. They are delineated in the more polished painting. However, in the Cartoon and lead up sketches, Leonardo successfully captures the mood arising from dynamic interplay of the characters. As onlookers we engage with the artist in a symbolically dense network layered with emotional, psychological and religious significance. Leonardo explicitly and implicitly played with this complex archetypal constellation through multiple preliminary sketches that convey fluidity of motion and a willingness to experiment with material expression of his internal experience.

Gombrich notes that

> Leonardo could induce in himself a state of dream-like loosening of controls in which the imagination began to play with blots and irregular shapes, and that these shapes in turn helped Leonardo to enter a kind of trance in which his inner visions could be projected onto external objects...the indeterminate has to rule the sketch ...to stimulate the mind to further inventions...The sketch is no longer the preparation for a particular work, but is part of a process which is constantly going on in the artist's mind; instead of fixing the flow of imagination it keeps it in flux.

> (Ibid. p. 61)

One is reminded, here, of the analyst's state of reverie or evenly hovering attention underscoring the importance of not foreclosing analytic experience with the fixity of premature interpretation. Play with image allows for dreaming the dream onward and this comes with a more phenomenal and descriptive approach. Through these images we are affected by the implicit domain and are brought into a moment of the transcendent function as we respond psychologically, physically and emotionally to the visual network of a complex archetypal system.

One sees a familiar image and is drawn in by the complexity of the interwoven relationships and, in a sense, we become part of the system depicted by virtue of our engagement with the gestalt and the particulars. We can zoom in for a closer look or move back in order to appreciate the whole which is something that also happens in analysis.

Leonardo's play with sketching seems to be his method for capturing what we would call a kind of implicit knowing. Language and interpretation are not required for an implicit understanding by the artist or the viewer. We come to semantic reflections secondarily to one's initial visceral response. This is similar to Leonardo's approach to sketching whereby he first captures a feeling through making an image and follows up with the technical know-how required for the finished work. Both an artist and an engineer, he was adept at coordinating right and left hemispheres.

As is well known, Freud wrote a small book called *A Childhood Reminiscence of Leonardo da Vinci* (1916) using it as a means to analyze Leonardo based on his great interest in the St. Anne painting at the Louvre. He did make cultural/historical leaps but evaluated the painting in relation to what he imagined to be Leonardo's personal psychology. Freud saw, in the drapery of the skirts of Anne and Mary, a vulture. This observation, he associated with a childhood description by Leonardo of being attacked in infancy by a vulture.

FIGURE 4. *St. Anne and
St. Mary with image of vulture.*

Jung (1959/1977, 9i, para. 93) has commented, as follows, on Freud's book:

> ...interwoven with the apparently personal psychology there is an interpersonal motif known to us from other fields. This is the motif of the dual mother, an archetype to be found in many variants in the field of mythology and comparative religion and forming the basis of numerous collective representations.

Jung argues that Leonardo "was in all probability representing the mythological dual-mother motif and by no means his own personal prehistory." Further, he asks: "What about all the other artists who painted the same theme? Surely not all of them had two mothers" (ibid., para 95)?

I would like to call attention to Leonardo's subtle method of painting called *sfumato* as it affects how we engage with his art outside conscious awareness. *Sfumato* comes from the Italian *sfumare* meaning "to tone down" or "to evaporate" or "to evaporate like smoke." In painting and drawing it has to do with "the fine shading that produces soft, imperceptible transitions between colors and tones" (http://www.britannica.com/search?query=sfumato, accessed March 19, 2013).

Gombrich notes that *sfumato* is:

> Leonardo's famous invention...the blurred outline and mellowed colors that allow one form to merge with another and always leave the viewer something to our imagination, (http://painting.about.com/od/oldmastertechniques/a/sfumato_chiar).

According to Alexander Nagel, *sfumato* "describes not merely the appearance of smoke but its disappearance, its imperceptible diffusion in the atmosphere" (1993, p. 7). This invention also had to do with the application of translucent glazes in delicate films no more than the thickness of a red blood cell, probably with his finger. With 30 of these films stacked one on the other, he "softened lines and color gradations until it seemed as if the entire composition lay behind a veil of smoke" (Pringle 2013, p. 38).

This refined method of transition from light to dark or dark to light engages our imagination and reminds us again of the liminal states well known to us in the practice of analysis. There is a holding together of the opposites with an almost imperceptible transition. This method may account for the minute, yet powerful expression of Mona Lisa's smile that could be likened to capturing a slight facial expression that implicitly registers and has an effect but is only consciously visible through a frame of micro-processed videotape such as the infant researchers use.

Through content, form, fluidity of movement, color and refined technique, *The Virgin and Child with St Anne* pictures came to symbolize for me the archetypal foundation of the therapeutic relationship as it emerged with Helena. This image entered my conscious awareness as a co-creation that floated through the therapeutic atmosphere of this particular relationship giving form and shape to unconscious and non-conscious interactions.

I didn't specifically talk about the pictures until six months into the treatment at a moment when Helena and I were feeling especially connected. In retrospect, I realize that I was waiting for her to feel a sense of attachment between us before talking about the St. Anne pictures. Otherwise, it could not have had an affective influence on her or could even have felt foreign and alienating. For a successful amplification, the image must match the archetypal pattern present in the dyad at a given moment and there must necessarily be an affective match with the story or image and an affective match in the therapeutic relationship. With such multi-level engagement comes a sense of coherency of self over time (Siegel 2007, p. 207). We could liken this process to a kind of multi-modal matching seen in infant research.

I was matching an unspoken state of being in a co-created atmosphere to an image that I felt carried a similar emotional valence. One is reminded here of the subtle atmosphere and liminality created between darkness and light with *sfumato*. I could see that this visual amplification had landed with a slight smile on Helena's face, not unlike that of the Mona Lisa. She was immediately curious and wanted to see the picture which I showed her in the following session.

The use of myth, story and imagery open possibilities for metaphoric, non-linear, ambiguous play in the space "in between." Moving from the personal to the collective is a move to another layer of the mutually influencing system.

When intersubjective matching is activated in the co-constructed dyad and there is a true sense of affective resonance (this is critical), the vibration reaches to and is felt at the archetypal level. The image that evolves "in between" represents a synthesis of the interaction of two minds, two bodies, two psyches meeting consciously, unconsciously and non-consciously in a "dyadic state of consciousness," a "moment of meeting," as the "transcendent function." We struggle to find words to describe the experience. Perhaps that is why the indirectness of metaphor is so valuable. Metaphor presents in pictures, possibilities, undefined images and allows for the mystery of the unknown.

Amplification when used well is itself an art. It is not necessarily employed with *explicit intentionality* but is instead an *emergent phenomenon* that captures the essence of a psychological constellation. It connects the personal and the archetypal and should be presented tentatively as an option—a possibility to be entertained, something to be played with. With careful attention to the analysand's explicit and implicit responses, engagement in metaphorical language and image has the potential to connect body and mind within the containing relationship.

Play with metaphor has an organizing effect and can regulate the two hemispheres of the brain. This is particularly important for patients who are survivors of trauma. My hope for the therapy with Helena, herself a survivor of early relational trauma, was that we could move toward earned security, a research term that seemed to me to have significant clinical implications.

Clinical Case

Helena enters each hour looking exhausted and immediately gets out a blanket from the sofa, wraps herself in it and frequently comments that she would like to stay in my office and sleep. It is as if she brings her baby self to be cared for and nurtured before again facing the demands of the academic world and the ongoing demands of mothering a toddler.

Disruptions have occurred around late cancellations and she has become furious with me; on one occasion when she was particularly stressed, she suggested that we discontinue the treatment. She has had to face that I, too, have limits and get frustrated. However, I have encouraged her to continue and have owned my participation in conflicts which has then freed her to reflect on her own participation. Successful disruption and repair has not been part of her relational repertoire. At one moment, I apologized to Helena and I could see a very slight smile as she looked down and took in what I said. A moment of connection ensued thus giving the feeling of a moment of meeting.

Through these moments of distress that are attended to and discussed, layer by layer, we have begun to build an earned securely attached relationship. I would like to talk about the value and some of the liabilities of using this concept clinically.

The move toward me as a safe haven began early in the therapy when Helena would become extremely dysregulated with volatile emotional surges and angry behavior towards James. She would leave the house sometimes with the baby and call me. In retrospect, she believes that these phone connections and availability laid the groundwork for a substantial trusting relationship between us. She could experience a secure base in the midst of terrifying fears and feelings. Through conversation and the archetypal presence of the holding symbolized by St. Anne, she could settle and return home because the screaming baby inside herself had found a place to land.

It seems to me that the content of what I said was not as important as my consistent presence in the implicit domain. The hope was that my ability to tolerate her screaming baby self helped her to cope with and better regulate Tanya. If so, the system could then move from fragmentation to coherency over time (Siegel, 2007, p. 207).

It has been important for Helena that I recognize not just her trauma, despair and depression all of which cause her great shame; she has needed me to see the alive, creative aspects of herself and her being. An interesting pattern has emerged between us that I would like to describe. At times when Helena has been in a very dark place tearfully describing painful childhood memories, she will look down, stop, then look up and ask me something about art or literature. I ask her about this surprising switch and she makes it clear that what she has been talking about is just too painful. Clearly, she needs a reprieve. On one occasion, she asked me if I had seen a show at the Metropolitan Museum of Art in New York called *The Steins Collect*. I responded that I had and a very animated conversation ensued. As part of the exhibit, the interior of the Stein's salon with all of its artwork was projected onto three walls giving the feeling of going back in time to see how the art was actually hung. I commented that it was as if we had gone to the museum together through the course of our conversation.

With the transition, we had entered another room, another kind of imaginal domain and way of being. Helena smiled in agreement. There was a moment of shared pleasure, recognition of each other through the medium of the artwork. We could say that the shift was defensive and that is true but it may have been appropriately defensive in that she and I both need to help her protect against becoming re-traumatized by overwhelming memories and affects. Most importantly, she could see herself in another light by watching me see her in this creative space between us. She could see me recognize healthy aspects of herself. Thoughts of the building of reflective function come to mind here. Also, through change in topic the system moved to a more regulated state and managed to stay within the Window of Tolerance developed by Siegel that Pat

Ogden talks about in *Trauma and the Body: A Sensorimotor Approach to Psychotherapy* (2006).

The St. Anne image emerged in the context of this particular relationship at a given moment in time. The fabric of the attachment has been woven with moments of meeting including disruption and repair. The BCPSG note that "A moment of meeting occurs when the dual goals of complementary fitted actions and intersubjective recognition are suddenly realized" (p. 33). The subtlety of the implicit domain that is primarily nonverbal has been balanced by more language based interpretation but like Leonardo's method of sketching, we need to fully experience the creative process affectively before technique or words can be found to fit the process itself.

Visual metaphor and use of amplification create an ambience, an atmosphere that allows for experience of both archetypal process and structure where there is room for the fluidity of change and the reliability of continuity (Sander 2002, 14-15). Helena and I continue on with connection, disruption and repair. We speak of trauma and art, her outer relationships and her internal experience. Together we tend both the transference/countertransference relationship along with here and now emerging, new and creative ways of being together within mutually influencing nested systems. Creativity seems to me to be an emergent property of interactions within individuals, with outer others and with the natural world.

References

Beebe, B. and Lachmann, F. (2002). *Infant Research and Adult Treatment*, Hillsdale, N.J.: The Analytic Press.

Boston Change Process Study Group (2010). *Change in Psychotherapy a Unifying Paradigm.* New York: W.W. Norton and Company.

Cain, A. C., and B. S. Cain. (1964). On Replacing a Child. *Journal of the American Academy of Child Psychiatry* 3, 443–456. Read more: http://www.deathreference.com/Py-Se/Replacement-Children.html#ixzz3whkdnk2o

Freud, S. (1916/1990). *Leonardo da Vinci and a Memory of his Childhood, Standard Edition.* New York: W. W. Norton and Company.

Fonagy Gombrich, E.H. (1966) Leonardo's Method for Working Composi-
tions in *Norm and Form: Studies in the Art of the Renaissance.* London: Phaidon Press.

Hesse, E. (2008). "The Adult Attachment Interview: Protocol, Methods of
Analysis, and Empirical Studies." in *Handbook of Attachment: Theo-
ry, Research, and Clinical Applications,* J. Cassidy and R. Shaver, eds.
New York: The Guilford Press.

Jung, C. G. (1959/1977). *CW* 9i.

Kohon, G. (1999). *The Dead Mother: The Work of Andre Green.* New York:
Routledge.

Lyons-Ruth, C. and Carlson, Nagel, A. (1993). Leonardo and Sfumato. *Res
24: Anthropology and Aesthetics. Autumn.* The Getty Center for the
History of Art

Ogden, P., et al. (2006). *Trauma and the Body: A Sensorimotor Approach to Psychotherapy.* New York: W. W. Norton and Company.

Pringle, H. (2013). The Origins of Creativity. *Scientific American: Mind.*
Vol.23, issue 1s.

Sander, L.W. (2002). Thinking differently: principles of process in living
systems and the specificity of being known, *Psychoanalytic Dialogues,* 12, 1:11-42.

Siegel, D. (2015). *The Developing Mind (Second Edition).* New York: The Guilford Press.

Tronick, E. (2007). *The Neurobehavioral and Social-Emotional Development of
Infants and Children,* New York: W. W. Norton & Company.

Butoh: the dance of being, a Jungian interpretation

by Anna Maria Costantino

Introduction

In this chapter some of *Butoh*'s features are compared to basic elements of Jung's thinking (shadow, antinomy, active imagination). Especially highlighted is how this dance can be considered a real path to individuation in Jungian terms. The *Butoh* dance can be conceived as the dance of being because dancing is necessary to look deep inside the self, into the unconscious, to confront the shadow. The shadow, as we shall see, is fundamental in Jung's thinking; it is the inferior layer of the personal unconscious, the dark and unknown aspects of personality. It embodies all we deny, or it is primitive, unsuitable in ourselves. It is by diving into these dark areas that the *Butoh* dancer begins his dance and regains the wholeness of the self.

The first time I witnessed *Butoh* dance the emotional intensity left me in tears. In front of me a convulsing figure slowly rose to the sky and collapsed violently back to the earth. Painted white and dressed in tatters, the figure looked like a ghost, like a being come undone. Every tiny movement sprung organically into the next; her finger, toes, arms and legs growing out into space, only to come shriveling back inwards as her life faded away. After a time, death seemed to have claimed the dance and all was still. I felt my heart beating slower, my limbs aching in sympathetic strain. But then the dancer stirred again transcending the pain to greet the dawn with a smile.

In time I realized I was witnessing the process of death and rebirth, of struggle and transcendence. I noticed my breath had slowed and a strange calm had descended. I started, unblinking, at the vision before me (Roquet, 2003 p. 1).

A *Butoh* dance performance is distinct from any other dance show. It makes even the audience transformed. Attending this intense art performance, the audience becomes deeply involved in an emotional atmosphere, in which both dancers and spectators share a unique experience free of intellectual ideologies and judgments.

> Even watching *Butoh* causes a deep sympathetic response in the depths of the body. Stilling the Ego, buried emotions rise up to trigger a deep, cleansing catharsis. The conscious mind is calmed and emptied, but the memories stored in the body awaken and vibrate with the energy of dancer on stage. (ibid., 2003, p. 3)

Butoh dance necessarily involves self-consciousness; it is not a body expression imposed by external rules, specific choreography or a quest for harmony in movements, it rather springs from the inner self disclosing its emotions. *Butoh* is an art form of undefined boundaries of great psychological interest.

History of *Butoh*

Butoh dancing started following the profound crisis that ravaged Japan after the Second World War. The country was war-torn, devastated by the atomic bomb. In just a few years its ancient culture was disrupted and its ethnic and religious values yielded to modernity. Facing new cultural western models young people abandoned their old identity.

In this new transition many artists did introspective work searching for their lost identity and opened themselves to the unknown trying to make contact with the world of the dead and with their own land, now made radioactive. In this *humus, Butoh* dance arose as opposition not only to the westernization tendencies but also to the traditional, conformist and reactionary Japanese culture.

Butoh dance scandalized Japan at the time it was developed. The anticonformist attitude of the dancers and the themes portrayed on stage (poverty, homosexuality, sodomy) caused this form of dance to remain on the fringes of Japanese society. Nevertheless, when in the 1980s *Butoh* was brought to Europe, it was a big success. Only in 1985 *Butoh* was officially accepted in Japan when the first *Butoh* festival was held in Tokyo.

When Tatsumi Hijikata and Kazuo Ōno in the 1950s began to improvise the first dances, they created a big turmoil. In 1959 the first *Butoh* performance was on stage: *"Kinji"* (Banned Colors). The title was taken from Yukio Mishima's book. The performance of just five minutes overruled all the accepted dancing conventional elements: just two scenes, no music, no lights, no rules or techniques and no aestheticisms.

The performance, addressing the issue of homosexuality, was a scandal. At that time homosexuality was absolutely taboo. It was the first time that a dance addressed this alternative side of human existence. *Butoh*, considered a countercultural dance, became the reference point of the avant-garde movements. It introduced a new sensitivity, offered a return to the origins, a more authentic way of being and feeling, opposing the affluent society.

Two are the founders of this dance: Tatsumi Hijikata, who in 1960 introduced the Ankoku *Butoh* (dance of darkness) creating a particular and unique method, and Kazuo Ōno who gave voice to light and consciousness. From their collaboration stemmed the first generation of *Butoh* dancers, of whom Ōno is the greatest interpreter.

Butoh dance

In *Butoh* the creative process and body conception, common to the traditional Japanese dance-theater and the classic western ballet, are irrelevant. *Butoh* is not concerned with the search for balance, the continuity of the movements, the search for beauty and aesthetics; nor does it comply with the conventional method used to guide the dance steps. In *Butoh* the dancer is not an executer and his body is not conceived as an interpreter of previously defined emotions. The body is no longer seen as an encumbrance. There is no need to improve technicality in order to achieve the style longed for.

The dance is not generated by the search for shape, beauty or harmony, but it is characterized by the loss of these features. It is conceived as the "natural body," the necessity to be. The movements are not adherent to stage directions but are determined by desire and instinct. They are not the result of practicing but come from within the self. It is very important for the body not to be tense but relaxed: an empty body, a dead body that warrants emotions to be revealed, ready for any metamorphosis.

> The body needs to be transparent to show how time has molded it...*Butoh* is the physical representation of the individual's traits, of the places he has lived in, of the influence of the environment on his behavior, education and life experiences. At a subconscious level the body's past experiences cannot be changed from the exterior. (D'Orazi, 2001, p. 18, p. 92)

The *Butoh* dancer is forced to look inside himself and listen to himself, express his Self through movements that may be considered to be horrible (Roquet, 2003). Tremors, tics, retroversion of the pupils, facial sprains, imbalanced and discontinuous movements are key instruments to analyze the unconscious.

Butoh dancers, often paint their bodies white: this color favors loss of form, of identity and gets rid of one's body boundaries. The dancers through their white painted bodies and their nakedness, want to undress themselves of everything and wear the cosmos, in an endless search for the "natural body," in harmony with the universe.

They don't want to escape gravity, but to descend into the earth vault to explore darkness, the mysteries of the earth and of existence.

FIGURE 1. *Photo of Anna Costantino taken at "Cantieri Culturali alla Zisa"* (Palermo, 2014) by photographer Alessandro D'Amico.

The body, no longer bound to "good manners" or social values, is free to expand. Through dance, shadows of hidden identities arise. Hijikata says: "the dancer, through the *Butoh* spirit, confronts the origins of his fears: a dance which crawls towards the bowels of the earth" (Viala & Masson, 1988, p. 188).

The Japanese psychologist Toshiharu Kasai, teacher of dance therapy based on *Butoh* principles, says that *Butoh* "is not only a performing art but also a way of exploring the mind/body relationship" (Kasai, 2000, p. 353). He proposed the "*Butoh* method for psychosomatic exploration" using some of the dancer's training exercises as a tool for psychosomatic exploration and integration. Kasai says that:

> *Butoh* may have liberating effects on the mind-body at various levels. On a very basic level *Butoh* promotes exploration of the impulses that we all (perhaps annoyingly, perhaps unwittingly) restrict: the need to scratch an inappropriately located itch,

the desire to sprawl out instead of sitting appropriately upright, or whatever one's particular culture may restrict or frown upon. On a deeper level, however, the psychosomatic exploration of *Butoh* exercises can have profoundly transformative effects; it allows people to live their naturally arising emotions such as anger, depression, sorrow, fear, joy, etc and it can be highly therapeutic. (Kasai, 2003, pp. 262-263)

In fact, psychologically, *Butoh* has transformative potentials that make it unique and different from other forms of art, placing it in an area of fuzzy boundaries but of considerable psychological interest.

I have proposed a Jungian interpretation of *Butoh* because of the many similarities with the Jungian theory. I will compare and examine in detail some of the elements of *Butoh* such as darkness, the *Butoh-Fu*, the dead body and other basic features of Jung's thinking, particularly antinomy, the transcendent function and the active imagination. *Butoh* dance can be considered a profound path toward individuation.

Dancing the darkness

The concepts of shadow and darkness, developed by Tatsumi Hijikata, underlie *Butoh* in its conception and method. With the term *Ankoku Butoh* or Dance of Darkness, Hijikata wanted to underline the belief that the dance, as the highest expression of vital energies, is "needed to search and find its roots in the dark depths of the body" (Salerno, 1998, p. 166).

In agreement with the avant-garde spirit common to the artists of that postwar period, Hijikata, opposing the traditional formalism, puts on stage everything that the dominant culture considers vulgar and therefore to be suppressed, repressed and hidden: people that dwell on the fringes of society, prostitutes, tramps, criminals, drunks, naked bodies painted in white, squats, close to the ground. He tries to retrieve the "humans' inherent ecological connection with the soil" (Roquet, 2003, p. 62).

Hijikata appears to give voice to what Jung calls "Shadow," that is the dark side of conscious life. In his research Hijikata begins to confront himself with his own shadow and goes back in time to the "unsocialized life of childhood" (ibid., 2003, p. 36). When the link between man and nature was still very strong "he became convinced that social conditioning contaminates the body and devised ways to work with the body and the body memory in order to eradicate this conditioning" (ibid., 2003, p. 32). His intention was to break all the schemes and to recover the more open and rational "natural body." Dancing allowed Hijikata to dive into the depths of anguish and into the deepest darkness to find the light; it was his way to be free from suffering, anxiety, fear, cultural contaminations.

Memories guide him to explore his body's memories: the harsh winters in Tohoku, the time that, as a child, he spent in lonely places in close contact with nature. He fell into a quagmire, experienced poverty and suffered pain following the loss of his older sister forced by his family into prostitution, followed by her death. Additionally, there was the death of all of his brothers in war. When Hijikata danced, all the violence he had known during his childhood and the devastation of war reappeared in his imagination. His sister danced with him, inside him and through him: "This sister he carried as a scar of the traumatic memories of his youth" (ibid., 2003, p. 36).

This is how he lived in relationship to death and defeated fear, creating a "corporeal dialogue" with his unconscious and with that shadow that Jung, in the text "The Self and the Unconscious" (*CW* 7, 1916-1928), describes as "the obscure brother," sometimes invisible, sometimes inseparable from ourselves and blended in as part of one's whole. In Hijikata's *Butoh* dance, as he strove to confront himself with the pains of his personal history and with the horrors of war, both the personal Shadow and the collective Shadow arise.

The personal Shadow enacts the shortcomings of one's own history and psychic traits that the environment tends to remove. The collective Shadow often is linked to the dark side of the archetypes and to evil.

FIGURE 2. *Photo of Sayoko Onishi taken at "Piccolo Teatro Patafisico"* (Palermo, 2014) by photographer Alessandro D'Amico.

Hijikata conceives dance as the need to break the shell formed by social habits which keep the body lagging behind the revolutions already accomplished. For him the body is not a means but an end not to be used to transmit ideas but, on the contrary, to question, to rethink, to recreate. Dance is not a linear composition, not a syntactical arrangement of body movements, but rather the exploration of the exemplary depth of the body itself; not a desire to pronounce a discourse, but to search for meaning. (Viala & Masson, 1988, p.64)

We find this connection between shadow and body in "The Psychology of Translation" (*CW* 16, 1946), where Jung says that knowing one's own Shadow makes a man corporeal. This statement, according to Marie von Franz (2004, p.29), suggests that discovering your own Shadow makes you earthly, more humble and less omnipotent. To dance the dance of Darkness it is necessary to dig into the unconscious, to confront ourselves with the Shadow; through dance the Shadows of hidden identities are revealed. The dance is not an end in itself, but it's a way to find one's self. In the light of all this, in Jung's *Psychology and Religion* (*CW* 11, 1938/1940), Jung says that:

> Each of us is followed by a shadow. The less it is built in the conscious life of an individual, the more black and dense it is... As such, this Shadow must be faced, it must be known even in its more painful and disturbing parts...We must accept it as our nocturnal side and...give her voice. By doing so, it will not act unconsciously and dangerously. (Jung, CWII, 1938/1940, pp. 82-84)

In some way Hijikata would say that we can dance with it. The shadow is, in fact, the first archetypal representation that we meet on the road of our inner life. Working with it opens the way to psychic transformation and the process of individuation.

The tension of the opposites

Antinomy or "the conflict between opposites that induces a superior synthesis" (Aversa, 1995, p. 62) is central to Jungian theory, but can also be found in the theories formulated by Ōno and Hijikata, as well as in the training techniques of the *Butoh* dancer. While Hijikata draws his inspiration from the suffering of his childhood, from the devastation of the war and perceives the world as being pervaded by darkness, obscurity and violence, Kazuo Ōno's dance draws the attention to light and consciousness and is characterized by the capacity to observe life. This way of thinking derives from his deep religiosity that makes him consider the dance as revelation of the Self. Through dancing he expresses the gratitude of being alive and part of this world.

Ōno sees unconscious God behind everything and his inspiration comes from his happy childhood memories, his mother, his hometown and the fish loving bears he used to see when he was a small child. Dance "highlights those simple features of life that we often disregard" (Salerno, 1998, p. 49). Starting from small details, from simple and everyday gestures, Ōno "is always in search of a link with the Universe making it possible for microcosm and macrocosm to meet" (Salerno, 1998, p. 49).

Butoh comes from the awareness that through dance it is possible to disclose the essence of nature. Ōno believes that it is impossible to describe a flower's beauty because nothing is more beautiful than the flower itself. It is possible, however, to express, while dancing, the astonishment in front of a flower: it is encountering life, it is the encounter with the flower's spirit. Dancing is not just a technique, it relates to our soul. Dancing is not moving the body but listening with our soul to the rhythm of the Universe, just as a child in the womb can hear the noises coming from outside (D'Orazi, 2001, pp. 39-40). For this reason Ōno calls his dance "the dance of the heart."

Ōno "lets in light and transparency in a world where death and pain are from the beginning the essence of one's life and finds...a road to redemption, in the deep appreciation of a man dancing because he is grateful to be alive" (D'Orazi, 2001, pp. 65-66). Hijikata's emphasis, instead, lies in his ability to transfer his long life pains into dance.

Thus, *Butoh* springs from the fusion between the "dance of darkness" and the "dance of the heart." Hijikata's and Ōno's beliefs and work, although profoundly antithetical, have bridged and found a synthesis of differing views and have created something more important. Without darkness there is no light and vice versa. Based on the same principle, Jung explains that confronting someone with his own Shadow brings out the light that is in one's Self.

The word *Butoh* is formed by two ideograms: *BU* and *TOH*. *BU* refers to the upper part of the body and is considered the link to heaven, to the Apollonian world. *TOH* refers to the lower part of the body, to the lower limbs, to the trampling of the feet on the ground and it is considered the link to the Earth and to the Dionysian world.

The first dichotomy that the dancer encounters is between mind and body. Only by going into a trance state the dancer can overcome this conflict, have access to the discovery of his body in relation to the Self, and then start dancing. To understand this process, the concept of "*Butoh-tai*" or "*Butoh Body*" is important. This is a state of consciousness that the dancer acquires progressively while dancing.

> It means acquiring a physical and mental attitude
> so as to integrate the dichotomized elements such
> as consciousness vs. unconsciousness and subject
> vs. object. The former is related to the multiplicity
> of our consciousness, and the latter to our "objecti-
> fying" mental function. (Kasay, 2000, p. 353)

Butoh-tai allows the integration of multiple aspects of consciousness and overcomes the conscious/unconscious dichotomy.

According to Jung, antinomy is the basis of all psychological processes and it is elaborated and over-ruled by the transcendent function that stays above the opposite poles of conscious and unconscious, favoring the passage from an old to a new attitude generating a synthesis. Antinomy, in fact, "makes it possible to the psychic flux to proceed, to transcend from one state to another, avoiding blockage, obstinacy, the impasse to the individuation process" (Aversa, 1999, p.62).

Similar processes are also present in *Butoh*: the work on the tension of opposite poles (mind/body, life/death, happiness/suffering, youth/senescence....) is completely overcome when the dancer reaches the state of trance and the dance really begins. Unlike other cultures, where trance is considered a way of dimming sensorial capacities, in the Japanese culture, Zen specifically, trance is considered a state when the increase in sensitivity makes the dancer very receptive and able to control his mind. In fact, before any performance, Hijikata and his followers used to endure a rigorous discipline of the body and a long starving period. This extreme physical condition allows to leave the state of conscience for an altered state of awareness, allowing the fusion of the objectified and the objectifying Self in a perturbed state of awareness.

FIGURE 3. *PHOTO TAKEN FROM THE VIDEO MEMORY OF THE PERFORMANCE "SAUDADE" OF ANNA COSTANTINO* (PALERMO 2015) BY VIDEOMAKER ROSANNA COSTANTINO

Hijikata explains that while he is about to sit, inside of him the ghost of his sister rises, generating in his body a conflict between opposite, antinomic tendencies. This condition, indeed, favors a state of trance: his dance begins.

Kazuo Ōno, instead, to allow his students to reach and have the perception of the unity between opposite poles, utilizes the metaphor of the spermatozoa. In a mother's uterus, in fact, only one sperm, among many, will be able to reach the egg. Therefore, at the origin of life, death and pain of the other spermatozoa occur. Ōno's dance expresses this tragedy and at the same time the joy of being alive.

> Sacrificing hundreds of millions of potential lives just for the only one able to complete its course, is something that stays with us, inside of us as memory, it is written in our DNA. (D'Orazi, 2001, p. 69)

> Transcendent function [Jung says] shall not be considered mysterious or suprasensorial or meta-physical, but just a psychological function resulting from the unification of conscious and unconscious contents. (Jung, CW 8, 1957/1958, p.83)

The transcendent function allows us to overcome the opposite poles and, as stated by Jolanda Jacobi, "it is like the psyche's transforming ability by mixing the opposite poles" (Jacobi, 1973, p.166). To reach this state the *Butoh* dancer must continuously confront himself with his Shadow, with "the vault of the Earth" and his body is in a state of crisis, suspended, in a continuous metamorphosis. For this reason "the condition that Hijikata was mostly interested in was the body in danger, the moment when the Self perception is at risk of dissolving" (Salerno, 1998, p. 38).

Hijikata states that while dancing it is very important to be tense and anxious so that the suspended body, while in crisis, is able to have tangible evidence of how fugacious life is, letting "the strong energies that influence the most obscure part of our Self flow: the desire to escape death" (ibid., 1998, p.38).

Being in crisis is also crucial in the psychological process. Facing the unconscious is not possible without undergoing a crisis. Jacobi affirms this,

> The flow of the unconscious into conscience...is a state of psychic disequilibrium, purposely induced in order to redeem any difficulty interfering with a

further development of the personality. It is an *ad hoc* disequilibrium, because...it allows the establishment of a new equilibrium only if the conscious will be able to blend and elaborate the impulses generated by the unconscious. (Jacobi, 1973, p. 157)

Butoh and Active Imagination

Active imagination is the method suggested by Jung to activate the transcendent function and favor a real dialogue between the conscious and the unconscious generating a new synthesis. Jung, in fact, as indicated by Andrew Samuels, believed in active imagination as "evidence of the transcendent function, or rather a collaboration between conscious and unconscious elements" (Samuels, 1987, p. 64).

The expression "active imagination"—as Renos Papadopoulos explains—"indicates an analytical method based on the underlying function of the psyche to produce images" (Papadopoulos, 2009, p. 339).

"The process implies focusing attention and curiosity in the interior world of the imagination and expressing it symbolically and, at the same time, searching for a psychological introspective viewpoint." The many creative figures of active imagination include the vision of the mind eyes, hypnagogic imageries emerging not only as visual impressions, but also as acoustic, motor or other somatosensory imageries; the interior dialog; the expression through one or more arts and the symbolic representation of the sand game and many others. (Papadopoulos, 2009, p. 331)

Papadopoulos indicates that the method is made of two parts. The first one is to let the unconscious emerge, the second is to come to terms with the unconscious. The process has a sequential nature even if there may be moments when the periods fluctuate back and forth or are present at the same time.

To favor the connection between the conscious and the unconscious, *Butoh* explores not only the trance state, *Butoh-tai* and other techniques, but also "the dead body" and "the dead gaze." The dead body is a way of allowing the self to come apart. To reach this condition it is possible to use the metamorphosis methodology from natural models which allow the dancer to reveal all what is human inside of him to become somebody different. Following this technique the dancer embodies different creatures or elements of nature in a never-ending variation of forms: now an animal, now a man, a tree, an insect, a fish, a flower, a spirit. Through a dynamic process the form is destroyed and re-created continuously. The body endures recurrent decompositions and reconstructions: changes involving at the same time the muscles and the mind.

Other techniques to reach the dead body state evoke the world of darkness (to which the unprivileged, ill-fated and unfit belong). Or one abandons one's own identity and self, to blend with the love for other human beings, being part of the cosmos.

The dead body is not a state of consciousness attempting to voluntarily express something. Its only aim is to free emotions without the interference of the rational mind. Dance movements are not voluntarily expressed as they occur in the live body. "The dancer is not to externalize inner feelings but to explore that area where the inner and outer feelings meet" (D'Orazi, 2001, pp. 58-59). Ōno compares the dead body dance to a dream: "You must dream. Ever unconscious. You must sleep, and suddenly, while you are sleeping, the dance begins. You don't know how" (Ōno, 1977).

In contrast, Hijikata compares the passivity of "the dead body" to a convict facing death on his way to the gallows:

> He is not walking but he is forced to walk; he is not living but he is forced to walk; he is not dying but

they make him die...Passivity as opposite to the energy intrinsic to life. (Tachiki, 1993, p. 62)

It is this mental condition that allows the unconscious, the deeper self and the painful memories to flow: "the body abandons the expressiveness and exposes himself as memory depository" (D'Orazi, 2001, pp. 70-71). While dancing, dancers have no perception of their movements but move like marionettes: "The being within the total void allows the body to discover the new strings that will move it" (Bergnark, 1991, p. 5).

The dead body relates to what Papadopoulos describes as the beginning of active imagination, that is letting the unconscious flow.

FIGURE 4. *Photo of Sayoko Onishi taken at Aurillac Festival 2015,* by photographer Jean Claude Chaudy

Another Butoh dancers' training technique, created by Ōno, is "the dead people gaze," an empty stare: "dead people see everything, but don't see anything" (D'Orazi, 2001, p. 112). The eye muscles relax and the blurred vision favors a state of consciousness that inspires the dancer to take an inner look. In this context Kazuo Ōno says:

> The eyes of the living observe, stare at a point, focus on an object and gaze on. When I dance the expression of my face is so absent because I'm trying to focus on every point, it is like I would drain my eyes from their reference point, from their target, in this way I use the dead gaze. (ibid., 2001, p. 113)

It is when eyes are in the blank that the soul unveils. It can happen that, while dancing, the *Butoh* dancer's eyes roll back becoming white. This is another method to isolate the Self and take an inner look. The dead gaze, the rolling back of the eyes or keeping them half open, so that the dancer is not completely in the inner or the outer world, allow him not to depend on his vision but to reawake other senses and explore what is usually hidden. In *Butoh*, the dance flows from the unconscious and starts moving the dancer's dead body as it happens in active imagination. Jung, in fact, explains "now the patients begin to draw, to paint, or to draw their images" (Jung, *CW* 15, 1935, pp. 177).

> The same occurs to the hand that guides a paintbrush, to the foot that begins to dance, to the eye-sight, to the hearing, to the speech, to the thought: it is an obscure inner surge that decides the configuration, an *a priori* unconscious impulse that determines the shape. (Jung, CW 8, 1947/1954, p. 221)

Not just a simple dance

Butoh is based on the confrontation of the Self with the unconscious expressing itself through the experience of dance balancing the body. *Butoh* dance contains similarities to Jung's process of individuation and it can be considered a path to the revelation of the Self. Through specific training and a long introspective path, the dancer abandons all superfluous unnecessary constraints to reveal his own identity. In *Butoh*, the dancer on stage always moves between the tension of the opposites with the aim to overcome polarity and to discover his own natural body. Similarly, Jung affirms that each individual aims at individuation, full personality and the Self.

Jung believes that it is possible to reach self completeness only when conscious and unconscious are bridged to achieve a symbolic synthesis through the transcendent function. It is through the concept of transcendent function that it is possible to find the connection between art and psyche. Art, as in *Butoh*, implies a search for the inner-self, and not for aesthetic formality.

Butoh, as the process of individuation, is a very profound process of transformation. For individuation to take place, Jacobi writes, "it is very important to concentrate exclusively on the intermediate point where creative transformation is found" (Jacobi, 1973, p. 158). This is the meeting point of mind and body from where the *Butoh* dancer, in trance, begins his or her dance.

Dance is a way of revealing the soul: to do so it is necessary for the dancer, descending into the darkness, to confront his unconscious and his fears in order to finally find light. Similarly, for Jung, individuation and the totality of the Self cannot be attained without confronting the archetypal figure of the Shadow.

The similarities between *Butoh* and Jung's thinking are numerous. *Butoh* might be considered as "the dance of being." Kasai affirms that "*Butoh* dance not only is an artistic performance but a path to find one's Self, lost and deeply buried in the unconscious as a result of various traumatic experiences."

In addition, Kasai affirms:

> What the performer experiences during the performance is like a dream during the night, afterwards

he/she gradually notices that there is spiritual calmness in the depth of his/her heart without clearly knowing why. It is evidence of a return from pilgrimage through the dissociated parts of the self and a recovery or creation of his/her own wholeness. (Kasai, 2000, p. 360)

Note: Jung's citations are from the Italian edition of the CW. Since paragraphs are not listed in the translations used the citations are listed by page no.

Bibliography

Aversa, L. (Ed.). (1999). *Psicologia analitica. La teoria della clinica.* Torino: Bollati Boringhieri Aversa, L. (Ed.). (1995). *Fondamenti di psicologia analitica.* Bari: Laterza.

Aversa, L. (1987). *Interpretazione e individuazione.* Roma: Borla.

Bergnark, J. (1991). *Butoh —Revolt of the Flesh in Japan and a Surrealist Way to Move.*

Mannen på gatan: Stockholm. website: http://www.surrealistgruppen.org/bergmark/butoh.html

Costantino, R. (2015). *Saudade // Artist Anna Costantino // Butoh,* Video memoria della performance *Butoh* di Anna Costantino. website: https://vimeo.com/128361182

D'Orazi, M.P. (2001). *Kazuo Ōno.* Palermo: L'Epos.

D'Orazi, M.P. (1997). *Butō. La Nuova Danza Giapponese.* Roma: Editori Associati.

Kasai, T., & Parsons, K. (2003). *Perception in Butoh Dance.* Memoirs of Hokkaido Institute of Technology, vol. 31, pp. 257-264. website: http://www.ne.jp/asahi/butoh/itto/method/announce.html

Kasai, T., & Mika, T. (2001). *Mind-Body Learning by Butoh Dance Method.* Proceedings from the 36th Annual Conference of American Dance Therapy Association. Raleigh, NC, U.S.A. website: http://www.ne.jp/asahi/butoh/itto/method/adta21.htm

Kasai, T. (2000). *A Note on Butoh Body.* Memoirs of Hokkaido Institute of Technology, vol. 28, pp. 353-360. website: http.//www.ne.jp/asahi/butoh/itto/method/announce.htm

Kasai, T. (1999). *A Butoh Dance Method for Psicosomatic exploration.* Memoirs of Hokkaido Institute of Technology, vol.27, pp. 309-316. http.// www.ne.jp/asahi/butoh/itto/method/announce.htm

Kasai, T. (May 1998). *A Peaceful Dimension of Mind-Body through Butoh Dance Method.* website: http://www.ne.jp/asahi/butoh/itto/method/kasait/ peters.htm

Keimling, C. *Butoh – Dance of Darkness?* Austin Downtown Arta Magazine. website: http://www.diversearts.org/old-site/ada/v9n3/adta_ dance.html

Klein, S. B. (1988). *Ankoku Butō the Pre-modern and Postmodern Influences on the Dance of Utter Darkness.* Cornell Est Asia Papers, Ithaca: Cornell University.

Kuwabara, T. (1996). *Going Back to the Origin of Life. Interview-Ōno Kazuo,* in <<Nikutaemo>>, n.2.

Jacobi, J. (1973). *Psychology of C.G. Jung.* New Haven: Yale University Press.

Jung, C. G. & Jaffè A. (Ed.). (1998). *Ricordi, Sogni, Riflessioni.* Milano, Rizzoli.

Novara, Red. (1971). Original title: *The Inferior Function. Jung's Typology,* Dallas, Spring Publication, Inc.

Ōno. K. (1977). Ōno Kazuo – Keido no kotob. Tokyo: Firumuātosha (Film Art Company).

Kasai, Toshiharu (2005). *Arm-Standing Exercise for Psychosomatic Training.* Bulletin of the Faculty of Humanities, N° 77, pp. 77-81. Sapporo Gakuin University. website: http.//www.ne.jp/asahi/butoh/itto/ method/announce.htm

Jung, C. G. (1957/1958). *Opera vol. 8.* Torino, Boringhieri, 1976

Jung, C. G. (1947/1954). *Opera vol. 8.* Torino: Boringhieri, 1976

Jung, C.G. (1946). *Opere vol. 16.* Torino, Boringhieri, 1993

Jung, C.G. (1938/1940). *Opere vol. 11.* Torino, Boringhieri, 1979

Jung. C. G. (1935). *Opere vol. 15.* Torino, Boringhieri, 1991

Jung, C. G. (1916/1928). *Opera vol. 7.* Torino, Boringhieri, 1983

Roquet, P. (2003). *Towards The Bowels of the Earth – Butoh Writhing in Prospective,* thesis in Asian Studies at Pomona College, Claremont, California.

Salerno, G. (1998). *Suoni del corpo, segni del cuore.* Genova – Milano: Costa & Nolan.

Tachiki, T. (Ed.). (1993). *Tennin Keraku*, Tokio: Seikyusha.

Viala, J., & Masson, S. (1988). *Butoh, Shade of darkness*. Tokyo: Shufunotomo.

Von Franz, M.L. (2004). *Tipologia psicologica: pensiero e sentimento, intuizione e sensazione*,

Waguri, Y. (1998). *ButōKaden*. Japan, Juatayatem.

FIGURE 1. *HEAD OR HEART*, DAVID HOSTETLER, OIL ON CANVAS, 36"H X 36"W.

Theatre and the Unconscious

by Kathryn Madden, PhD

> [T]he theatre is a vehicle, a means for self-study, self-exploration; a possibility of salvation. The actor has himself as his field of work.... Seen this way, acting is a life's work—the actor is step by step extending his knowledge of himself through the painful, ever-changing circumstances of rehearsal and the tremendous punctuation points of performance.

> — Peter Brook, *The Empty Space*

Prologue

Alone at the edge of the proscenium, the actor begins her pre-performance ritual by stepping onto the darkened stage. Most nights, but especially on opening night, she likes to wander off from the dressing room before the house is opened to the public. The smells from the stage—its velvet curtains, the floor, the stale or fresh paint—always summon her before these performances. The only light in the otherwise darkened hall emanates from a single, bare bulb on an iron pole, center-stage, partially illuminating the audience seats, performance space, and the wings backstage.

Standing center stage, she inhales the sight of the still vacant theatre. She roams down into the arena of soon-to-be-filled seats and, for a few moments, sits in the back row, then in the middle of the house, and finally in the front row. Gazing down into the orchestra pit, she notes how deep it is. She takes in the arrangement of chairs and scattered scores. She imagines how these perspectives will soon be experienced by those now scuffling to get their tickets in the lobby, waiting in anticipation, not knowing.

Here, at this time, she is still no one, no-thing, without make-up, wig, costumes, words, music, the intense bodily engagement and eye-contact with her fellow actors. She is still free. Or is she? Perhaps, she thinks, real freedom occurs only when she makes her entrance onto a stage replete with props, furniture, painted sets—or sometimes onto a stark stage with nothing on it at all, an empty space. For, in a strange sort of way, it is there, in that space of emptiness or fullness, that her soul at last feels free—free from herself; from her daily persona; from the mundane world; from lingering moods, memories, and projections; from developmental wounds; and from the past. More than any other time of the day, it is when she is here that she feels most alive.

Regardless of how long or arduous the rehearsal time had been, on opening night something truly exciting and transformative always seemed to happen. Always, when she is working deeply, it is like an alchemical journey. She and her colleagues would now, for the first time, be joined together with an audience. It didn't matter if it was a small gathering in a tiny off-Broadway theatre or in a vast, open-air amphitheater of several thousand people; the phenomenon was always the same. It is then that time, itself, is metamorphosed from the quantitative "chronos" of the mundane world into the qualitative "kairos" of the world of the play. It is there—in that alchemical vessel— the leaden "materia" of the commonplace is transmuted into the gold of the sublime. It is then and there that the new creation comes to life.

Imagination and Play

Play is one of the ways that, as children, we begin to learn who we are as well as who we might become. That process of becoming has elements that are both unconscious and archetypal. We may identify with the Hero, the Trickster (jester), the Healer, or the Great Mother (nurturer). Maybe we act out shadow elements of our young identities in our play with friends, expressing ourselves in ways that would be unacceptable at home.

Good guys and bad guys. Cops and robbers. Doctors, nurses, patients, housewives. We unconsciously assume archetypal roles in spontaneous play with our peers. As Jung says, "The creation of something new is not accomplished by the intellect but by the play instinct acting from inner necessity. The creative mind plays with the objects it loves" (1971, para. 197).

I was drawn to the more heroic roles that I first encountered on television who, at that time, tended to be played by men. I became Davy Crockett, the Swamp Fox or Zorro. Later, I wrote a story recalling those days called "Zorro of Starcrest Drive," named for the street we lived on at the time. Perhaps I acted out what I intuited to be the characteristics of the boy my father had wanted but never got. Questing. Fighting. Achieving. Winning.

Jung says in "The Psychology of the Child Archetype,"

> The hero's main feat is to overcome the monster of darkness: it is the long-hoped-for and expected triumph of consciousness over the unconscious. The coming of consciousness was probably the most tremendous experience of primeval times, for with it a world came into being whose existence no one had suspected before. (1981, para. 284)

At times I still find myself operating under that hero archetype, but now I am more conscious of this than when I was a child of five or six and was unconsciously drawn to playing these roles. Maybe we are all drawn to playing the hero in our own life stories, if only to develop into our potential by first becoming aware of that potential and then striving for it against all obstacles, overcoming our own "monster[s] of darkness."

How, then, do we draw a connection between play as children and the role an actor plays on stage? Anthropologist, Victor Turner, sheds light on this subject in his book, *From Ritual to Theatre: The Human Seriousness of Play.*

> In Western languages, action has...the flavor of contestation. Action is "agonistic." *Act, agon, agony,* and *agitate* are all derived from the same Indo-European base *ag-, "to drive," from which came the Latin *agere,* to do, and the Greek *agein,* to lead. In Western (Euro-American) culture, work and play both have this driving, conflictive character.... In those genres of *cultural* performance which predated Greek theatre...wars and feuds between groups of deities or clans and lineages headed by well-armed heroes, as well as competition for position, power, or scarce resources...were vividly portrayed, carried out in mimicry. (1982, p. 103)

So in our imaginative play as children as well as acting in the theatre, we typically find a protagonist (the "good guy" of the story) and an antagonist (the "bad guy or guys"). The quest for resolution of the conflict or conflicts between these opposites—these "actors"—is what drives the play forward to its dénouement.

The Historical Roots of Modern Theatre

Every character in a play has an aim, a purpose in the unfolding drama. She leaves her dressing room and opens the door to the vast arena of scrims, poles, widgets, moving sidewalks, and actors racing to change costumes. She listens for her orchestra cue above the general back-

stage bustle. It will be her first contact with the audience, although her character will come to life behind an invisible "fourth wall" of liminal space that, in this show, will not be broken.

Her adrenaline rises, her pulse builds, her concentration is keen, as if readying an arrow to shoot with her bow. Her intention is extremely focused and precise. She holds a certain desire and intent, so well-rehearsed as to be embodied in her every movement. Once inside this door, all of her own persona has vanished, while that of the character she inhabits comes into being. She swings her cape and steps into the light. Her role in the story has begun, and the audience delights in watching what happens as the story unfolds.

When we consider the origins of modern theatre in the West, two sources usually come to mind: liturgical dramas of the medieval church and Greek tragedy. As to the first, we know that a form of theatre was performed in the medieval church to convey the drama of the central story of the Christian religion—the life, death, and resurrection of Christ. But, as Turner reminds us, "The Mass, the Eucharist, itself was, of course, a drama with a scriptural script long before it gave rise to the 'Passion Plays'" (1982, p. 103).

In much the same way as the development of liturgical dramas was drawn from the Mass itself, we believe that Greek theatre had its roots in the rituals celebrated at the altar of the Greek god, Dionysius. As the Canon of the Latin Mass in the medieval Roman Church told the story of Jesus' death, burial and resurrection, so the hymn (known as the *dithyramb*) sung at the Dionysian altar told the stories of his "life and mythos." These early rituals "expanded to embrace not only Dionysian tales, but also those of gods, demigods, and heroes, some of whom were regarded as the founding ancestors of the Hellenes and their Mediterranean neighbors" (Ibid., p. 103).

These dramas were much more than celebrations of the Dionysian myth and other mythological stories so integral to the culture of ancient Greece. They were also cathartic and therapeutic to the audiences who attended them. As Edward Edinger tells us in his book, *The Eternal Drama: The Inner Meaning of Greek Mythology*:

> Aristotle described the effect of watching tragedy as a catharsis in which one has the opportunity to release the emotions of pity and fear. Just as a possessed person is calmed by the playing of frenzied music, so sad and anxious people are relieved by seeing the emotions that grip them acted out. Thus, the play functions as a mirror that provides an image to objectify the inner affect. [1994, pp. 123-124]

Edinger's quote is reminiscent of one of Jung's few statements regarding the theatre to be found in the *Collected Works*: "One might describe the theatre, somewhat unaesthetically, as an institution for working out private complexes in public" (1977, para. 48). Clearly, Jung was willing to acknowledge the potential for an unconscious connection between audience and actors on stage. But Edinger, takes the idea to an even deeper and transformative level.

> While watching the drama, the spectators became identified with the mythical happening being portrayed, which allowed them to participate briefly in the archetypal level of reality. We know from psychotherapeutic experience that an encounter with the archetypal dimension can have healing and transformative effects, and in this respect drama has many parallels to dreams, serving something of the same purpose for the collective psyche that dreams do for the individual. [1994, p. 123]

For theatre to have this kind of cathartic impact suggests that these connections must be located on a much deeper level than even the personal unconscious. They seem to stem from what Jung called the "collective unconscious." They seem built into the DNA of our humanity.

While the roots of modern Western theatre can be traced to both ancient Greek rituals as well as the liturgical dramas of the medieval Roman Church, there is yet one more source to consider. Turner reminds us, in *From Ritual to Theatre*, that there is evidence to show that it may be the original expressive form to communicate the stories of one of the most significant events in the lives of aboriginal peoples, and that is—the hunt.

Contemporary playwright and screenwriter, David Mamet, drills down into this idea in the chapter "Hunting Instincts," from his book on theatre, simply called, *Theatre*. Mamet says,

> Man is a predator [and] as predators we close out the day around the campfire with stories of the hunt. These stories like the chase itself, engage our most primal instinct of pursuit: The story's hero is in pursuit of his goal.... In the hunt story, the audience is placed in the same position as the protagonist: The viewer is told what the goal is and, like the hero, works to determine what is the best thing to do next.... How may he determine what is the course toward the goal? Through observation.... This is the essence of the story around the campfire: "And you'll never guess what happened next...." (2010, pp. 17-18)

Theater, Mamet believes, engages "the same portion of the brain that we use in the hunt: the ability to spontaneously process and act upon information without subjecting the process to verbal (conscious) review" (Ibid., p. 17). It fulfills a more basic need than the presentation of information (e.g., a lecture) because it engages us at a more visceral and primal level. "This is the apparent paradox of dramatic writing," Mamet continues. "It is not, though it may appear to be, the communication of ideas but rather the inculcation in the audience of the instincts of the hunt. These instincts precede and, in times of stress, supersede the verbal; they are spontaneous and more powerful than the assimilation of an idea" (Ibid., p. 17).

We experience theatre communally, as a member of an audience. A successful drama (or comedy, for that matter) will cause this audience to suspend its analytical faculties—what you may have heard as the "willing suspension of disbelief." In other words, my rational brain knows that I, along with many strangers, have traveled to this building, paid for passes to gain entrance to a now darkened room where we observe other strangers, on a lighted, elevated platform, who do things, move around and talk to each other, but pay me not the slightest attention. If the play is good, however, if it is able to draw me into its world, I forget (become unconscious of) the "real world" and become absorbed in the drama (or comedy) and, along with the strangers all around me, can't wait to see "what happens next."

Actor and Audience

In the final pages of this chapter, we will consider the unconscious inspiration of the playwright. But for now, we will continue to focus—as we have been doing—primarily on two separate but related components: 1) the actor and 2) the audience. For these are the only two elements that are absolutely indispensable to theatre. As legendary stage and film director, Peter Brook says in his seminal and critical work about contemporary theatre, *The Empty Space*:

> I can take any empty space and call it a bare stage. *A man walks across this empty space whilst someone else is watching him, and this is all that is needed for an act of theatre to be engaged.* Yet when we talk about theatre this is not quite what we mean. Red curtains, spotlights, blank verse, laughter, darkness, these are all confusedly superimposed in a messy image covered by one all-purpose word. We talk of the cinema killing the theatre, and in that phrase we refer to the theatre as it was when the cinema was born, a theatre of box office, foyer, tip-up seats, footlights, scene changes, intervals,

music, as though the theatre was by very definition
these and little more. (1996, p. 9)

So—except for the part about "a man walking across an empty space
on a bare stage"—Brook starts out by describing what theatre is not.
Yet in 1968, when he originally wrote these words, this is what much
of theatre had become and still is to this day: theatre as business, as
commercial enterprise, as spectacle, as entertainment.

Before the development of the box office and the all-powerful
critic who, with a thumbs up or thumbs down, can cause a fledgling
show to die in a night or become a hit, theatre, as we have seen, was
once a much different enterprise, but that theatre still lives. Why
in this age of film, television, and streaming video—when, from
our living rooms, we can even tune into a "live broadcast" of a play,
musical, or opera—does live theatre survive?

In *Jung's Advice to the Players: A Jungian Reading of Shakespeare's
Problem Plays*, Sally Porterfield provides some insight into that question. She says,

> The extraordinary power, the numinosity of great
> art stems from its ability to speak to the unconscious,
> that part of us which Jung tells us communicates not
> in words, but in symbols. Theatre, which combines
> verbal and visual arts, works on both levels in a
> particularly potent way. The words, which appeal to
> the conscious mind by their intellectual, emotional,
> or aesthetic content, also speak to the unconscious,
> calling up personal and archetypal associations the
> conscious mind cannot recognize but can experi-
> ence, sometimes in bewilderingly powerful ways.
> (1994, pp. 1-2)

True, the passage above could just as easily pertain to the medium
of film which, in some ways, is even superior to the stage in its
ability to manipulate the verbal and visual (especially the symbolic)
to great effect upon the audience. But Porterfield has more to say

about the singular quality of theatre that no other story-telling medium can approach.

> From where does the magic emanate that suffuses this art form and elevates it into something very closely resembling a religious calling for so many people? If we accept the premise that great literary characters derive their power from the archetypes they invoke, then we can take that belief one step further. In drama, the power is intensified by the merger of character and actor, which brings the archetype, quite literally, to life. Perhaps after all, this is the power that enthralls most in theatre, the fusion of unconscious and conscious reality, not on a page or on canvas, but in the flesh. The merger might be regarded as part of that alchemical process which Jung believed to be a symbolic search for the self. The word becomes flesh, and we realize that we are in the presence of the divine. (ibid., pp. 2-3)

The key point is that there is an immediacy of live theatre that can never exist in viewing a film. What you experience in theatre is happening now in front of you—*in the flesh*—revealing moments of brilliance which may be different each show. Actors are not machines, after all, and no two performances of any show—however tightly-directed and well-rehearsed—are identical.

What happens in the theatre—or at least has the potential to happen—recalls what Jung said about "the meeting of two person-alities." He likened it to "the contact of two chemical substances: if there is any reaction, both are transformed" (2005, pp. 49-50). In this case, the "two personalities" are the actor and the audience.

"But wait," you say, "I don't go to the theatre to be 'treated' or 'transformed' but for entertainment." Interestingly, the etymolog-ical derivation of the word *entertainment* is "held-in-between." In other words, entertainment is "a liminal phenomenon" that occurs in the "liminoid time of leisure between the role-playing times of 'work'" (Turner, 1982, p. 114). But liminal, or this state of "betwixt and between," could be applied as equally to the neophyte in a rite of passage ritual to adulthood, as to what happens in the theatre between actor and audience.

Culture, Turner explains in *The Ritual Process,* (1969, vii. ff.), is forever dynamic and changing as influenced by the primordial energies of deep, underlying myths that are mobilized in moments of crisis and during transitional periods. Focusing upon the emotional-experiential underpinnings of ritual, Turner concludes significantly that in traditional societies ritual served the function of alleviating social turmoil. Yet, even though much of contemporary theatre may have distanced itself from its function in religious or social ritual, according to Turner, it still

> claims to be a means of communication with invisible powers and ultimate reality, and can still assert, particularly since the rise of depth psychology, that it represents the reality behind the role-playing masks, that even its masks, so to speak, are "negations of the negation." They present the false face in order to portray the possibility of a true face. (1982, p. 115)

Echoing Jung's remarks on theatre from *Symbols of Transformation,* "as an institution for working out private complexes in public," the great American playwright, Arthur Miller, said in his introduction to his volume of *Collected Plays,*

> My conception of the audience is of a public, each member of which is carrying about with him what he thinks is an anxiety, or a hope, or a preoccupation which is his alone and isolates him from mankind; and in this respect at least the function of a play is to reveal him to himself so that he may touch others by virtue of the revelation of his mutuality with them. If only for this reason I regard the theater as a serious business, one that makes or should make man more human, which is to say, less alone. (1958, p. 11)

There is a power for a given culture in the enacted representation of important and transformative stories. How theatre accomplishes this feat can best be explained by another glance at its historical roots in ritual and catharsis.

As referenced above, the hunt, which provides nourishment to the tribe, becomes also the source of "entertaining" stories of fearless heroes pursuing and overcoming ferocious wild animals by their cunning and superior force. This ritual enactment also confirms and teaches the young boys that it is the men who perform this role in the tribe and that, someday, when they are ready, they will be called upon to do so.

The medieval Christian Church's "mystery plays" depicting the events before, during, and after the death of Christ, moved the faithful, and perhaps even converted more than a few non-believers through their power to bring to life the Biblical stories, which most of the audience couldn't read anyway. Thus, they served the society—or, at the very least, the church—as a recruitment vehicle and as a means whereby the faith of believers was deepened and strengthened.

These two examples show how ritual and theatre can act to preserve the status quo of the social fabric. Below are two examples that demonstrate how the cathartic impact of theatre upon audiences, far from exemplifying Turner's concept of ritual serving to alleviate social turmoil, can actually "stir it up" by giving embodiment to yearned for ideas or states of being. By making the unconscious conscious.

First, the popular 1778 play by Pierre Beaumarchais, *Le Mariage de Figaro* touched a collective nerve in pre-revolutionary France and was so popular with audiences that three theatre goers were crushed to death at the overly packed opening night performance. This play, better known today in the form of Mozart's opera, *Le Nozze di Figaro* (*The Marriage of Figaro*), with its mockery of aristocratic privilege has been characterized as foreshadowing the French Revolution. Who can say that this popular play didn't help to galvanize and give form to unconscious or unexpressed feelings of the people who had had enough of the dominant cultural complex of the aristocracy?

And then, about one hundred years later, Nora's final slamming of the door as she leaves her bewildered and weeping husband, Torvald, setting off on her own journey at the end of Ibsen's *A Doll's House*, foreshadowed the liberation of women in the 20th century from their 19th century roles as either housekeepers or old maids.

Embodiment and the Senses

The notion of "embodiment" and "making the unconscious conscious" reminds me of what Peter Brook says about the invisible becoming visible on the stage. He places this idea in the context of how many aspects of our lives escape our senses and adds that we only begin to recognize their manifestation when they become rhythms or shapes that emerge when we realize that actors are not the creators of their characters, of their being. A conductor, for example, when open and relaxed, does not make the music. Instead, it is the music that makes him. "The invisible takes possession of him;" says Brook, "through him it will reach us" (1996, p. 42).

I think of some of the training we received as young actors in the late 1960s. It was an age of "sensitivity sessions," EST, and Gestalt therapy. One of my drama professors at the University of Maryland once took our acting class down to the Agricultural Barn for some work on "actors' senses." We entered a huge cow barn strewn with hay in the middle and manure at the outskirts of about a 50-foot arena. There were no lights in the barn, and the door was to be shut. Even in this darkness, we were told that each of us would be blindfolded. The goal was to find each other, using our senses, but without speaking or making a sound. Any signals were taboo; yet, one-by-one, we were to form a circle of the entire class.

Our senses were intensified by the strong smell of manure (over-activated for those who, like myself, were allergic to hay). We shuffled around, some over the hay to the edges of the manure and stumbled into it, groaning as they pulled themselves upright, now laden with cow-droppings. Hands flailing in the stenchy abyss, we groped for another. What might have been excitement related to facing the unknown, became a feeling of helplessness and abandonment. The barn was a vast space. Ah! Two people must have connected, since, even without verbal sound, the sound of two bodies finding each other could be sensed through the emission of breath. During the twenty or so minutes of this "sense exercise," I could feel rage and frustration ebbing up in my body. It was beginning to feel an impossible task, especially when I ended up walking in the wrong direction right into a pile of manure. But just then, I felt the presence of a hand reaching out. I grabbed around in the air and found it. So grateful to find and to be found in this morass of excrement, I immediately hugged the body of whomever I had encountered. Together, we worked as a team to find our way toward what was becoming a more evident shuffling of multiple feet. Task finally accomplished, we took off our blindfolds as the doors were opened and sunlight streamed into the barn. It was then I saw that my "foundling" was a young African-American woman—the only one in our class. We had held onto each other, lost in a darkened cow barn in 1968.

The entire exercise took on a deeper meaning as again we reached out for each other, bodies soiled, souls opened. The actor needs to begin with facing the invisible in a way that transcends his/her experience in life and then to translate that experience onto the stage. This, at least, is one way in which the unconscious can be activated into being in the preparation of young actors.

At best, the actor's "aliveness of being"—in touch with the richness of unconscious material and open to the invisible becoming visible—can shake the audience awake from the emotional dullness of their daily humdrum existence. The audience member would likely be riled at the notion of being dumped into a pile of manure or to see such an enactment onstage. So part of the actor's offering is to have journeyed into territory that few can fathom and probably should not attempt. By holding up a mirror to the audience so that they may more readily see into their own psyches, theatre begins to take on a ritual, liminal, and transformative function. What lies invisible in the collective unconscious has a greater chance of breathing, of circulating, of being seen.

Acting as a Path Toward Individuation

One aspect of the unconscious and the theatre that we have not covered here, and that most "civilians" (as actors often refer to all non-theatre people) probably have little to no knowledge of, is that of the personal, emotional, even spiritual development of the actor—e.g., acting as a path toward individuation. Jung referred to the concept of individuation in the chapter entitled, "Conscious, Unconscious, and Individuation," in *The Archetypes and the Collective Unconscious*, "to denote the process by which a person becomes a psychological 'in-dividual,' that is, a separate, indivisible unity or 'whole'" (1990, para. 490). The concept is strikingly similar to the quote that began this chapter: "[T]he theatre is a vehicle, a means for self-study, self-exploration; a possibility of salvation" (1996, p. 59). This statement appears in *The Empty Space* as Brook introduces the reader to the work of Jerzy Grotowski, then the artistic director of the Thirteen Row Theatre—later known as the Laboratory Theatre— in Poland. Grotowski undertook to create an avant-garde theatre that also became a center for research into the theatre arts, focusing largely on the "the relationship between the stage and audience and, consequently, between the actor and the audience" (Mokrzycka-Pokora, 2002). Grotowski's book, *Towards a Poor Theatre* (1968), was published in over a dozen countries, becoming something of a workbook for the international experimental theatre movement of the 1960s and 1970s.

> Fascinated with the thoughts of Carl Jung, he [Grotowski] sought out archetypes that would prove helpful in building roles and turn his actors' efforts into an act of sacrifice. The ecstatic acting techniques of the Laboratory Theatre were not aimed at achieving a state of trance, but rather on

nurturing precise acting in a state of sharpened consciousness. (ibid., 2002)

Grotowski's approach to acting embraced deeply psychological self-study. It was concerning the methodology of the "poor theatre" that Peter Brook observed, "the actor has himself as his field of work" (1996, p. 59). The actor, he says,

allows a role to "penetrate" him; at first he is all obstacle to it, but by constant work he acquires technical mastery over his physical and psychic means by which he can allow the barriers to drop.... So that the act of performance is an act...of sacrificing what most men prefer to hide—this sacrifice is his gift to the spectator. Here there is a similar relation between actor and audience to the one between priest and worshipper.... The priest performs the ritual for himself and on behalf of others. Grotowski's actors offer their performance as a ceremony for those who wish to assist: the actor invokes, lays bare what lies in every man—and what daily life covers up. This theatre is holy because its purpose is holy; it has a clearly defined place in the community and it responds to a need the churches can no longer fill. (ibid., pp. 59-60)

Despite evidence of an ancestral connection between contemporary theatre and the liturgical dramas of the medieval church, however, the words Brook uses above to describe Grotowski's approach to theatre and acting—priest, worshipper, holy—still strike in us a strange and unfamiliar ring. Yet, if we side-step just a bit and allow ourselves to think of the actor assuming the role of a shaman, we begin to draw closer to the concepts of "theatre and the unconscious," Grotowski's "poor theatre," and Brook's "holy theatre." Appearing throughout many cultures for millennia, a shaman is one whose role it is within a tribe or village to mediate between the spirit and the human worlds. The shaman performs this mediation through ritual, trance, and then bringing back to this world the spiritual knowledge gained for purposes of healing or teaching. "Shamans, like Grotowski's actors," says George Home-Cook, "experience a *calling*," one, he says that is "often brought about by a personal crisis." Theatre, for Grotowski, "has a very real sociological function: to liberate the participants from their own socio-psychological complexes by engaging in the self-sacrificial experience and process of acting thus bringing about a general increase in their mental, physical and spiritual well-being" (2001, pp. 3-4).

A Conversation About Creativity

You always look for the thing that's out of place, and you move in the direction of the strangeness.

— Rinde Eckert

To close, I would like to share an excerpt from a recent conversation with friend and former theatre colleague, Rinde Eckert. Rinde and I first met in 1977 during our collaboration on *Viva Reviva*, an experimental, feminist musical with lyrics by Eve Merriam and music by Amy Rubin. It was produced at the Lenox Arts Center in Lenox, MA and later played off-Broadway. Since then, Rinde has developed a highly-regarded and much-awarded international career in what he calls "interdisciplinary performance art." More than any other performing artist I know personally, Rinde has dedicated himself to creating an opus of work that is unique, deeply personal but also universal, challenging (both to performer and audience), visionary, thought-provoking, and, of course, entertaining. As you will see, his process of creation is open to the unexpected, to the unconscious. His performances draw you into a strange, yet somehow familiar, world in which you become completely engrossed. As you experience the performance unfolding before you, you find yourself asking a question, but realize you have no idea what the answer will be: "What in the world is going to happen next?"

John Rockwell, writing of Rinde's work in *The New York Times* on November 17, 1988, said that "Best of all was the duet with Ms.

Jenkins, *Shorebirds Atlantic*. It was eerie yet touching, a tale of two people who meet at the edge of an abyss. Mr. Eckert's text, spoken by both performers, skirted pretension but rose handsomely above it, and Ms. Jenkins's movements for the two of them admirably complemented the poetry and Mr. Eckert's spare, folk-flavored music" (Rockwell, 1988). Ben Brantley, also of *The New York Times*, said, in a review of *Horizon* on June 6, 2007, that Rinde, "finds vivifying parallels between the theological quest of one man and the theatrical quest to capture and illuminate life" (Brantley, 2007).

The conversation picks up after first discussing Rinde's background, his college days at the University of Iowa in which he decided to major in music after trying out the theatre program (for the record, both of his parents were classically trained singers), his initial steps into forging a career in new music theatre, and whether there is a methodology or approach that he uses in the creation of his works.

KM.   Let's go back to the question of where these ideas come from. With *And God Created Great Whales*, for example, it almost sounded like the ideas came from an intellectual analysis of Melville's original *Moby Dick*.

RE.   It feels like that, but I don't think that was actually what went on. I think I come to these things afterwards when I try to rationalize why I'm doing it. While I'm "taking the trip," it's very often unclear to me what the answer is, but I've learned to ask follow up questions about dreams I have.

I think one of the clearest is a piece I did called *Shorebirds Atlantic*. It's about a 20-minute piece. It was with Margaret Jenkins, a dancer in California. A beautiful little piece—a duet.

We decided to just go into the studio and start working with what we had. What we had was a roll of paper. We started playing around, and I put up—typically I give myself physical problems to solve. In this case, we put up a series of pieces of paper. I scrunched it up so it had little waves in the paper. We laid several of them out and created little corridors. You'd have to jump over these little loopy things, and the paper was very thin. So you had to dance on it in a very particular way because it would move underneath you. And so we just played around with that for a while.

Then one day we came in, and I said, "Ah, let's go for coffee. Let's work at the café and have a conversation." We went to the café, and she started talking about what it was to be an older dancer, how she couldn't do the things that her company could do. She was facing that inevitable moment when she wasn't going to be able to dance anymore, when she wasn't really a dancer anymore in her mind. She was facing the end of her career, and it was frightening. She was having physical problems with her back and her knees. So she was going to have to stop soon. What she created for *Shorebirds* was really beautiful, but she had to figure out a very different way of dancing for this piece.

KM: Was there a story for this piece?

RE: Well, that was my responsibility—narrative is what I do— and I sort of just "went away" and had this little daydream. I remembered Atlantic City, of being a boy and visiting Atlantic City with my parents and a friend of mine.

Now anybody else who didn't know that they were looking for something, and didn't credit their subconscious as an ally, would probably ignore it. I mean, it was just a daydream. It wasn't any "big dream." It was just a little daydream that popped into my head. But it was something. I remembered Atlantic City, and I found myself thinking about that and my friend Johnny Stewart.

So I'm thinking about this trip to Atlantic City and the beach—but I know I'm looking for something because I'm on the "hunt" right now. I'm in hunting mode. And when you're in hunting mode, you are careful to note any difference in the environment because you're looking for something that's unusual. A broken twig is going to tell you the deer went that way. A spot of blood—anything unusual. And this was unusual. Why would I be thinking about that? I hadn't seen anybody from that time. It was a long time ago. Atlantic City.

Then a certain amount of analysis goes into it. What is Atlantic City? Well, Atlantic City is a gambling town sitting on a coast of the ocean. So, there's the ocean, and then there's the gambling town. What is gambling? Gambling is the illusion that you control your fate. It promises to be a mystery, but there is no mystery. The odds are known. The house knows exactly who's going to win, and it ain't gonna be you!

KM.   ...at least not very often.

RE.   That's right! Not very often. If you gamble long enough, you will lose. That's just the way it is. And if you win consistently, they won't let you play. So there's no question about what's going to happen. If you win at the blackjack table over and over, eventually they're going to accuse you of counting cards, no matter whether you're lucky or not. If your winning goes beyond what they think are reasonable odds, then in their mind you are cheating because you have defied the odds.

So I was thinking there's this thing that purports to be a mystery but which is no mystery at all. And then there's this other thing which I know as the Atlantic Ocean—but that is a real mystery. And then there's this strand between them. Then I thought about the pieces of paper and waves, and there was something in the pieces of paper that reminded me of waves and ocean. Then Margaret was talking about facing the inevitable reality, facing the failure of her body which was going to break down. It was a machine that was going to break down.

Then I thought about gambling, and that it's all about machines. This huge machine is going on, the machine of that gambling culture. It just keeps going on and on, and it does the same thing over and over again. All these spinning wheels and one-armed bandits rolling and tumbling and so on. So you have some of the energy and physicality of that natural environment where you have waves and cycles.

I thought that these two things were really interesting together. So I just put that up. I said to myself: "Okay, this is a good thing to bear in mind." Then I came into rehearsal and said, "Let's dance on the shore for a while." We're on the shore of Atlantic City. On the one hand, we've got the neon lights and the big wheels, and on the other, we've got this huge expanse—this big thing that we don't understand and we can't live in, and it's this grand mystery. So we have this grand mystery and this other thing that is lying to us all the time telling us that we can win, but at a certain point in the process, we will lose. Just as your body, at a certain point, is going to break down.

So I said, "let's dance, let's be shore birds." And we started doing bird things. The movement was like going into the surf and back out again. Margaret choreographed these little hand movements. And then I thought, "Oh man, I want to be in a skirt—a white skirt. Let me dress myself up as much like a bird as possible." So we ended up looking like these swimming creatures, but we had on white robes, white caps, white skirts, and high-top black sneakers—you know, these little feet—and dark goggles.

Then at a certain point, I got into crisis with it. I've got to now know why and what we're actually doing here. I'm not comfortable with just being these birds. I need a crisis of some kind. Why are we here? And that's when the certain art comes into play where you know where you're standing, you have a vocabulary of movement, you know you like this place. This is a good place to be. I just need to take this one step further. I need to ask one more question about this.

But then it came to me. It just so happened that at the same time we were building this, there was an AIDS crisis, and a lot of dancers were dying, gay dancers were dying. So it was natural for me at that moment to be thinking about death and about that "wheel of fortune." All of a sudden, I came up with this: "This guy is dying. He's here because he's dying. What is he doing? Ah, he wants to commit suicide. He's going to swim out into the ocean and keep on swimming until he tires and drowns. But what's she doing there? What is her role in this? They're strangers. They just met. But he was looking at her in some way." So then it became this thing of, "Oh yeah, he wants to swim out, but he wants to—just before it becomes inevitable, he wants to turn back, and he wants to see someone waving at him from the shore. Then he turns for the final push and is gone."

KM.　But what happens to her?

RE.　Well, it became a piece about a guy who goes to Atlantic City, who's dying of some incurable disease. And he goes to bars, looking for a very particular woman who will help him—and he explains what he is doing and what he wants her to do. She asks, "What if I try to save you?" And he says, "It's very important that you stand your ground. You have to let me go. You have to let me do this. You have to let me go." And she agrees, finally, that she will do this for him. Then they have this final moment where they're dancing together on the shore, and then he swims out, and the robes come off, the skirt comes off, and he's in black swimming trunks. And finally you see him disappear. There's a whole movement vocabulary of his finally—the head comes up before the last gulp, and you see him sink. He sinks like a stone monkey. He calls himself a stone monkey. He's going to be a mythic creature. He sinks into the mythic ocean as a mythic creature.

And we see her sitting on a bench. She's taken off her bathing cap and her glasses. You see her face suddenly, and the hair comes out. She's taken off her robe, and you see her now as a woman. She's been kind of unisex up until that point. Her last words were, "I could have saved him—and ruined everything." And then the lights go down.

The rest of her company used to sit and watch—these were guys who were losing friends—and they would just be sobbing. It was just this amazing thing.

So the progression of that idea is: it's partially knowing that you're hunting, and you look at the world differently—

KM.   You're ready for the message from the dream or the daydream.

RE.   Yes. You're looking for news of a difference. Something that is out of place. And you go there. You always look for the thing that's out of place, and you move in the direction of the strangeness.

[Excerpt from *Shorebirds Atlantic*: https://www.youtube.com/watch?v=69uwiofwI5w]

FIGURE 2. *COINCIDENTAL GATHERING*, COLETTE CALASCIONE.

I like this conversation because, without planning to, it recaps most of the major themes of this chapter. We talked about theatre as mythology—a modern mythology involving mysteries that aren't mysteries (gambling), known things that are giant mysteries (the ocean), as well as death, loss, and regret. We talked about the cathartic effect of the play on the audience, given the timeliness of the narrative (AIDS epidemic). Most importantly, and in a way not previously explored in this chapter, we talked about the spontaneous, unconscious roots of the creative process itself.

The creative impulse produces a daydream. The daydream is taken seriously because the playwright is "on the hunt" for something, and, as he says: "You move in the direction of the strangeness." The daydream leads to an amplification and an analysis of the images that emerged. Playing with the images and symbols then causes a eureka moment that becomes the narrative. Significantly, it didn't start with a rational idea, "let's write a play about loss and grief that will be cathartic and healing for people experiencing the loss of friends and family to an epidemic."

Epilogue

The actor takes her bow along with the other actors and sings a reprise of the leading musical number of the show. Curtain call begins her movement back into the mundane world. Another bow. As the final curtain falls, the actors scurry like lemmings toward the stairs or the elevator that leads to dressing rooms. Amid the noise and clamor of the soul's release back into the routine of everyday life, she also feels a strange duality of fulfillment and melancholy. This week there will thankfully be seven more performances. For seven more times this week, she will be mesmerized by the stark, bright bulb that paradoxically leads her into darkness, then into the light, and, then, home again.

The artist stands with one foot in the imaginal realm of the unconscious and one foot in the conscious world of the ego. From the unconscious surface images in visions, dreams, and daydreams. The artist who surrenders to the unconscious, who is in touch with the imaginal realm, is able to retrieve a rich source of material for use in whatever creative medium she or he works. The theatrical artist is no exception. Acting, when taken seriously, is a life's work, full of the exploration of self and relationship. It is soul-work. The conception, narrative, characters, and *mise en scène* of the theatrical work engage the conscious and unconscious of participants and audience alike—not for its own sake, but for the transformation and enlightenment of all involved.

> Why do we sacrifice so much energy to our art? Not in order to teach others but to learn with them what our existence, our organism, our personal and repeatable experience have to give us; to learn to break down the barriers which surround us and to free ourselves from the breaks which hold us back, from the lies about ourselves which we manufacture daily for ourselves and for others; to destroy

the limitations caused by our ignorance or lack of courage; in short, to fill the emptiness in us: to fulfill ourselves...art is a ripening, an evolution, an uplifting which enables us to emerge from darkness into a blaze of light.

Jerzy Grotowski

Bibliography

Brantley, B. (June 6, 2007). "The Eternal Vaudeville of the Spiritual Mind," *The New York Times*

Brook, P. (1996). *The Empty Space*. New York: Touchstone

Edinger, E. (1994). *The Eternal Drama: The Inner Meaning of Greek Mythology*. Boston: Shambala

Home-Cook, G. (2001). "Shamanizing with Grotowski: Understanding Grotowski's Theatre as a Shamanic Phenomenon." Unpublished PGDip Dissertation. East 15 Acting School, Loughton, UK.

Jung, C.G. (1981). *The Archetypes and the Collective Unconscious*. CW 9i. Princeton, NJ: Princeton University Press.

Jung, C.G. (1977). *Symbols of Transformation*. CW 5. Princeton, N.J.: Princeton University Press.

Jung, C.G. (1972). *Two Essays in Analytical Psychology*. CW 7. Princeton, N.J.: Princeton University Press.

Jung, C.G. (1971). *Psychological Types*. CW 6. Princeton, N.J.: Princeton University Press.

Miller, A. (1958). *Collected Plays with an Introduction*. London: The Cresset Press

Mokrzycka-Pokora, M. (Oct. 2002). "Jerzy Grotowski." (http://culture.pl/en/artist/jerzy-grotowski)

Porterfield, S.F. (1994). *Jung's Advice to the Players: A Jungian Reading of Shakespeare's Problem Plays*. Santa Barbara, C.A.: Praeger.

Songline / Tonefield Productions website. (http://www.songtone.com/artists/eckert_link.htm)

Rinde Eckert website. (www.rindeeckert.com)

Rockwell, J. (Nov. 17, 1988). "Jack of All Stage Arts." *The New York Times.*

Turner, V. (1982). *From Ritual to Theatre: The Human Seriousness of Play.* New York: PAJ Publications.

Turner, V. (1969). *The Ritual Process: Structure and Anti-Structure.* Ithaca, NY: Cornell University Press.

Contributors

Linda Carter, MSN, CS, IAAP

Linda Carter, Jungian analyst, is a graduate of Georgetown and Yale Universities and the C.G. Jung Institute-Boston. She has been in private practice for over 30 years seeing children, adolescents and adults. She is the founder and chair of the Art and Psyche Working Group, an organization dedicated to developing and producing international conference experiences that bring together members of the arts communities with psychotherapists committed to a depth psychological approach.

Anna Maria Costantino

Clinical Psychologist and candidate at the Italian Center for Analytical Psychotherapy (CIPA). Expert in Butoh dance-theater; she received the European Diploma of Butoh at the International Academy of Butoh Dance at "New Butoh School" in Palermo, studying with Master Sayoko Onishi. She has participated in various other laboratories with other masters as Yoshito Ono, Tadshi Endo, Marie Gabrielle Rotie, and Ken Mai. She has presented performances in Italy and abroad, using Butoh technique to interact with various artistic expression forms. Dr. Costantino has served as a psychologist at the Center for the Care of Victims of Trauma and Abuse. She is the psychologist at Centro Armonia of the ASP in Palermo, carrying out clinical activities and participating in prevention of violence in schools. She has worked as a volunteer psychologist at the non-profit association Onlus "La danza delle ombre" for the homeless in the city of Palermo.

Carol Thayer Cox

Carol taught for many years for the art therapy programs at George Washington University, Vermont College of Norwich University, and Pratt Institute. She continues to offer workshops on color, imagery, and symbolism as reflected by different states of consciousness across the life span. Mentored by Joan Kellogg from 1979 to Joan's death in 2004, Carol is a founding board member and former officer of the Association of Teachers of Mandala Assessment. In her private practice Carol consults about psychological assessment through art and has worked in various psychiatric and psycho-educational settings. She served on the editorial board of *Art Therapy: Journal of the American Art Therapy Association* for ten years. She has conducted and supervised numerous art therapy research studies and has authored and co-authored professional journal articles and book chapters. Co-author with Barry Cohen of *Telling Without Talking: Art as a Window into the World of Multiple Personality Disorder* and co-editor with Peggy Heller of *Portrait of the Artist as Poet*, Carol is also founder of MUSE, a performing arts troupe that presented for years teaching psychological theory through art, dance, music, and poetry.

Leonard Cruz, MD

Leonard Cruz, MD, maintains a busy practice of psychiatry and is also the Editor-in-Chief of Chiron Publications, co-founder of the Asheville Jung Center and Chairman of the Mission Institutional Review Board. He co-authored *DSM-5 Insanely Simplified* and is a contributor to a newly released Chiron book, *A Clear and Present Danger: Narcissism in the Era of Donald Trump*. He is currently at work on a short story collection and a nonfiction work on globalization, sustainability and human rights.

Lisa Raye Garlock, MS

Ms. Garlock is a registered, board-certified, and licensed art therapist; certified art therapy supervisor; member of the Jung Society of

Washington, DC; and Assistant Professor and Clinical Placement Coordinator in the Graduate Art Therapy Program, The George Washington University, Washington DC. She teaches Jung in her Process of Counseling and Art Therapy Theory class at GW, where she also requires students to illustrate and process psychological theories through art making. She became consciously aware of Jung while taking a course during her graduate training at Nazareth College in 1995. Her artwork unconsciously illustrated many of Jung's concepts, particularly regarding symbols, archetypes, anima/animus and the shadow. She has further explored unconscious artistic processes through meditation painting, begun as a healing practice after hand surgery.

James Hollis, PhD

James Hollis is a Zurich-trained Jungian analyst in practice in Washington, D. C. where he is also Executive Director of the Jung Society of Washington, and author of fourteen books. James taught Humanities 26 years in various colleges and universities before retraining as a Jungian analyst during 1977-1982. He has also served as Executive Director of the Jung Educational Center in Houston, TX for many years and is a retired Senior Training Analyst for the Inter-Regional Society of Jungian Analysts. He was the first director of Training of the Philadelphia Jung Institute, and is Vice-President Emeritus of the Philemon Foundation. His books have been translated into minimally 18 languages.

Ian Livingston

Ian pursued his formal education at the University of Wisconsin in Stevens Point, and at the University of South Dakota. His labors have taken him from work in underground mines in Wyoming to the tops of old-growth redwood trees in California. His studies have been ongoing in diverse areas and span the life inquiry from Plato to Lacan, and from Patanjali to Feynman. He has studied

Buddhism, Taoism, and Hindu thought alongside his studies in Western philosophy and psychology. His primary devotion has been to the life of the mind and plumbing the depths outlined by the mystics of Christianity. He lives in California's Gold Country in the foothills of the Sierra Nevada mountain range.

Naomi Ruth Lowinsky, PhD

Naomi is an analyst member of the San Francisco C.G. Jung Institute, a frequent contributor to and poetry editor of *Psychological Perspectives*, and a widely published poet. She is the co-editor, with Patricia Damery, of the essay collection: *Marked by Fire: Stories of the Jungian Way*. Her memoir about the creative process is called *The Sister from Below: When the Muse Gets Her Way*. She has four published poetry collections including *Adagio and Lamentation*—an offering to her ancestors—and her latest, *The Faust Woman Poems*. Lowinsky won the 2015 Blue Light Poetry Prize for her chapbook *The Little House on Stilts Remembers*.

Kathryn Madden, PhD

Kathryn is the Editor of *The Unconscious Roots of Creativity,* and has been the Editor-in-Chief of *Quadrant: The Journal of the C. G. Jung Foundation for Analytical Psychology* for 12 years. She is a licensed psychoanalyst of Jungian and psychodynamic focus in private practice in NYC. Kathryn is the author of *The Dark Light of the Soul* (Lindisfarne), and was co-editor of *The Encyclopedia of Psychology & Religion* (Springer). Her 15-year tenure with *The Journal of Religion & Health: Psychology, Spirituality & Medicine,* (Springer) was honored, along with her staff, with The Distinguished Research & Writing Award presented by the American Association of Pastoral Counselors. Kathryn teaches as Associate Faculty at UTS/Columbia University and at Pacifica Graduate Institute in CA.

Jordan S. Potash, PhD

Dr. Potash is a registered, board-certified and licensed art therapist; registered expressive arts therapist; and Assistant Professor in the Graduate Art Therapy Program, The George Washington University, Washington D. C. began his studies of Jungian thought in 2000 when he trained in Joan Kellogg's theory The Archetypal Stages of the Great Round of Mandala. He remained in supervision for 5 years refining his learning with Kellogg's main disciple Carol Thayer Cox. Since then, he has published on the theory as it pertains to aesthetics, professional burnout, and self-awareness. In addition, he has taught related courses and workshops in the U.S., Hong Kong and Israel. His keen interest in Jungian and archetypal studies centers on its application for respecting personal and cultural symbolism while still appreciating universal themes as a foundation for peaceful multicultural societies.

Susan Rowland, PhD

Dr. Rowland is the Chair of Engaged Humanities & the Creative Life at Pacifica Graduate Institute, has degrees from the Universities of Oxford, London and Newcastle, UK, and was the first Chair of the International Association of Jungian Studies (IAJS). She is author of many studies of Jung, literary theory and gender including *C.G. Jung and Literary Theory* (1999), *Jung: A Feminist Revision* (2002), *Jung as a Writer* (2005) and also edited *Psyche and the Arts* (2008). Another recent book is *C.G. Jung and the Humanities* (2010), showing how Jung's work is a response to the creative, psychological, spiritual, philosophical and ecological crises of our age. In 2012, Her book, *The Ecocritical Psyche: Literature, Complexity Evolution and Jung* was published by Routledge, showing how the Jungian symbol is a portal to nature. Susan's work is not so much "about" Jung as an attempt to develop his special insights into myth, technology, the feminine, nature and the numinous for today's wounded world.

Murray Stein, PhD

Dr. Stein was president of the International Association for Analytical Psychology (IAAP) from 2001 to 2004 and President of the International School of Analytical Psychology in Zurich from 2008-2012. He has lectured internationally and recently published two new works, *Minding the Self* and *Soul-Retrieval and Treatment*. He lives in Switzerland and is a Training and Supervising Analyst with ISAPZurich. He has a private practice in Zurich.

Tjeu van den Berk

Dr. Tjeu van den Berk worked at the Catholic Universities of Amsterdam and Utrecht. He has published extensively on the relationship between religion and art. His books include such works as *Jung on Art: The Autonomy of the Creative Drive, Die Zauberflöte, Mystagogy: Initiation into the Symbolic Consciousness, The Mystery of the Brainstem, The Numinous.*

Robin van Löben Sels, PhD

Dr. van Löben Sels is a Jungian analyst, teaching and supervising in the Albuquerque-Santa Fe area of New Mexico. She is the author of *A Dream in The World: Poetics of Soul in Two Women, Modern and Medieval* and *Wanting a Country for this Weather*, a book of poetry. She has also published articles in *Spring, Quadrant*, and *Psychological Perspectives*.

Ann Belford Ulanov, MDiv, PhD, LHD

Dr. Ulanov is the Christiane Brooks Johnson Professor of Psychiatry and Religion, Emerita, at Union Theological Seminary, a psychoanalyst in private practice, and a member of the Jungian Psychoanalytic Association, New York City, and the International Association for Analytical Psychology. With her late husband, Barry Ulanov, she is the author of *Religion and the Unconscious; Primary Speech: A Psychology of Prayer; Cinderella and Her Sisters: The Envied and the Envying; The Witch and The Clown: Two Archetypes of Human Sexuality; The Healing Imagination; Transforming Sexuality: The Archetypal World of Anima and Animus;* by herself she is the author of *The Feminine in Christian Theology and in Jungian Psychology; Receiving Woman: Studies in the Psychology and Theology of the Feminine; Picturing God; The Wisdom of the Psyche; The Female Ancestors of Christ; The Wizards' Gate; The Functioning Transcendent; Finding Space: Winnicott, God, and Psychic Reality,* 2001; *Attacked by Poison Ivy, A Psychological Study,* 2002; *Spiritual Aspects of Clinical Work,* 2004; *The Unshuttered Heart: Opening to Aliveness and Deadness in the Self,* 2007; *The Living God and Our Living Psyche,* 2007; *Madness & Creativity,* 2013; *Knots and Their Untying,* 2014.

Heidi Sylvia Volf, MA

Heidi is a multimedia designer, researcher, and actor enchanted by the creative endeavor as a means of transformation. She has written several short stories, plays, and poems, as well as composed many images echoing mythic themes. She wishes to further explore the archetypal images of the unconscious dreamscape, the gnarled roots of depression, and metaphysical discomfort in general, becoming more aware of the gentle pulsing of the collective heartbeat heard and felt throughout.

Permission Acknowledgments

The editor and publishers are grateful to Norah Pollard for permission to republish her poem, "She Dreamed of Cows," from *Death and Rapture in the Animal Kingdom* (originally published by Antrim House, 2009). We thank HarperCollins Publishers for permission to republish excerpts from "Kaddish" [5 l.] and "The Lion for Real" [4 l. As epigraph] from COLLECTED POEMS 1947-1997 by ALLEN GINSBERG (Copyright ©2006 by the Allen Ginsberg Trust) and an excerpt from "Ars Poetica" [4 l.] from THE COLLECTED POEMS 1931-1987 by CZESLAW MILOSZ (Copyright © 1988 by Czeslaw Milosz Royalties, Inc). We thank Schocken Books (an imprint of the Knopf Doubleday Publishing Group, a division of Penguin Random House, LLC.) for permission to republish excerpt(s) from THE COMPLETE STORIES by Franz Kafka, (Copyright © 1946, 1947, 1948, 1949, 1954, 1958, 1971). We thank Mark Richardson for permission to publish his illustration entitled *The Pillar of Isis*. We thank The National Gallery, London, for permission to publish the Leonardo da Vinci drawing known as *The Burlington House Cartoon* and the Louvre in Paris for permission to publish the painting *Virgin and Child with St. Anne* by Leonardo da Vinci We thank the artist, Colette Calascione for permission to include three of her paintings in this volume: *Internal Landscape, Coincidental Gathering,* and *Traveling Hermit.* We also thank Susan Crehan-Hostetler for permission to include in this volume her late husband, David Hostetler's, painting entitled *Head or Heart.*

www.ingramcontent.com/pod-product-compliance
Lightning Source LLC
Chambersburg PA
CBHW050803270326
41926CB00025B/4516